Injustice on Appeal

Injustice on Appeal

The United States Courts of Appeals in Crisis

William M. Richman

Distinguished University Professor of Law
The University of Toledo College of Law

William L. Reynolds

Jacob A. France Professor of Judicial Process
University of Maryland Francis King Carey School of Law

OXFORD
UNIVERSITY PRESS

OXFORD
UNIVERSITY PRESS

Oxford University Press is a department of the University of Oxford. It furthers the University's objective of excellence in research, scholarship, and education by publishing worldwide.

Oxford New York
Auckland Cape Town Dar es Salaam Hong Kong Karachi Kuala Lumpur Madrid
Melbourne Mexico City Nairobi New Delhi Shanghai Taipei Toronto

With offices in
Argentina Austria Brazil Chile Czech Republic France Greece Guatemala Hungary
Italy Japan Poland Portugal Singapore South Korea Switzerland Thailand
Turkey Ukraine Vietnam

Oxford is a registered trade mark of Oxford University Press in the UK and certain other countries.

Published in the United States of America by
Oxford University Press
198 Madison Avenue, New York, NY 10016

Library of Congress Cataloging-in-Publication Data

Richman, William M.
Injustice on appeal : The United States Courts of Appeals in Crisis / William M. Richman,
William L. Reynolds.
p. cm.
Includes bibliographical references and index.
ISBN 978-0-19-534207-9 ((hardback) : alk. paper)
1. Appellate courts—United States. 2. Appellate procedure—United States.
I. Reynolds, William L., 1945- II. Title.
KF8750.R53 2013
347.73'8—dc23

2012022806

Printed in the United States of America on acid-free paper

Note to Readers
This publication is designed to provide accurate and authoritative information in regard to the subject matter covered. It is based upon sources believed to be accurate and reliable and is intended to be current as of the time it was written. It is sold with the understanding that the publisher is not engaged in rendering legal, accounting, or other professional services. If legal advice or other expert assistance is required, the services of a competent professional person should be sought. Also, to confirm that the information has not been affected or changed by recent developments, traditional legal research techniques should be used, including checking primary sources where appropriate.

(Based on the Declaration of Principles jointly adopted by a Committee of the American Bar Association and a Committee of Publishers and Associations.)

For Carol, for always.
W.M.R.

To my children, Bill, Megan, and Sarah
W.L.R.

CONTENTS

PREFACE

This book examines the background and consequences of shortcuts in case processing adopted by the federal circuit courts over the past forty years. These shortcuts, which we call collectively "Appellate Triage,"[1] include unpublished opinions that lack precedential value and that could not be cited (until 2006); reduction in the frequency of oral argument; and the delegation of great quantities of decision-making authority to central staff. Today, the vast majority of cases resolved by the circuit courts are decided using those shortcuts. The burden of those changes has fallen largely on the disfavored in our society.

We began writing in this area more than a third of a century ago. We started by examining unpublished opinions, their nonprecedential status, and the prohibitions on citation to them. Soon, we realized that the problem also included the elimination of oral argument and the growth of central staff. We then wondered why the obvious solution to the caseload problem—more judges—had not been adopted. That led us to examine the judges' arguments for their refusal to ask Congress for additional judgeships and the reasons they have systematically discounted the large body of empirical evidence that refutes those arguments. More recently we began to notice that the judges, having succeeded in restricting the size of the bench, have ceased even to discuss the issue in public. Our thirty-plus years of study have left us with anger and despair over the creation and jealous maintenance of a system that underserves the nation and shortchanges the poor and powerless.

1. We have written about the changes in the United States Courts of Appeals many times. *See* William L. Reynolds & William M. Richman, *Justice and More Judges*, 15 J. Law & Pol. 559 (1999); William L. Reynolds & William M. Richman, *The New Certiorari Courts*, 80 Judicature 206 (1997); William L. Reynolds & William M. Richman, *Studying Deck Chairs on the Titanic*, 81 Cornell L. Rev. 1290 (1996); William M. Richman & William L. Reynolds, *Elitism, Expediency, and the New Certiorari: Requiem for the Learned Hand Tradition*, 81 Cornell L. Rev. 273 (1996); William M. Richman & William L. Reynolds, *Appellate Justice, Bureaucracy, and Scholarship*, 21 U. Mich. J.L. Reform 623 (1988); William M. Richman & William L. Reynolds, *The Supreme Court Rules for The Publication of Opinions: A Critique*, 46 Ohio St. L.J., 243 (1985); William L. Reynolds & William M. Richman, *An Evaluation of Limited Publication in the United States Courts of Appeals*, 48 U. Chi. L. Rev. 573 (1981);William L. Reynolds & William M. Richman, *The Non-Precedential Precedential Limited Publication and No-Citation Rules in the United States Courts of Appeals*, 78 Colum. L. Rev. 1167 (1978).

We thank both of our schools for generously supporting our work on this book and the studies that preceded it. That support has been both intangible and tangible, with the latter in the form of research grants and research assistance. We are also grateful to the many scholars and judges around the country who have contributed to the body of commentary in the area; many of them have also have had kind words to say of our work.

Special thanks to Susan McCarty, Senior Research Librarian at the University of Maryland School of Law for her splendid editorial assistance, and to Yvonne McMorris, also of Maryland, for her cheerful and patient assistance. Also thanks to University of Toledo College of Law students, Wyatt Holliday, Sydney Leavitt, and Michelle Tussing, for valuable help in the final stages of preparation of the book, and to Diane Bohn for patient administrative assistance. We are grateful, as well, to our editors at Oxford University Press for their patience and support. Finally, we express our gratitude to our families for their patient encouragement and support during the preparation of this book and the thirty-some years of study that preceded it.

INTRODUCTION

This book treats a metamorphosis—actually, a deterioration—of one of the nation's great legal institutions, the United States Circuit Courts of Appeals. These courts hear appeals from the United States District Courts, and they are reviewed in turn only by the Supreme Court, at its discretion by writ of certiorari. The courts are organized into twelve geographic circuits and one specialty circuit (the Federal Circuit).

The importance of these courts would be hard to overstate. They decide over fifty thousand cases per year, out of which the Supreme Court usually chooses to review fewer than one hundred. From the litigant's point of view, the decisions of the Courts of Appeals are, for all practical purposes, final—the last stop in the judicial system. The Courts of Appeals are also important from the point of view of the law's development and for the same reason. The Supreme Court hears so few cases—and they typically deal only with questions having important public policy implications—that the Courts of Appeals supply the definitive answer to the vast majority of the nation's legal questions. Thus, for nearly all constitutional and federal statutory issues, all questions dealing with the jurisdiction of the federal courts and the interpretation of the Federal Rules of Evidence and the Federal Rules of Civil, Criminal, and Appellate Procedure as well as all issues dealing with judicial authority over the vast administrative machinery of the federal and state governments, the courts of appeals supply the last word.

Any significant change in so important an institution would be noteworthy, but the change that this book treats is remarkable for additional reasons. First, it happened so quickly—over a span of only thirty years, one legal generation. That might seem gradual by many standards, but the institutions of government and especially the courts are, by nature, conservative and slow to change. Hence the change that is this book's subject is truly radical. Second, the shift occurred entirely at the impetus of the courts themselves, with no executive and very little legislative input. In other words, the radical shift is entirely of the judges' making. The third reason flows from the second; when stripped of all rhetoric, the reason for the change in the circuit courts is that the judges prefer the new arrangement. The fourth reason is that the change in the courts of appeals represents a major reallocation of government benefits, draining them from the routine middle-class litigants and lavishing them on the wealthiest and most powerful litigants. Finally, the revolution has attracted little attention from the legal profession and even less from the public and, amazingly, even less from the judges themselves.

This book's organizational plan is typical for a scholarly work chronicling a major institutional disruption. First, chapter 1 treats the history of the courts of appeals since their beginning with the Evarts Act until about 1965, when the metamorphosis began. It pays special attention to the character of the courts and their procedure for deliberative decision making. That procedure, which we call the Learned Hand tradition, garnered for the courts an enviable reputation as one of the world's most distinguished judicial bodies.

Chapter 2 then discusses the change in the courts' workload and the avalanche of cases that forced the courts to choose how to increase their decision-making capacity. The increase in caseload was unprecedented and huge—ultimately an increase of more than 1500 percent in a generation. The courts might have responded to the caseload glut in any number of ways: they could, for instance have directed urgent pleas to Congress for a proportional increase in appellate judgeships. Or they might have reduced proportionally the time and effort spent on each appeal. In fact, they did neither. Instead, they gradually instituted a system that we have labeled the "Appellate Triage model" or the "Two-Track system." The basic plan of the system is that the caseload is divided up into two groups. On one group, less than 15 percent of the total, the courts lavish attention, treating them personally, in accordance with the central values of the Learned Hand tradition. They hear oral argument, confer at length, prepare multiple drafts of opinions, exchange those draft opinions with their colleagues, and eventually issue one or more long, scholarly, heavily footnoted opinions crafted personally by the judges with the help of a few personal law clerks. Furthermore, they publish those opinions, and in the common law tradition, treat them as binding future decisions until overruled or modified by the Supreme Court or the entire circuit sitting en banc.

The other portion of the caseload is treated differently via a system of appellate expediting devices. There is no oral argument, and conferences may occur en masse (as many as fifty in a day), and thus the judges often devote only a few minutes to each case. Nearly all of the work on that portion of the caseload is done by a relatively new cadre of para-judicial personnel—staff attorneys or "the central staff." Unlike the traditional law clerk who worked at the judge's elbow, this group is concentrated in the circuit headquarters and is thus often physically separated from the judges. They are hired and supervised not by the judges but by supervisory staff attorneys. They transmit their work product, typically memoranda and draft opinions, to the judges' chambers by ordinary or electronic mail, and seldom confer in person with the judges. Very little is known publicly about the work or status of these para-judges.

Opinions in these cases—the vast majority of the total—are typically issued *per curiam*. Moreover, they are usually short, sometimes only a few lines, and not formally published; the judges show their disdain for those opinions by denying their value as precedent, feeling free to disregard them when deciding future cases. Perhaps, most frighteningly, the decision on which track a particular cases fits—a decision which, after all, represents an important question of distributive justice—is typically not made by the judges themselves, but rather by the staff.

Chapters 3 through 8 treat in turn each of these appeal-expediting devices—denial of oral argument, reliance on central staff attorneys, withholding formal publication, and denial of precedential status. The arguments for implementing each are probed and found to rely on questionable premises and faulty logic. Further, we consider the costs that each of the expediting devices imposes on the legal system.

Chapter 9 then discusses the cumulative impact of the several appeals-expediting devices, arguing that the courts have transformed themselves in the teeth of their enabling statute from courts of mandatory jurisdiction to certiorari courts. That is a change of major proportion. Despite the statutory guarantee, average litigants are denied a meaningful mandatory appeal heard by the judges, and instead must petition the staff to have their cases included in the select few that receive the traditional appellate treatment and the attention of the judges. The chapter also notes that the impact of the expediting devices is not class neutral; it falls disproportionately on the poor and middle class, whose appeals are deemed less momentous than the "big" cases brought by or against the government or major private economic actors.

The book then makes a digression in chapter 10 to discuss a generation's worth of proposals and studies, conducted by a confusing, albeit impressive array of councils, committees, and commissions assigned to consider the plight of the circuit courts and recommend solutions. Remarkably, these repetitive studies typically either ignore the central question of the propriety of the Appellate Triage regime, or, if they address it, make recommendations for relatively minor alterations, which then are ignored by the policy makers.

Finally, chapters 11 through 14 recommend our own obvious solution: a radical increase in the size of the federal appellate bench. This is not a solution that has been rejected after serious consideration. Rather an increase in the number of circuit judgeships has been lobbied *against* forcefully for many years by elements of the judicial establishment. This final portion of the book considers in detail the arguments that have been made against the most obvious solution and exposes them as so weak as to cast doubt on the sincerity of their advocates. Finally we speculate, based on the language used in many of the anti-expansionist arguments, that the real reason that the courts have rejected radical increases in judgeships has been the judges' desire to avoid diluting their own prestige and their desire to maintain their own job satisfaction.

CHAPTER 1

A Brief History of the Circuit Courts

This chapter provides a brief discussion of the history of the circuit courts of appeals. For the first hundred years of our history, there was no separate set of intermediate courts of appeals, though Congress had experimented with various court configurations to perform their function. Then in the Evarts Act (1891) and the Judges' Bill Congress created the current appellate court system, intending that the circuit courts of appeals would perform the traditional functions of a common law appellate court—the correction of trial court error and the incidental law-giving function needed to explain the error correction results. The courts functioned this way for nearly eighty years until an explosion of appellate litigation required that these courts change in primary function, staffing, and internal operating procedure.

A. BEFORE THE CASELOAD EXPLOSION

An understanding of the Appellate Triage system requires a brief review of the history of the federal courts. Although the Constitution provided for the establishment of a Supreme Court, the framers left the rest of the federal judiciary to the wise discretion of Congress. In the Judiciary Act of 1789,[1] Congress established the federal judicial system. For more than a century after that notable achievement, however, Congress continually experimented with the federal court system, and it is probably not too strong to say that it took Congress a long time to make sense out of the federal judiciary.[2]

1. Act of September 24, 1789, 1 Stat. 73.

2. The standard work on the subject up through the passage of the Judges' Bill, told in numbing detail, is FELIX FRANKFURTER & JAMES M. LANDIS, THE BUSINESS OF THE SUPREME COURT: A STUDY IN THE FEDERAL JUDICIAL SYSTEM (1928). Paul Carrington, *Crowded Dockets and the Court of Appeals: The Threat to the Function of Review and the National Law*, 82 HARV. L. REV. 542 (1969), brings the story forward into the period we cover in this book.

Although the federal judicial system always consisted of the Supreme Court, trial courts, and intermediate appellate courts, the allocation of responsibility among those tribunals changed as the new nation grew and its economy expanded. For the first century, the nation's appellate system often looked a bit odd, at least from a modern perspective. At the beginning, for example, following the English practice, "the federal system mingled appellate and *nisi prius* work . . . ."[3] That system remained in place for a long time; the system of federal courts looked markedly different than it does today.[4]

Although Congress made many changes in the jurisdiction and composition of the different levels of courts, it was not until 1891 with the adoption of the Evarts Act[5] that the present system of circuit and district courts was adopted, and it was not until 1925, with the passage of the Judges' Bill[6] (so-called because it was adopted largely at the urging of the judges themselves, especially Chief Justice Taft) that the courts fully assumed their current definition. In that way, the mingling of trial and appellate functions ended, and the various courts assumed their current well-defined roles.

The system that Congress created has lasted for more than a century. It was a remarkable edifice that brought order and justice to the ever-increasing realm of federal interests, which grew with both the economy and the increasing assertion of personal rights. The new system did more than organize the different levels of the judiciary; the reforms also changed the allocation of responsibility among them. By making the Supreme Court's jurisdiction largely discretionary, Congress sought to free it from the burden of handling routine matters of error correction. The idea was that the Court would then be able to focus on matters of constitutional law and the exposition of federal law generally. The day-to-day judicial business of the federal appellate courts—supervising the work of the district courts—could then be entrusted to the circuit judges.[7] Thus, the primary role of the circuit judges was to supervise the dispute resolution in the trial courts and not to expound the law. Paul Carrington has described the system at its inception this way:

> The perceived role of the appellate court was to correct the errors of the trial court in applying the law to the facts . . . . Certainly it was very far from the minds of those who adopted the Evarts Act that the intermediate courts of the United States would ever be taken seriously as sources of federal law.[8]

3. FRANKFURTER & LANDIS, *supra* note 2, at 17.

4. *Everything* was different. Before passage of the Evarts Act in 1891, for example, "no appeals were allowed in criminal cases, and none were available in civil cases where the amount in controversy did not exceed five thousand dollars." Carrington, *supra* note 2, at 550.

5. Circuit Court of Appeals Act of 1891, 26 Stat. 826.

6. Act of February 13, 1925, 43 Stat. 936.

7. *See* Carrington, *supra* note 2, at 560.

8. Paul D. Carrington, *The Function of the Civil Appeal: A Late-Century View*, 38 S.C. L. REV. 411, 416–17 (1987).

Thus, the circuit courts were created to serve the modest end of policing the trial courts. Law making was not their task. Instead, the newly created *certiorari* jurisdiction of the Supreme Court was supposed to give that Court the time to serve as the primary expositor of federal law.

The received and perhaps idealized tradition of the operation of the circuit courts harks back to the example of the Second Circuit in the 1940s. That court, which has become known as the Learned Hand Court, serves as the exemplar of how an appellate court should operate (the "Learned Hand Treatment"). The model is the one taught in law schools in classes in appellate procedure and endless rounds of moot court competitions. Thanks to a wonderful history of the Second Circuit by Marvin Schick,[9] we know much about the way that court functioned. The process was radically different from today's. Oral argument was heard in practically every case; "a small number of appeals" were decided from the bench following argument, and about 20 percent of the appeals were resolved in brief *per curiam* decisions.[10] The court took its responsibilities very seriously; law clerks, for example, had very little influence. It was said by Judge Medina that Learned Hand "wouldn't even let a law clerk write a sentence, not one sentence."[11] There is no evidence that central staff existed, or if they did, their functions were purely ministerial.

B. THE CASELOAD EXPLOSION

The courts began to change in the late 1960s and early 1970s in response to a vast increase in their caseloads. The caseload explosion produced some truly staggering numbers. In 1960, 3,899 cases were filed in the geographic circuit courts; by 2010, the there were 56,790 filings. *Thus, over the past fifty years, the circuit courts' caseload has increased by 1436 percent, a more than fourteenfold increase.*[12] What caused this explosion in litigation? The twentieth century saw a dramatic increase in both population and economic activity. Those developments led to exponential growth in federal law as the modern administrative state was born and grew quickly. Thus, a substantial part of the docket growth was the natural result of large increases in population and economic prosperity. That part of the growth should be easy to

9. Marvin Schick, Learned Hand's Court (1970).
10. *Id.* at 93–94. This was true of the court as late as 1960.
11. *Id.* at 107 n.92.
12. For the 1960 total, see Comm'n on Structural Alternatives for Fed. Courts of Appeals, Final Report 9, table 2–4 (Dec. 18, 1998), *available at* http://www.library.unt.edu/gpo/csafca/final/appstruc.pdf. For the 2010 total, see Admin. Office of the U.S. Courts, 2010 Judicial Business of the U.S. Courts 83, table B (2010), *available at* http://www.uscourts.gov/uscourts/Statistics/JudicialBusiness/2010/JudicialBusinespdfversion.pdf. For table only, see http://www.uscourts.gov/uscourts/Statistics/JudicialBusiness/2010/appendices/B00Sep10.pdf.

understand—more people generate more litigation and more economic activity, which in turn creates more and more complex litigation.

But another reason for the increase in filings was largely unrelated to demographic and economic growth. The Warren Court's revolutions in constitutional law in the 1950s and 1960s play a large role here—in particular, the dramatic changes in civil rights law and constitutional law governing criminal procedure in state and federal courts. The lower federal courts, of course, were generally responsible for implementation of the newly favored guarantees of the Bill of Rights and the Fourteenth Amendment. Habeas corpus and other post-conviction filings proliferated dramatically,[13] a development that required, at least at first, an inquiry into cases long since decided.[14] Civil rights cases also exploded with federal courts forced to assume supervisory authority over state schools, federal and state prisons, and mental hospitals.

At the same time, Congress was continually adding to the apparatus of the regulatory state, asserting new control over the environment, workers' rights, the employment and educational rights of minorities, the rights of the handicapped, and the allocation of funds by colleges, universities, and primary and secondary schools. Moreover, the caseload increased not only in numbers, but also in complexity. The Learned Hand Court, for example, did not have to deal with legislation governing the thermal pollution of lakes and rivers by nuclear power plants. Later years added still other burdens to the federal judicial system. One study in the late 1990s, for example, identified the adoption of sentencing guidelines as the cause of a substantial increase in caseload.[15] Recent years have also seen great increases in the number of immigration appeals.

All of these substantive legal developments placed great pressure on the circuit courts. Not only did their new tasks require widespread supervision of the greater volume of litigation in the district courts (and even, sometimes in state court), but the necessary exegesis of all of this new law also consumed a lot of time. It had been recognized since the Evarts Act that the courts of appeals served two functions, as indeed any common law appellate court must. Their decisions served not only to correct error in the district courts but also, secondarily, to expound the law that governed their decisions. Thus, forty years ago, Dean Carrington described the

13. Fred Cheesman II, Roger A. Hanson & Brian J. Ostrom, Nat'l Ctr. for State Courts, A Tale of Two Laws: The U.S. Congress Confronts Habeas Corpus Petitions and Section 1983 Lawsuits 4 (Mar. 1999), *available at*http://www.ncsconline.org/WC/Publications/Res_CapPun_TaleTwoLawsPub.pdf.

14. Many of the new decisions in criminal procedure were applied retroactively. As a result, the lower federal courts were faced with large numbers of claims for habeas corpus relief. The passage of time had often made these difficult to resolve. The impact of these developments on the advent of limited publication is traced in Penelope Pether, *Inequitable Injunctions—The Scandal of Private Judging in the U.S. Courts*, 56 Stan. L. Rev. 1137, 1142–65 (2004).

15. Comm'n on Structural Alternatives for Federal Courts of Appeals, Final Report 15 (1998), *available at* http://www.library.unt.edu/gpo/csafca/final/appstruc.pdf (also discussed in detail *infra* chapter 10).

modern role of the court of appeals this way: "In addition to serving as a check on the power of district judges and administrative agencies, the Court of Appeals have a related function in helping to create a stable body of national law."[16] In other words, the courts of appeals had to perform both jobs—supervisor *and* law-giver.[17] The vast increase in the domain of law, however, turned the Evarts Act's allocation of function on its head; the law-giving function of the courts began to overwhelm the primary error-correction mission.

At the same time, it became impossible for the Supreme Court (even with its now almost completely discretionary jurisdiction) to keep up with the law-making necessary to harmonize and develop the burgeoning body of federal law and insure justice throughout the system. The Court has made matters worse in recent years by limiting itself to hearing only about eighty cases a year. The combination of all of these developments has caused profound changes in the role of the circuit courts, for now it is they, and not the Supreme Court, that must do most of the heavy lifting of maintaining federal case law.

The circuit courts necessarily changed as a result of their new role. The extra complexity of their enhanced law-giving role has added significantly to their burdens. Opinion writing, the source of the new law, became an increasingly burdensome task as the judges labored to explain the law that they were creating. Moreover, the opinions themselves have changed; in the past several decades, they have become significantly longer, more complex, more scholarly—in other words, more like Supreme Court opinions, adding still greater burdens to the judicial workload.

Often, an institution stressed by too much work will fall behind, but that has not happened; the courts' dockets, while grotesquely swollen, remain current. The median time between submission and disposition—between six and nine months in 1980—is still only 11.7 months today.[18] With the courts remaining current despite an exponential growth in the size and complexity of their caseloads, one would expect to see a similarly dramatic increase in the number of judgeships, but that has not happened either.[19] The result, of course, is that the individual judges' workload has ballooned. In 1960, 68 judges dealt with 3,899 appeals

16. *Id.* at 551.

17. The district courts have undergone a similar evolution, adding their own appellate function as they review the work of magistrate and bankruptcy judges.

18. For 1980, see Federal Judicial Workload Statistics During the Twelve-Month Period Ended December 31, 1980, at 4, *available at* http://www.llmcdigital.org/docdisplay.aspx?textid=17267490&type=pdf. For 2010, see http://www.uscourts.gov/uscourts/Statistics/JudicialBusiness/2010/judicialbusinespdfversion.pdf.

19. The number of circuits has grown, albeit very slowly: the Tenth Circuit was carved out of the Eighth, and the Eleventh was created out of the Fifth. On the other hand, the Ninth Circuit, the largest circuit measured by the number of judges, remains intact, despite numerous (and controversial) efforts to change it.

filings; fifty years later, 167 judges handled 56,790 cases. Thus, while judgeships have increased only 250 percent, filings have increased fifteenfold.[20] That means that in 1960, there were 57 filings per judgeship, and today there are 327 filings per judgeship; in the intervening fifty years, judicial workload has increased by nearly 600 percent!

Obviously, judicial capacity is not keeping up with workload, and the courts remain current only by managing staggering increases in each judge's workload. A very obvious solution to the problem would be a radical increase in the number of judges, yet that option has not even been considered by the political branches for the simple reason that the judiciary refuses to ask for the number of judgeships its own staffing formula suggests it needs. Rather, the courts have adopted internal solutions: they publish only 15 percent of their opinions;[21] they deny oral argument in 75 percent of the cases,[22] and they have hired about five hundred staff attorneys,[23] para-judges to prepare cursory nonprecedential opinions in the vast majority of cases. The result is that the concept of an "appeal of right" no longer means what it once did.

These changes have been noted by others. The White Commission, a blue-ribbon group headed by the late Justice White, said much the same thing a decade ago.

> This obligatory review was sharply distinguished from the concept of discretionary review, under which an appellate court has a choice as to whether it would consider the case on its merits. Up until three decades ago this right to appeal was assumed to include an opportunity to file briefs, to present oral argument to the court, and to receive from the court a written opinion explaining the decision. That conception of an appeal, however, has undergone modification as the appellate courts have adopted screening and tracking procedures through which a large proportion of appeals are decided by the court without oral argument and by judgment orders or unelaborated opinions.[24]

20. *See* sources cited *supra* in note 12; *see also* Diarmud F. Scannlain, *Striking a Devil's Bargain: The Federal Courts and Expanding Caseloads in the Twenty-First Century*, 13 Lewis & Clark L. Rev. 473 n.1 and sources cited therein.

21. *See* Admin. Office of U.S. Courts, 2010 Judicial Business of the U.S. Courts, table S-3 (2010), http://www.uscourts.gov/uscourts/Statistics/JudicialBusiness/2011/tables/S01Sep11.pdf.

22. See Admin. Office of U.S. Courts, 2010 Judicial Business of the U.S. Courts, table S-1 (2010), http://www.uscourts.gov/uscourts/Statistics/JudicialBusiness/2011/tables/S01Sep11.pdf.

23. *See infra* chapter 8.

24. Comm'n on Structural Alternatives for Fed. Courts of Appeals, Final Report, *supra* note 12, at 70.

When these appeal-expediting procedures began to be implemented, only a small minority of the cases received the truncated process; today it accounts for more than 80 percent of the docket.[25]

In other words, the judges have created their own solution to the caseload problem, a system of shortcuts that we refer to as "Appellate Triage." Although the history we have detailed shows that some members of Congress, the Executive Branch, and the bar must have been aware of what was happening, the change in age-old procedures excited the attention of no one, including the judges themselves. Amazingly, the profound changes wrought by these new procedures were adopted with little more apparent consideration to their consequences than would have been given to a proposal to change the margin requirements on briefs.

Further, the judges adopted the procedures without serious internal reflection on the consequences of what they were doing. There are no in-depth studies and reports debating the options available and their costs and benefits. With only a very few exceptions, the judges themselves reflected very little on the new role of the circuit courts in our system of justice. In short, radical change has come about with little fanfare and less thought about how to accommodate the new role of the circuit courts with the needs of justice.

The changes we discuss in this book have resulted from the activity of the courts, not Congress. Apart from appropriating money for the newly created central staff positions, Congress has left the circuit courts to fend for themselves since 1925.[26] Not surprisingly, perhaps, the judicial establishment seems happy enough with that neglect. They have asked Congress for very little during that time (apart from pay raises and fancy new courthouses). That abstinence is quite remarkable given the developments that we discuss.

C. THE NUMBERS

The changing workload can best be captured by putting the numbers in tabular form.

The most striking thing about these numbers is the dramatic increase in filings per judge. The average judge in 2010 had six times as many cases to resolve as did a judge in 1960. But a second look reveals something equally dramatic—the number of authorized judgeships has not changed in recent years. In fact, the last increase in

25. The appellate courts of several states have gone through the same general evolution. We do not specifically address state courts and their problems in this book, however. We also do not discuss the somewhat related problem of publication in the federal trial courts. On that topic, see generally Hillel Y. Levin, *Making the Law: Unpublication in the District Courts*, 53 VILL. L. REV. 973 (2009).

26. Congress has spent a good bit of time discussing whether to break up the Ninth Circuit, but even that debate has not led to any action.

Table 1 JUDICIAL WORKLOAD

Yearly	Filings[27]	Authorized Judgeships[28]	Filings per Judgeship[29]
1960	3,899	68	57.3
1970	11,662	97	120.2
1980	23,200	132	175.8
1990	40,898	167	244.9
2000	54,697	167	327.5
2010	56,790	167	340.1

their number occurred in 1990. In other words, a significant increase in caseload has *not* been met by an increase in judges. The result, of course, was a dramatic increase in caseload for each judge. And yet the courts are current in their workload

How have they accomplished that feat? They have done so by the use of the Appellate Triage regime that we discuss in the following chapters.

D. A CONCLUDING NOTE

This chapter has traced the evolution of the circuit courts from their confused origins through their role as supervisor of the trial courts to their present role as primary law-giver within the federal judiciary. There has been another revolution, however, one that has been much less obvious. The circuit court judges have forsaken much of their role as judges and become, instead, bureaucrats, nominal supervisors of large numbers of civil servants who do the real work that Congress has assigned to the judges (and that most everyone believes is still done by the judges).

27. *Source*: uscourts.gov. Table B-1. The data distinguish between "filings" and "terminations." In recent years, the latter number has been about half the former. Filings in 2009 declined 6 percent from the previous year, a drop that "stemmed mainly from a drop in administrative agency appeals involving the Board of Immigration Appeals." John Roberts, 2009 Year-End Report on the Federal Judiciary 2 (2010).There was a further decline in the number of appeals in 2010.

28. *Source*: United States Courts, Judges & Judgeships, *available at* http://www.uscourts.gov/JudgesAndJudgeships/Viewer.aspx?doc=/uscourts/JudgesJudgeships/docs/allauth.pdf. Elsewhere in this book, we use the number 179 as the current number of circuit judges because that is the number used by the Administrative Office of the Courts and by most scholars in the area. Here we use 167 as the current number; the difference between the numbers (179 as opposed to 167) is the 12 judges of the Federal Circuit. We use the smaller number here to compare current workload with that of 1960 because the Federal Circuit did not exist in 1960, its caseload having been handled by other courts.

29. *Source*: *Id.*

The adoption of the Appellate Triage regime by the circuits has caused the current state of affairs. At first, the judges used the triage devices to deny argument and issue shorter opinions in cases the judges did not really want to hear. Gradually, they realized that shorter opinions could be written by persons who worked for the court at large, rather than in the chambers of a single judge. The judges next realized that they did not have to supervise actively those who wrote the unpublished opinions; after all, those opinions were, in the infamous words of Chief Judge Kozinski, "garbage."[30] That ability to delegate meant that they did not need to ask for more judges, additions they believed would undercut their status.

We now turn to an examination of the several pieces of the Appellate Triage system, how they work in practice, and the costs that they impose on our system of justice.

30. William Glaberson, *Ideas & Trends: Unprecedented; Legal Shortcuts Run into Dead Ends*, N.Y. Times, Oct. 8, 2000 ("More garbage is not better."), *available at* www.nytimes.com/2000/10/08/weekinreview/ideas-trends-unprecedented-legal-shortcuts-run-into-some-dead-ends.html.

CHAPTER 2
The Publication Plans

One of the most important strategies of the Appellate Triage regime is limiting the publication of circuit court opinions. This chapter examines the steps that led to the adoption of that strategy and the effects of limited publication on the courts, the bar, and the litigants. The chapter concludes with a look at the publication rates in the courts of appeals as well as the contents of their Publication Plans today.

A. THE HISTORY OF PUBLICATION PLANS

Dissatisfaction with the volume of published opinions is not a new phenomenon; indeed, it might be said that the complaining about the number of published opinions has been timeless.[1] As early as 1915, a prominent judge noted that the federal and state courts of last resort had produced over 65,000 opinions, filling 630 volumes, in the five years between 1908 and 1913.[2] Another writer noted that in the year ending June 30, 1915, 175,000 pages of law reports from the American state and federal systems were added to the library of the Harvard Law School.[3] These figures were alarming because it was thought that no lawyer, judge, or law professor could possibly remain current with the avalanche of decisional law. One commentator lamented:

> Looking ahead a half century to the time when there shall be two or three times as many inhabitants within our borders and a corresponding increase in our litigation, what are

1. For good summaries of the early literature favoring limitations on opinion writing, see Leah F. Chanin, *A Survey of the Writing and Publication of Opinions in Federal and State Appellate Courts*, 67 LAW LIB. J. 362 (1974); J. Myron Jacobstein, *Some Reflections on the Control of the Publication of Appellate Court Opinions*, 27 STAN. L. REV. 791 (1975). These efforts were not overwhelmingly successful. *See* Eugene B. Prince, *Law Books, Unlimited*, 48 A.B.A. J. 134, 136 (1962).

2. John B. Winslow, *The Courts and the Papermills*, 10 ILL.. L. REV. 157, 158 (1915).

3. Edward H. Warren, *The Welter of Decisions*, 10 ILL. L. REV. 472, 472–73 (1916). *See also* Prince, *supra* note 1, at 134 for alarming statistics in terms of the number of "miles" of law reports in our large libraries.

> we to expect if the present rate of production of precedents be maintained? The law library of the future staggers the imagination as one thinks of multitudes of shelves which will stretch away into the dim distance, rank upon rank, and tier upon tier, all loaded with their many volumes of precious precedents. One shrinks from the contemplation of the intellectual giants who will be competent to keep track of the authorities and make briefs in those days; they, as well as the judges who pass upon the briefs, must be supermen indeed.[4]

Recognition of the problem led to the consideration of methods to streamline the appellate process, including examination of whether the number of opinions published should be reduced. Early commentators suggested that not all decisions merit reasoned opinions and surely not all opinions merit publication. They crystallized their suggestions into proposed sets of standards for determining which cases deserve written opinions and which of those should be published.[5]

Limited publication has been actively considered by the federal judicial establishment since the end of World War II.[6] By that time, some state courts had already experimented with limited publication, and the earliest efforts to limit publication of judicial opinions in the federal courts of appeals had occurred in the Third and Fifth Circuits.[7] Later, the subject was raised at the 1964 meeting of the Judicial Conference of the United States. The Conference, concerned with "the ever increasing practical difficulty and economic cost of ... maintaining accessible private and public law library facilities"[8] resolved "[t]hat the judges of the courts of appeals and the district courts authorize the publication of only those opinions which are of general precedential value and that opinions authorized to be published be succinct."[9]

4. Winslow, *supra* note 2, at 158.

5. *See, e.g.*, Francis P. Whitehair, *Opinions of Courts: Fifth Circuit Acts Against Unneeded Publication*, 33 A.B.A. J. 751 (1947); Winslow, *supra* note 2, at 161.

6. This resolution did not produce the systematic limited Publication Plans that the circuits have since adopted. However, some of the circuits had already begun selective publication as part of their screening procedures. The Fourth Circuit took the additional step of urging that unpublished decisions not be cited. *See* Jones v. Superintendent, Va. State Farm, 465 F.2d 1091 (4th Cir. 1972). As a result, the Fourth Circuit has been called "the probable mother of the non-publication system." Remarks of John P. Frank, Ninth Circuit Judicial Conference (July 29, 1976).

7. *See* John J. O'Connell, *A Dissertation on Judicial Opinions*, 23 TEMP. L.Q. 13 (1949); Whitehair, *supra* note 5; Note, *Opinions of Courts: Should Number Published be Reduced?* 34 A.B.A. J. 668 (1948) (a report to the Judicial Conference for the Third Circuit of the United States). Concern over the number of opinions can be traced back even further. *See* David Greenwald & Frederick A. O. Schwartz Jr., *The Censorial Judiciary*, 35 U.C. DAVIS L. REV. 1133, 1144–45 (2002).

8. ADMIN. OFFICE OF U.S. COURTS, REPORT OF THE PROCEEDINGS OF THE JUDICIAL CONFERENCE OF THE UNITED STATES 11 (1964), *available at* http://www.uscourts.gov/judconf/64-Mar.pdf.

9. *Id.*

The increase in the number of appeals discussed in chapter 1 had caught the attention of the judicial establishment. Worried about the pressures of a caseload growing rapidly as a result of the Warren Court revolution in civil rights, habeas corpus, and criminal procedure (much of which was applied retroactively and led to many post-conviction appeals), the Judicial Conference chose limited publication as the antidote.[10]

In 1971, the effort to restrict publication began to accelerate; the Federal Judicial Center's Annual Report for that year noted a "widespread consensus that too many opinions are being printed or published or otherwise disseminated."[11] The report failed to explain that conclusion in any detail, and it did not mention, much less address, alternative remedies for the workload problem, including the creation of additional appellate judgeships. The report proposed no comprehensive solution to the caseload problem, but it noted that the Judicial Center would continue to compile information on federal and state court approaches to limiting publication.[12]

These brief "studies" (if that is the right word) ended in a short report made by the Board of the Federal Judicial Center to the Judicial Conference of the United States;[13] that report stated that the needless proliferation of published decisional law had created serious problems for the courts. The board recommended that the Judicial Conference direct each circuit council to review its publication policy and implement the following modifications:

a. Opinions will not be published unless ordered by a majority of the panel rendering the decision;
b. Nonpublished opinions should not be cited, either in briefs or in court opinions;

10. Penelope Pether has made a strong argument that limited publication was conceived in sin. She contends that the system was adopted in reaction to a new wave of appeals perceived by the circuit judges to be frivolous and unsavory. Spawned by Warren Court decisions, a large part of the increase consisted of post-conviction and civil rights cases. In particular, Pether traces the popularity of unpublished opinions to efforts by the Fourth Circuit, beginning in the late 1950s, "to find a satisfactory process for disposing of *pro se* post conviction appeals without the appointment of counsel, without hearing, and via unpublished opinions ...." Penelope Pether, *Inequitable Injunctions: The Scandal of Private Judging in the U.S. Courts*, 56 Stan. L. Rev. 1435, 1460 (2004). In making that argument, Pether relies primarily on a talk given by Judge Margaret McKeown to the American Association of Law Schools in 2001 and on *Jones v. Superintendent, Virginia State Farm*, 465 F.2d 1091 (4th Cir. 1972). She tells the story at length in Pether, 56 Stan. L. Rev. at 1442–64.We agree with Professor Pether that the distaste for various types of appeals, including post-conviction, not only played a large role in instituting limited publication, but also played a significant part in its continued maintenance. Nevertheless, caseload pressures, regardless of their source, surely played a major role in the proliferation of unpublished opinions; original sin cannot be the only explanation.

11. Federal Judicial Center 1971 Annual Report 7–8 (1971).

12. *Id.*

13. Bd. of Fed. Judicial Ctr., Recommendation and Report to the April 1972 Session of the Judicial Conference of the United States on the Publication of Courts of Appeals Opinions (1972).

c. When an opinion is not published, the public record shall be completed by publishing the judgment of the court.[14]

The critical component of the board's recommendation lay in linking nonpublication with the effective denial of precedential status through a prohibition on citation. At its October 1972 session, the Judicial Conference approved the circulation of the Center's report to all circuit judges and requested that each circuit develop an opinion Publication Plan.[15] The report failed to explain the reasons for the Conference's recommendation.

Meanwhile, work on drafting model standards continued at the Federal Judicial Center.[16] The Advisory Council for Appellate Justice,[17] a distinguished group of lawyers, law teachers, and judges brought together by the Judicial Center, produced a draft report that considered standards for publication, procedures for deciding which opinions should be published, and the desirability of allowing citation of unpublished opinions.[18] After further revisions, this report was published in pamphlet form by the Federal Judicial Center under the title, Standards for Publication of Judicial Opinions.[19]

14. *Id.* at 1.

15. Admin. Offices of U.S. Courts, Report of the Proceedings of the Judicial Conference of the United States 33 (1972), *available at* http://www.uscourts.gov/uscourts/FederalCourts/judconf/proceedings/1972-10.pdf. Originally, the plans were to be submitted by January 1, 1973. The deadline was later extended to December 31, 1973. Admin. Offices of U.S. Courts, Report of the Proceedings of the Judicial Conference of the United States, 1971, Communication from Chief Justice of the United States Transmitting Proceedings of the Judicial Conference of the United States, Apr. 5–6, 1973, at 5 (May 21, 1973), *available at* http://www.uscourts.gov/uscourts/FederalCourts/judconf/proceedings/1973-04.pdf.

16. Federal Judicial Center 1971 Annual Report 6 (1972), *available at* http://www.uscourts.gov/uscourts/FederalCourts/judconf/proceedings/1972-07.pdf.

17. The most succinct explanation for the origin and purpose of the Advisory Council for Appellate Justice appears as a preface to its pamphlet, Advisory Council for Appellate Justice, Federal Judicial Center Research Series No. 73-2, Standards for Publication of Judicial Opinions (1973) [hereinafter Standards for Publication of Judicial Opinions]:

> The Federal Judicial Center brought together on September 24–25, 1971, a group of distinguished lawyers, law teachers and judges for the purpose of commencing a study in depth of the appellate systems of the United States, both state and Federal. The work was undertaken in the realization that present-day appellate processes are already under dangerous pressure and that the case-loads to be anticipated in the near future cannot be handled without basic changes in the staffing, structure, organization and work habits of the appellate courts. Those who attended the first conference named themselves the Advisory Council on Appellate Justice and selected as Chairman Maurice Rosenberg, Nash Professor of Law at Columbia University.

18. This report, Limiting Publication of Judicial Opinions (1973), was the work of the Committee on Use of Appellate Court Energies, a sub-unit of the Advisory Council for Appellate Justice. As far as we know, this report is unpublished and unavailable except in the National Archives. It can be found there in the files of the Commission on Revision of the Federal Court Appellate System—Document #454.

19. Standards for Publication of Judicial Opinions, *supra* note 17 (report of Committee on Use of Appellate Court Energies of the Advisory Council for Appellate Justice).

The Model Rule[20] suggested by the report has been the template for many of the rules subsequently promulgated by the United States Courts of Appeals. It, too, provides that not all opinions need be published and that opinions "Not Designated for Publication, shall not be cited as precedent by any court or in any brief or other materials presented to any court."[21] Once again, precedent and publication were yoked together.

By its spring 1974 session, the Judicial Conference had received from the circuits the proposed plans that it had requested. The report of the Conference revealed its satisfaction with the progress made by the circuits' efforts at limiting publication. Although the proposed plans were not identical, the Conference thought their divergence a useful experimental tool in arriving at a settled position on publication.[22]

20. The Model Rule provides:

> 1. Standard for Publication
>
> An opinion of the (highest court) or of the (intermediate court) shall not be designated for publication unless:
>
> a. The opinion establishes a new rule or law or alters or modifies an existing rule; or
> b. The opinion involves a legal issue of continuing public interest; or
> c. The opinion criticizes existing law; or
> d. The opinion resolves an apparent conflict of authority.
>
> 2. Opinions of the court shall be published only if the majority of the judges participating in the decision find that a standard for publication as set out in section (1) of this rule is satisfied. Concurring opinions shall be published only if the majority opinion is published. Dissenting opinions may be published if the dissenting judge determines that a standard for publication as set out in section (1) of this rule is satisfied. The (highest court) may order any unpublished opinion of the (intermediate court) or a concurring or dissenting opinion in that court published.
> 3. If the standard for publication as set out in section (1) of the rule is satisfied as to only a part of an opinion, only that part shall be published.
> 4. The judges who decide the case shall consider the question of whether or not to publish an opinion in the case at the conference on the case before or at the time the writing assignment is made, and at that time, if appropriate, they shall make a tentative decision not to publish.
> 5. All opinions that are not found to satisfy a standard for publication as prescribed by section (1) of this rule shall be marked, Not Designated for Publication. Opinions marked, Not Designated for Publication, shall not be cited as precedent by any court or in any brief or other materials presented to any court.

Id. at para. 5.

21. *Id.*

22. The Conference Report noted:

> While the plans of each circuit generally follow the basic recommendations of the report of the Federal Judicial Center to the April 1972 meeting of the Judicial Conference, each circuit, to a limited extent, is experimenting with respect to some phases of its plan. There are in effect 11 legal laboratories accumulating experience and amending their publication plans on the basis of that experience. Because the possible rewards of such experimentation are so rich, the Conference agreed that it should not be discontinued until there is considerably more experience under the diverse circuit plans.

ADMIN. OFFICE OF U.S. COURTS, REPORT OF THE PROCEEDINGS OF THE JUDICIAL CONFERENCE OF THE UNITED STATES 12 (1974), *available at* http://www.uscourts.gov/uscourts/FederalCourts/judconf/proceedings/1974-03.pdf.

While the Federal Judicial Center and the Judicial Conference of the United States were studying the problem, the powerful blue-ribbon Commission on Revision of the Federal Court Appellate System conducted a separate inquiry. The so-called Hruska Commission[23] was made up of members of Congress, judges, law professors, and lawyers. Its congressional mandate was, first, to study and report on the present division of the United States into the several judicial circuits, and, second, to study and report on the structure and internal procedures of the courts of appeals. As part of the latter endeavor, the Commission considered opinion writing and publication in those courts. The Commission held hearings in 1974 and 1975 and issued its final report in June 1975. Concerning the problem of limited publication, the Commission first recommended that "in every case there be some record, however brief and whatever the form, of the reasoning which impelled the decision."[24] In other words, the disposition had to include some explanation of how the court got to its decision. A majority of the Commission then recommended that the circuits adopt both selective publication and no-citation rules.[25] The Commission as a whole, however, reserved judgment on those issues and left the problem for the Judicial Conference.[26]

The stage was thus set for the circuits to adopt their own procedures, and they promptly did so. Within a few years, every circuit had adopted "Publication Plans," which set forth the criteria for determining which opinions would be published. Although the original plans did not identify the precedential value of unpublished opinions and merely limited citation to them, within a few years, most circuits had also limited their precedential effect.[27]

One of the curious things about unpublished opinions is that although a good bit of attention was paid by the federal judicial establishment to their initial development—an amount that shows their importance to the federal courts—the actual implementation of limited publication was left up to the individual circuits.

23. Named for its Chair, Senator Roman Hruska, the Commission's work is treated in greater detail in chapter 10.

24. COMM'N OF REVISION OF FED. COURT APPELLATE SYS., STRUCTURE AND INTERNAL PROCEDURES: RECOMMENDATIONS FOR CHANGE 50 (1975), *reprinted in* 67 F.R.D. 195, 201 (1976) [hereinafter HRUSKA REPORT].

25. *Id.* at 51, *reprinted at* 201.

26. The Commission concluded:

> We have not attempted to exhaust the range of solutions, or to choose between them. The Judicial Conference of the United States retains a continuing interest in the resolution of these problems; experimentation in the various circuits is continuing; empirical data are being collected; a range of alternatives is being explored. We recognize the Judicial Conference as an appropriate forum and do not believe that it would serve a useful function for the Commission to attempt, by specific recommendation, to foreclose that further study which the problem deserves.

Id. at 52, *reprinted at* 259.

27. Robert J. Martineau, *Restrictions on Publication and Citation of Judicial Opinions: A Reassessment*, 28 U. MICH. J. L. REFORM 119, 121 (1994).

No federal rule has ever addressed the appropriate criteria for the publication of opinions or the precedential value of those not published. Indeed, it was not until the adoption of Federal Rule of Appellate Procedure 32.1 in 2006 that the judicial establishment "for the first time, acknowledged the existence of non-precedential opinions in the national rules."[28] There still is no system-wide rule on the issues of precedent and publication,[29] and no one in a position of authority has ever attempted to explain why.

Although the Judicial Conference hoped the circuits could function as legal laboratories, there is little public evidence of correspondence among the courts about their own experience with limited publication. Moreover, the federal judicial establishment has not examined the issue since the study made in the late 1970s, reported below. In other words, although the several circuits have revised their plans from time to time, they have said little or nothing in those revisions to explain why they believe those changes make sense and what the experience has been in circuits with similar rules.

B. THE FEDERAL JUDICIAL CENTER STUDY

In the late 1970s, the Federal Judicial Center commissioned the authors of this book, based on our previous work in the field, to conduct a study of unreported opinions in the federal circuit courts to find out how the various Publication Plans were working. The study examined nearly one thousand opinions issued by the courts of appeals during the 1978–79 reporting year.[30] We did both a qualitative and quantitative analysis of the opinions. Below is a summary of our results in the latter category:

> We first examined whether the content of the Plans, especially the specificity of the criteria for publication, affected the rate at which opinions went unpublished. We found it likely that Publication Plans with vague standards "enhance[d] the possibility of publication."[31]
>
> Circuits whose Plans contained a presumption against publication published about the same portion of their opinions as did circuits operating under plans that did have such a presumption.[32]

28. Amy E. Sloan, *If You Can't Beat 'Em, Join 'Em: A Pragmatic Approach to Nonprecedential Opinions in the Federal Appellate Courts*, 86 NEB. L. REV. 895 (2008).

29. The American Bar Association recommends that all decisions be published and that citation be freely permitted. Criminal Justice, Torts, Ins. Practice, & Senior Lawyers Div., A.B.A. Report to the House of Delegates, Res. 01A115 (Aug. 1. 2001).

30. The methodology for the study is described in William L. Reynolds & William M. Richman, *An Evaluation of Limited Publication in the United States Courts of Appeals: The Price of Reform*, 48 U. CHI. L. REV. 573, 584–86 (1981) [hereinafter *An Evaluation*].

31. *Id.* at 590.

32. *Id.* at 591, table 4.

> Unpublished opinions were markedly shorter than published ones. Because shorter opinions are presumably easier to write than longer ones, it seemed plausible to infer from that fact that unpublished opinions do save judicial time.
>
> Nevertheless there was no obvious connection between productivity and non-publication rates. In other words, there is no evidence to confirm the intuition that curtailing opinion publication increases judicial productivity.[33]
>
> A significant cost of limited publication was the very low level of quality of the unpublished opinions. In three circuits, at least 59 percent of the unpublished opinions gave "no discernible justification" for the decision, and in two circuits at least 23 percent of the opinions were affirmed simply on the basis of the opinion below. Expressed differently, the percentage of unpublished opinions decided by a reasoned opinion ranged from 13.6 percent to 79.6 percent; the median figure was 57.9 percent.[34]
>
> There was no positive correlation between judicial productivity and the percentage of opinions that failed to meet minimal quality standards. In other words, "the most productive circuits were not the ones that produced the most sub-standard opinions."[35]

The qualitative evaluation of the plans also proved instructive. First, we looked for "suppressed precedent," unpublished opinions that should have been published. The reason for that inquiry was that some of the early commentators on the subject had worried that panels would hide their decisions from scrutiny by not publishing them. Not long after our study, Judge Wald expressed similar concerns about courts hiding certain decisions.[36] In our sample, however, we found "no widespread 'hiding' of law-declaring opinions."[37] We did find, however, some instances where unpublished opinions were used to hide defects in judicial administration, including improper behavior by trial judges,[38] decisions that certainly should have been published under any reasonable criteria.

Our study was completed more than thirty years ago. Amazingly, it remains the only significant study of the Publication Plans and their workings ever done by or for the federal judiciary.[39] That statement needs to be repeated: in the *three decades* since our study was completed, the judicial establishment has not sponsored

33. *Id.* at 597, table 7.

34. The numbers, methodology, and explanations of the terms can be found *id.* at 600–04. One telling but hardly surprising set of data showed how many unpublished opinions were shorter than fifty words. The range among the circuits was from 6.0 percent of unpublished opinions shorter than fifty words to 70.3 percent; the median figure was 42.9 percent. *See id.* at 607, table D. Those data are very disturbing, of course.

35. *Id.* at 606.

36. Patricia M. Wald, *The Problem with the Courts: Black-Robed Bureaucracy or Collegiality under Challenge?* 42 Md. L. Rev. 766 (1984).

37. Reynolds & Richman, *An Evaluation, supra* note 30, at 608.

38. *See* discussion *id.* at 610–11.

39. Nor do we know of a comparable study done by private sources.

a single comprehensive study of limited publication—a critical component of the Appellate Triage system. We can only guess at the reason for such a lacuna. Our findings and those of nearly every other academic commentator failed to confirm the merits of the limited publication strategy, so one obvious possibility is that the judicial establishment failed to conduct additional studies because the results were unlikely to be positive.[40]

C. THE PUBLICATION PLANS TODAY

This section examines the way the Publication Plans work today. First, we look at their content and then at the various publication rates under the plans.

1. Content

When the circuit courts adopted Publication Plans for the first time in the mid-1970s, they adopted variations on the Model Rule that had been promulgated by the Federal Judicial Center. The Model Rule, as noted earlier, provided guidance on criteria for opinion publication and the precedential value of unpublished opinions.[41]

Our early study of limited publication found that the Plans of the individual circuits differed in only three significant components: whether there was a presumption in favor of publication, who decided whether to publish (the majority or a single judge), and the level of specificity in the plan. Even with those differences, the Plans bore a great deal of similarity to one another, a hardly surprising fact given their then recent and common birth. More surprising is that the close family resemblance persists. An examination of the current version of the Plans reveals that similarity, but it also shows that some circuits have made substantial changes to their plans and that, as a result, real differences do exist today among the circuits' Publication Plans.[42] Those differences concern three variables.

40. The effort to eliminate non-citation rules that we discuss in chapter 5 was accompanied by several smaller studies sponsored by the Federal Judicial Center. Those studies provided fodder for critics of both non-citation practices and limited publication generally.

41. The Model Rule is quoted *supra* note 20.

42. The discussion of the contents of the Plans draws heavily on a fine article, David R. Cleveland, *Local Rules in the Wake of Federal Rule of Appellate Procedure 32.1,* 11 J. App. Prac. & Process 19 (2010).

a. What to Publish?

About half of the circuits follow the Model Rule in listing categories of cases where publication should take place. Perhaps, the most expansive is that of the Fifth Circuit, which provides:[43]

> The publication of opinions that merely decide particular cases on the basis of well-settled principles of law imposes needless expense on the public and burdens on the legal profession. However, opinions that may in any way interest persons other than the parties to a case should be published. Therefore, an opinion is published if it:
>
> (a) Establishes a new rule of law, alters, or modifies an existing rule of law, or calls attention to an existing rule of law that appears to have been generally overlooked;
>
> (b) Applies an established rule of law to facts significantly different from those in previous published opinions applying the rule;
>
> (c) Explains, criticizes, or reviews the history of existing decisional or enacted law;
>
> (d) Creates or resolves a conflict of authority either within the circuit or between this circuit and another;
>
> (e) Concerns or discusses a factual or legal issue of significant public interest; or
>
> (f) Is rendered in a case that has been reviewed previously and had its merits addressed by an opinion of the United States Supreme Court.

An opinion may also be published if it:

> Is accompanied by a concurring or dissenting opinion; or reverses the decision below or affirms it upon different grounds.

An enumeration of categories of cases for publication serves the admirable purpose of directing the panel's attention to appropriate considerations in deciding whether to publish.[44] Six circuits, on the other hand, give little or no guidance concerning the decision to publish. It is not clear why these courts have abandoned the Model Rule. It is not the practice of the circuits to explain their preference for one type of plan over another, but we suspect that one reason for deviation from the Model was judicial indifference to the question of publication, perhaps caused by a belief that the judges would do as they wished regardless of the content of the Plans. Bolstering our

43. 5TH CIR. R. 47.5.1.

44. Moreover, there has been a recent surge of interest in other areas, including medicine, in the value of lists as a way of insuring that essential steps have not been omitted. *See, e.g.*, Atul Gawande, *The Checklist: If Something so Simple Can Transform Intensive Care, What Else Can It Do?*, THE NEW YORKER, Dec. 10. 2007, *available at* www.newyorker.com/reporting/2007/12/10/071210fa_fact_gawande.

suspicion is the fact that publication rates for individual judges vary widely, revealing that *individual* judges pay little attention to the "paper rules" contained in the Plans.

Only the First Circuit does things differently. It turns the enumeration of factors on its head. Its list focuses on when an *unpublished* opinion, rather than a published one, may be issued.[45] This rule, as David Cleveland suggests, "is firmly pro-Publication."[46] In that feature, it is unique among the circuits' plans.

b. Precedential Value

The circuits also differ on whether unpublished opinions have any precedential value. Eight circuits follow the Model Rule and expressly deny precedential effect to unpublished opinions. Two circuits (the Fourth and Sixth) take no position on the question, and two more (the Fifth and D.C. Circuits) give precedential effect depending on date of issuance of the opinion. They do so bizarrely, however, because the Fifth Circuit only gives precedential effect to opinions issued *before* 1996, and the D.C. Circuit gives it only to those issued *after* 2001.[47] Of course, there is no explanation offered for this very strange dichotomy.

c. Citations

Before the promulgation of Appellate Procedure Rule 32.1, the circuits diverged on the citation of unpublished opinions. The new rule, which generally forbids prohibiting the citation of unpublished opinions, was adopted to accomplish uniformity.[48] It should come as no surprise that the circuits have differed sharply on how to implement it.

2. Publication Rates

The most significant variation in implementation is the widely differing publication rates of several circuits. Although the composition of the federal appellate caseload differs from circuit to circuit, the wide range of publication rates suggests that something more than the number of federal and state prisoners housed within a circuit's borders influences the decisions on publication.

In this regard, Lauren Robel has made an important point. She first noted that although 58 percent of federal appellate judges believed they had produced

45. 1st Cir. L. R. 36.0. The rule also—uniquely—gives an example of a category of appeals that will typically go unpublished (e.g., certain Social Security cases).
46. Cleveland, *supra* note 40, at 37.
47. *See id.* at 25.
48. We discuss this topic in chapter 5.

published opinions in almost all of those cases where they "should be written," another 30 percent believed they "sometimes" did not write opinions for publication in those cases where they "should be written."[49] That observation led her to conclude that those numbers, when combined with the widely divergent publication rates for circuits and individual judges, suggest that different local norms determine what cases meet the criteria for publication contained in the various appellate courts' plans. This divergence exists despite the striking similarity among the plans themselves and the fact that each contains criteria for predicting which cases are likely to have sufficient lasting value as precedent to justify the additional thought and effort required for a published decision.[50]

Robel's insight that "local norms" explain the difference in publication rates among circuits with similar Publication Plans, suggests that judges are using different criteria to determine whether an appeal is worthy of the Learned Hand treatment. If they were using the same criteria, we would expect a strong convergence among publication rates. The only discrepancies in publication rates would result from either the differences in the types of appeals heard and/or from the weak differences among the Plans. There is no evidence that either is the case, however. The large differences in publication rates, therefore, strongly support Robel's insight.

Robel's insight also squares with the results of our study three decades ago of the effect of Publication Plans on publication rates.[51] Among the findings in that study of nearly one thousand unpublished opinions was that there was at most a weak correlation between a circuit's publication rate and the content of its Publication Plan.[52] In short, the differences among publication rates are explained by factors extraneous to the content of the Plan. The meaning of these findings is clear: despite many protestations to the contrary, either the circuit judges do not consider the potential of an appeal as precedent to be the only consideration in deciding whether to publish the decision, or they do not agree on the meaning of precedent.

49. Lauren Robel, *The Practice of Precedent: Anastasoff, Noncitation Rules, and the Meaning of Precedent in an Interpretive Community*, 35 Ind. L. Rev. 399, 403 (2002). Robel drew her data from the 1990 Report of the Federal Courts' Study Commission.

50. *Id.* at 404 n.52.

51. Reynolds & Richman, *An Evaluation, supra* note 30, at 584–93.

52. *Id.* at 587–93.

CHAPTER 3

The Premises of the Argument for Limited Publication

This chapter examines critically the several premises of the limited publication regime, and the next chapter advances some counter-arguments against that system. In making those arguments, we are reminded of the plight of the litigant who must construct the argument of an unskilled opponent in order to demolish it: Inevitably, the party with more skill will make the argument better than his opponent ever has. Our problem is not that the proponents of limited publication are unskilled—indeed, they are very able,[1] but that no one has set forth a complete case in support of limited publication. Thus, in laying out the case for limited publication, we necessarily make the creation of that system sound more thoughtful and careful than it was. In fact, not much concerted, coherent effort went into the theoretical justification for its creation, and its later defenses have been ad hoc and piecemeal. More surprisingly, there has been no defense of its geometric growth. The paucity of justification is really quite remarkable because the regime represents a fundamental deviation from the common law tradition and a set of high order decisions about the distribution of a scarce resource—the time and attention of the circuit judges.[2]

The studies that led to the implementation of limited publication a half century ago were, as we have discussed, somewhat vague concerning its justification. Basically, the authors of those studies saw a problem—too many appeals—and adopted a solution—limited publication—without giving the problem or its solution much apparent thought. Although academic criticism of limited publication began almost immediately,[3] no judges felt a need to respond. Occasionally, an

1. We know of no academic who supports limited publication enthusiastically. *But see* Carl Tobias, *The New Certiorari and a National Study of the Circuits*, 81 CORNELL L. REV. 1264 (1996) (calling for more study of the issue).

2. It is also astonishing how few defenders of that system there are, defenders willing to attach their names to a system that they must believe contravenes much of what they learned defines a good judge.

3. We published our first article on limited publication in 1978.

attempt at justification would be made in passing, but the judicial establishment largely continued to ignore the problem.

A decade ago, however, two events changed the game. First, the long and bitter debate over proposed Federal Rule of Appellate Procedure 32.1 led to a number of thoughtful commentaries on limited publication.[4] Second, Judge Richard Arnold's constitutional attack on the nonprecedential nature of unpublished opinions along with Judge Alex Kozinski's response[5] prompted thoughtful discussions of many of the issues.

Nonetheless, no one has made a complete case for limited publication since we presented arguments in support of the system when we examined the problem in 1978.[6] In the third of a century since then, defenders of limited publication have apparently abandoned some arguments and advanced others not thought of until recently. Critics of limited publication, in other words, face a constantly moving target: slay one dragon and another emerges.

Moreover, some of the premises of limited publication have *never* been set forth by its defenders, even though they are logically necessary to justify that system. The closest thing to a formal justification for limited publication was made in 1973 in Standards for the Publication of Judicial Opinions, a report by the Committee on Use of Appellate Court Energies.[7] In this chapter we address the policy arguments made by the report and note that they lack supporting data and arguments, leading to the suspicion that they were offered to provide cover for a decision reached on other grounds. Nevertheless, it is helpful here to restate the proffered reasons to make analysis more coherent. What follows, therefore, is our understanding of the several premises that underlie limited publication and our critique of each premise.

A. THE FOUR ASSUMPTIONS THAT SUPPORT LIMITED PUBLICATION

The first assumption supporting limited publication is that substantial judicial time can be saved if not all judicial opinions are published (that is, if they are denied precedential value). Second, the argument goes, very little will be lost; not all appellate opinions need to be published because not all of those opinions have public value. The third and most problematic premise is that those appeals that do not need to be resolved in a published opinion can be identified at an early stage of the proceedings. The final assumption is that full publication is too costly, both for the producers of the opinions (the judicial system) and for their consumers (the

4. Rule 32.1 permits the citation of unpublished opinions. *See infra* chapter 5.

5. Both of those opinions are discussed *infra* chapter 6.

6. *See* William L. Reynolds & William M. Richman, *Non-Precedential Precedent—Limited Publication and Non-Citation Rules in the United States Courts of Appeals*, 78 Colum. L. Rev. 1167(1978).

7. STANDARDS FOR THE PUBLICATION OF JUDICIAL OPINIONS: A Report of the Committee on Use of Appellate Court Energies of the Advisory Council on Appellate Justice (1973).

litigants, the bar, and the public).[8] We begin, however, with a brief digression concerning the law of the circuit doctrine because it determines what is at stake in the precedent/nonprecedent debate. Remarkably, the pervasive doctrine, which is so crucial to the limited publication debate, seems to be taken for granted and has received very little attention in the debate.

B. THE LAW OF THE CIRCUIT

In order to understand fully the context in which unpublished opinions operate, it is necessary to consider the modern-day concept of the law of the circuit. Amy Sloan explains the rule this way:

> In the federal appellate courts, the law of the circuit rule implements the policy of horizontal *stare decisis.* The law of the circuit rule provides that the decision of one panel is the decision of the court and binds all future panels unless and until the decision is reversed or overruled by the Supreme Court or by the appellate court sitting *en banc.* Every circuit follows the law of the circuit rule.[9]

Thus, a panel decision on a new topic binds all future panels of that circuit until the first decision is changed by the Supreme Court or en banc review. The effect is to give "hyper-precedential" effect to the first panel decision.[10]

The law of the circuit doctrine is relatively new in its connection with unpublished opinions;[11] the first mention of the link seems to be a reference by Judge Patricia Wald in a 1986 article.[12] The relation between the two is all too obvious: the law of the circuit rule, combined with a full *precedential effect regime,* would make every decision crucial, and the judges would feel pressure to weigh carefully the wording in everything they write in order to ensure that the case fits nicely within the warp and woof of existing decisional law in the circuit and that the opinion is worthy of hyper-precedential effect. Doing that task properly, the proponents of

8. Until the adoption of Federal Rule of Appellate Procedure 32.1 in 2006, there was a fifth premise: cost savings would be reduced and unfairness would result if opinions could be freely cited. This premise is discussed in chapter 5.

9. Amy E. Sloan, *The Dog that Didn't Bark: Stealth Procedures and the Erosion of Stare Decisis in the Federal Courts of Appeals,* 78 FORD. L. REV. 713 (2009). Each circuit has a formal en banc review process; nine circuits also have an "informal" en banc review. Professor Sloan's article contains an excellent discussion of both types of en banc review.

10. William M. Richman, *Much Ado about the Tip of the Iceberg,* 62 WASH. & LEE. L. REV. 1723, 1726 (2005).

11. Nowhere in the discussions leading to the adoption of the Publication Plans discussed in chapter 2 is there any mention of the law of the circuit rule. That is not surprising because the rule had not yet been developed.

12. Patricia M. Wald, *Changing Course: The Use of Precedent in the District of Columbia Circuit,* 34 CLEV. ST. L. REV. 477, 500–02 (1986).

limited publication argue, takes a good bit of time and skill. It is not a job that can be foisted off on a distant and minimally supervised central staff. Thus, the law of the circuit rule, combined with full precedential publication of all opinions, would force judges to give every appeal something resembling the full Learned Hand treatment, something that cannot be done at current staffing levels. In short, judges lack the time to make sure that all opinions square with existing precedent and are fit to serve as precedent for all future cases.

That is a remarkable argument, for it ignores the most basic duty of a common law court. A judge's duty is *always* to follow precedent, unless she explains why she is not doing so. Otherwise the court violates the central imperative that like cases be treated in like fashion. If the judges lack the time to do the job they have agreed to perform, they should demand the resources they need to do it properly. They have not done so, a failure that we explore in chapter 11.[13]

That failure is bad enough, but there are two additional disturbing possibilities raised by the intersection between unpublished opinions and the law of the circuit rule. First, a panel unhappy with the result called for by an existing precedent can ignore the precedent and reach the result it wants simply by deciding the appeal in an unpublished decision. By doing so, the panel has not overruled a law of the circuit, something that could be done only by an en banc court. At the same time, the panel has managed to achieve the desired result by manipulating the process without doing something about the "bad" law that forced it to be dishonest in the first place. In other words, the panel has used the unpublished opinion route to mask concern over the correctness of circuit precedent. Needless to say, this impedes the growth and development of the law and means that other cases raising the same problem might be decided differently, because the panels in those cases might be more honest and follow the troubling circuit precedent.

The second disturbing possibility involves a panel unsure of the *law* it wants to adopt, but sure of the *result* it wants to reach in the case at hand. That panel can finesse the problem by issuing an unpublished opinion—that is, an opinion that will have no precedential value. Once again, a desired result will have been reached by violating a fundamental precept—cases must not be decided ad hoc, but only under law that will be applied to all similar cases.

Both possibilities raise serious questions about judicial behavior. Among the many virtues of the doctrine of precedent is that it prevents judges from treating similarly situated litigants differently. In turn, that reduces concern about unprincipled judicial behavior and unpredictable outcomes.

Although the regime of limited publication was widely accepted long before the law of the circuit doctrine was adopted (indeed, that doctrine is not even mentioned in the early discussions about limited publication), it has nevertheless become the

13. Specifically, chapter 11, sections A and B detail the process that the judges have used to keep their numbers small.

centerpiece of principled objections to the reform of that system. Later in this book we examine how best to reform the system;[14] for now, the law of the circuit doctrine must be understood as a brooding omnipresence over the debate. We turn now to the premises that support the limited publication of circuit court opinions.

C. FIRST PREMISE: LIMITED PUBLICATION SAVES JUDICIAL RESOURCES

The whole Appellate Triage apparatus revolves around the notion that it conserves the time and energy judges spend deciding cases. In order to resolve those cases, given the caseload volume, however, they must delegate much decision-making responsibility to subordinates. Limiting publication and limiting precedential value are required to ensure the safety of that delegation. In this sense, the system works. The average appeal processing time in 2010 was 11.7 months; in 1980, when the Publication Plans had gone into full operation, the comparable figure was 8.9 months.[15]

The trains do come in on time, however. Elsewhere we discuss the costs that this entails, but it is worth noting three points at the outset. First, those savings can be realized only if the circuit courts make snap decisions about which track an appeal belongs on; the more reflection on that question, the less time will be saved. Second, the time savings for the circuit judges are apparent. But other players in the legal system may find that limited publication significantly *increases* their costs. Finally, the savings in judge-time does not mean the limited publication regime has been cost-free. The delegation of decision making to central staff has led to the creation of a large, expensive bureaucracy. Currently, the circuits employ a total of about five hundred staff attorneys . They must be paid, and they need office space and an administrative hierarchy. They must be interviewed, hired, and supervised. We do not know how expensive this bureaucracy is, but it must run into the many millions of dollars. To our knowledge, no administrator has bothered to do the arithmetic, but it is a substantial sum to offset against any savings realized by limiting publication.

A far more important cost, of course, is not financial. Rather, it is the cost to society of not dealing openly and honestly with the problems caused by caseload glut. Instead, to keep up with the flood, the judicial establishment has perverted the common law's method of deciding cases.

14. *See infra* chapters 11–14.
15. Management Statistics for United States Courts 1980, at 13.

D. SECOND PREMISE: NOT ALL APPELLATE OPINIONS NEED TO BE PUBLISHED

At one time, publication meant that the opinions would be printed in a bound volume labeled "Federal Reporter" and that they would constitute precedent that could be cited to any court as authority. Limited publication changed all that and made most opinions nonprecedential and unciteable. Reaction to the limited publication and non-citation rules took the form of informal publication (ultimately publication in the Appendix of the Federal Reporter) and Rule 32.1, which prohibits citation bans. Thus, assigning opinions to the unpublished category today really means only that the judges have predicted that those opinions will have little value to the public and that they have determined that those opinions will not be treated as precedent.

1. The Two Types of Appellate Decisions

Scholars have long distinguished between two different functions of appellate opinions: declaring the law (that is, they serve as precedents) and resolving disputes. A classic statement of this dichotomy comes from a distinguished jurist, Shirley Hufstedler:[16]

> Appellate courts serve two quite different functions: First, appellate courts review the trial record for error in the particular case. We can call this the review for correctness. Second, appellate courts use the cases before them as vehicles for stating and applying constitutional principles, for authoritatively interpreting statutes, for formulating and expressing policy on legal issues of system-wide concern, for developing the common law, and for supervising each level of the system below them. We can call the second set of tasks the institutional functions—the business of Government.

The decision not to publish represents the judges' determination that the opinion does no more than ensure that the proceedings and result in the court or agency below were correct. An opinion that does no more is a "dispute-settling" opinion because its only function is to review the fairness of what happened below, to see if the lower court's opinion was reached correctly. Other opinions—a small minority it turns out—also do more: they create law in some fashion. These opinions may establish new law, criticize or modify existing law, explain the law better to the

16. Shirley M. Hufstedler, *New Blocks for Old Pyramids: Reshaping the Judicial System*, 44 S. Cal. L. Rev. 901, 910 (1971). *See also* Paul D. Carrington, *Crowded Dockets and the Courts of Appeals: The Threat to the Function of Review and the National Law*, 82 Harv. L. Rev. 542, 550 (1969); Robert Leflar, *Sources of Judge-Made Law*, 24 Okla. L. Rev. 319 (1971).

various judicial constituencies, or otherwise contain material of interest to persons other than the litigants. We can call these "law-declaring" opinions.

This distinction between opinions that correct error and those that make law is critical to the limited publication regime. If an opinion only corrects for error below, there is no need for the rest of the world to see it; it has value *only* to the litigants and to the trial judge, and, as such, it might be styled a "private" opinion. By contrast, an opinion has "public" value and hence needs to be published *only* when it makes law.

There are two concerns about that dichotomy. The first problem is that it is not clear that it is easy or even possible to spot the difference between appeals that call for law declaration and those that require only review for error. In other words, an appeal does not come clearly labeled. How can a court know, therefore, which category an appeal falls under unless it has worked hard on the case before making the classification? But if it does that, how much time will it save by taking the unpublished opinion route? And if much time is spent answering that question, then what has been gained by not publishing the decision? We shall return to this question later in this chapter.

The second problem with the dichotomy between "law-making" and "dispute-settling" opinions is that it assumes the two functions can be separated easily, if they can be separated at all. That assumption reveals a transformation in thinking about the nature of precedent, a transformation that is a basic underpinning of the limited publication regime.

When a court thinks of itself as entitled to concentrate on the law-making aspects of its decision, it is, of course, beginning to think like a legislature.[17] The published opinions of the circuit courts show this all too clearly. Over the last few decades, circuit court opinions have become more complex and more focused on the law rather than on the decision itself. Joan Shaughnessy has observed that part of the problem courts face today is that they have undertaken an "immense burden" in examining "every possible nuance" of their decision; opinion writing has become, as a result, a far more demanding occupation than it was a generation ago.[18] She notes that a few years ago then Judge Samuel Alito found the typical opinion of the 1960s was "much shorter and less complex than those published by the Third Circuit today."[19] Similarly, Peter Tiersma has described the change in recent years from a "case-law" system, where the facts and outcome are the focus of the analysis, to an "opinion law" process which centers on "a careful scrutiny of the words written in the opinion."[20] Finally, Steven Cappalli has likened the contemporary appellate opinion to a law review article that seeks to generate rules rather than elucidate

17. *See* Joan M. Shaughnessy, *Unpublication and the Judicial Concept of Audience*, 62 WASH. & LEE L. REV. 1597, 1601 (2005).

18. *Id.*

19. *Id.* at 1603.

20. Peter M. Tiersma, *The Textualization of Precedent*, 82 NOTRE DAME L. REV. 1189 (2007).

the principles required for the decision.[21] Cappalli believes there is a direct linkage between the change in appellate opinion writing styles and the increase in unpublished opinions.[22]

The implication for the limited publication regime is this: Opinion writing has become a more difficult task because today's judge must weigh each word carefully. She is not merely setting forth basic principles and showing how they work in the context of a set of facts. Instead, she is setting forth a rule that reads much like a statute, and, as a result, the judge must be very careful in her choice of words. This takes time to accomplish. Thus, as the burden of writing each published opinion has increased, there has been corresponding pressure to publish fewer opinions. Part of the pressure to maintain the limited publication regime, therefore, can be traced to the collective felt need of the judiciary to become more of a law-making, rather than a dispute-resolving body.[23] More generally, the institution of unpublished opinions has accompanied the judicial evolution from Learned Hand to Alex Kozinski—the progression, in other words, from judge to scholar.

2. Error-Correcting Opinions Can Be Short

There is an important corollary to the premise that some opinions only correct for error and, therefore, have no public value. This corollary is that dispute-settling opinions can be short. The argument is simple to state: an opinion that has only private value—that is, an opinion of concern only to the litigants, their counsel, and the tribunals below—need not contain a full recitation of the facts, arguments, or the application of the law to the truncated statement of facts. That recitation is unnecessary because the parties, counsel, and lower tribunals know the relevant facts, arguments, and law. All that is needed in the opinion is some explanation of why one side has prevailed. And because the court does not have to worry about carefully fitting the decision within the existing body of law, that explanation does not have to be elaborate.

This line of reasoning leads to an all-too-inevitable slippery slope. If full development of the facts and law is not needed in the opinion, what is the minimum description and explanation a court can get away with? How little can the judges

21. Richard D. Cappalli, *The Common Law Case against Non-Precedential Opinions*, 76 S. Cal. L. Rev. 755 (2002).

22. *Id.*

23. Although we do not pursue this topic here, it would be a fertile field of study for someone. We also note that more complex opinions might have something to do with the increase in the number of highly qualified law clerks. They are hard-working and ambitious and often have been trained as academics in graduate schools; surely they are looking for outlets for their intellectual energy and training, an outlook that is unlikely to rejoice in the handling of the more mundane cases.

provide the litigants (and the public) and still satisfy their own consciences? As we shall see, the answers to those questions can be quite perturbing.

In any event, not all unpublished opinions are short and sweet. Some commentators have written about unpublished opinions containing long discussions of the law, replete with multiple citations, which look very much like opinions that should have been published. Although we found such opinions—sometimes referred to as "suppressed precedent"—to be relatively rare in our Federal Judicial Center Study of three decades ago,[24] a more recent scholar has found many lengthy and contentious opinions in the pages of the Federal Appendix.[25]

More disturbing is the fact that unpublished opinions, even if short and lacking in any substance, can still be controversial or reflect an inherent bias.[26] In an intriguing study done twenty years ago, three scholars tested a set of unpublished opinions to see whether a judge's political affiliation affected publication rates.[27] It did. The authors found statistical significance in the difference in publication rates of Democratic and Republican judges involving opinions reaching "liberal" results.[28] This finding of "implicit bias" in making the decision whether to publish led the authors to conclude that many unpublished opinions appear in cases in which judges perceived themselves as having significant discretion, and as a result were free to decide the case in accordance with their personal values. The data suggest that a number of the unpublished cases may have been decided differently if heard by a different panel of judges.[29]

3. The Lesson of Reversals

An easy test case for determining whether an opinion should be published is whether it reverses or otherwise substantially modifies the result in the trial court. After all, a reversal means the circuit court has found significant error in what happened below, and all of the circuit Publication Plans provide for publication of opinions when it would be in the public interest. It would seem that any opinion that reverses the tribunal below is, by definition, in the public interest.

24. *See* William L. Reynolds & William M. Richman, *An Evaluation of Limited Publication in the United States Courts of Appeals: The Price of Reform*, 48 U. Chi. L. Rev. 573, 606–10 (1981) [hereinafter *An Evaluation*].

25. Brian P. Brooks, *Publishing Unpublished Opinions: A Review of the Federal Appendix*, 5 The Green Bag 259 (2002).

26. For early studies noting inconsistencies in unpublished opinions, see William L. Reynolds & William M. Richman, *Limited Publication in the Fourth and Sixth Circuits*, 1979 Duke L.J. 807, 809 n.13.

27. Donald R. Songer, Danna Smith & Reginald S. Sheehan, *Non-Publication in the Eleventh Circuit: An Empirical Analysis*, 16 Fla. St. U. L. Rev. 963 (1989).

28. *Id.* at 983. Curiously, Republican judges were more likely to publish their liberal decisions, an apparent anomaly that the researchers did not attempt to explain. *Id.*

29. *Id.* at 984.

There are several reasons for this thinking. First, if the lower court was so wrong that its error needs no explanation, it is quite possible other courts will tread the same erroneous path. Trial judges in the federal system are not chumps. If they make a mistake so basic that it needs no serious explanation, then something very fundamental is wrong. The basic error committed by the trial court is surely a signal, in other words, that the law needs to be clarified publicly, even if the reviewing court thinks otherwise. Thus, formal publication of the reversal would call attention to the correct state of the law.

Second, reversals in seemingly routine cases may reflect battles within the judiciary over the correct legal standard to be applied. If neither the lower nor the appellate court publishes an opinion about the problem, the dispute may go unnoticed for a long time. Again, publication is needed so that the problem gets noticed.

Third, by calling the attention of the whole world to the reversal, the published opinion helps keep the trial judges on their toes. No one likes to be told in public that he is wrong, and the threat of public rebuke is, therefore, a very important disciplinary tool (as anyone who has ever clerked for a trial judge knows all too well). Because the first part of an appellate court's job is to supervise the trial courts, one would expect that the panel would recognize the virtues of public correction and that more reversals would be published.

When all of these reasons are considered together, the case for publishing virtually all reversals seems very strong.[30] Such has not been the case, however. In our study of the problem conducted thirty years ago for the Federal Judicial Center, we found that 14 percent of the unpublished opinions we reviewed had reversed the court below.[31] That significant numbers of reversals go unpublished suggests once again that the nonpublication game is one the judges play without following their own rules.

Further confirmation that the judges do not follow the rules they set up can be found in observations from two veteran circuit judges. Judge Patricia Wald has written that: "Due to the pressure of accelerating caseloads, the majority of federal cases now get this unpublished treatment. Many would have been the subject of full-fledged opinions a few decades ago."[32] Judge Harry Edwards made a similar observation more than twenty-five years ago that circuit courts were deciding a significant number of cases without opinions even though those cases would have been decided by a published opinion two decades earlier.[33]

30. A few reversals might not need to be published; an example would be an intervening change in statutory law. *See* Reynolds & Richman, *An Evaluation*, *supra* note 24, at 519–20.

31. *Id.* at 617, table 13.

32. Patricia M. Wald, *The Rhetoric of Results and the Results of Rhetoric: Judicial Writings*, 62 U. Chi. L. Rev. 1371, 1373 (1995), *cited in* William M. Richman & William L. Reynolds, *Elitism, Expediency, and the New Certiorari: Requiem for the Learned Hand Tradition*, 81 Cornell L. Rev. 273, 284 (1996).

33. Harry T. Edwards, *The Rising Work Load and Perceived "Bureaucracy" of the Federal Courts: A Causation-Based Approach to the Search for Appropriate Remedies*, 68 Iowa L. Rev. 871, 895 (1983).

4. Facts Matter

Another problem with the premise that appeals that do not need the Learned Hand treatment can be readily identified is it assumes there is no public value in seeing how an appellate court handles the fact-application question. That is, even though the court may be applying well-settled law, the application of that law to different fact situations by an appellate court can be helpful to lower courts, litigants, and advisors.

David Cleveland uses the area of qualified sovereign immunity to illustrate this point.[34] The law of qualified immunity, he contends, is well settled; we know this because many immunity cases are resolved by unpublished opinions—which, by definition, involve settled law. Because immunity law turns on whether certain constitutional rights were established at the time of the alleged offense, the case law must provide government employees with clear guidance.This, of course, is what can be found in the unpublished opinions dealing with qualified immunity, where the appellate court applies settled law to claims based on different facts. Unfortunately, those unpublished opinions cannot be used to provide guidance because they are not precedential. "[D]rawing only from the relatively small number of published decisions means that the contours of the rights and government officials' knowledge of the lawfulness of their conduct is less clear. Fewer cases yield fewer applications of the law, which means a greater level of abstraction and lesser certainty about the scope of constitutional rights."[35]

Qualified immunity is not the only area where appellate guidance is needed to settle recurring questions of law application. Immigration law surely provides another example.[36] Although the basics of immigration law are well settled, they must be applied in countless different fact settings. Lower courts and litigants surely would benefit from seeing how those application questions are decided on appeal.

The need for more published opinions—that is, for more *law* in areas such as qualified immunity and immigration—shows that it is not enough for a circuit court to decide that an opinion should not be published simply because it does not make new law. The court must also realize that litigants and trial judges need guidance on law application questions.

Judge Danny Boggs and Brian Brooks have written about the need to have case law showing how a general rule is fleshed out in subsequent fact-specific cases.[37]

34. David R. Cleveland, *How the Uncertain Precedential Status of Unpublished Opinions Muddles Qualified Immunity Determinations*, 65 U. MIAMI L. REV. 45. (2010).

35. *Id.* at 76.

36. *See, e.g.*, Lauren Robel, *The Myth of the Disposable Opinion*, 87 MICH. L. REV. 940 (1989); Shruti Rana, *"Streamlining" the Rule of Law: How the Department of Justice is Undermining Judicial Review of Agency Action*, 2009 U. ILL. L. REV. 829 (2009).

37. Danny J. Boggs & Brian P. Brooks, *Unpublished Opinions*, 4 THE GREEN BAG 17, 20 (2000).

They illustrate this need using a series of cases involving nursing homes in the Sixth Circuit where a broad statement had to be applied in different contexts.

> [T]he evolution of the law—meaning not only the general rule stated in the first case, but *the degree of additional detail required to breathe life into the general rule*—frequently depend on the willingness of the court to publish additional decisions in later cases that differ from the first only in their facts .... The moral of this story is that highly general statements of legal rules often are insufficient by themselves to ensure consistent results in future cases.[38]

Any good first-year law student could have given the same answer. The common law depends on facts—and multiple fact patterns—not just recitations of doctrine to be understood. Limited publication deprives us of those patterns.

5. The Cumulative Effect of Precedent

Each decision tells us something about the law. The totality or weight of the case law also tells us something. Many cases in an area suggest the problem might need to be revisited, that the solutions judges and legislators have attempted might not be working. On the other hand, the plethora of decisions might simply reflect the fact that although the law is clear, there are a lot of disputes in the area. Unfortunately, the poor quality of so many unpublished opinions does not help anyone—academics, litigants, or the judges themselves—distinguish between those two possibilities.

It is easier to overrule a decision that has been followed only once than one that has been followed a thousand times. Thus, the number of decisions on a single point also helps determine how easy it is to change the case law in an area. Again, the disdain for close legal analysis (or any at all) in unpublished opinions makes it much harder to determine just how much opinion has hardened on a particular point.

In addition to cumulative *weight*, each judicial analysis of a precedent tells us a bit more (or a lot more) about what that earlier decision means. Karl Llewellyn taught us that we cannot know the meaning of a precedent until it has been commented upon by later judges.[39] Those later comments can help us learn about problems with existing law that might lead to its modification, reworking, or even overruling. It is also useful to learn that there are no problems and that the law in an area is working well. Limited publication, however, denies us most of those comments and thus hampers our more complete understanding of the meaning of precedents.

38. *Id.* (emphasis added).
39. Karl Llewellyn, The Bramble Bush 68–69 (4th prtg. 1973).

E. THIRD PREMISE: EARLY IDENTIFICATION OF OPINIONS THAT NEED NOT BE PUBLISHED IS POSSIBLE

The limited publication regime was designed to save judicial time and effort. In order to maximize those savings, it is necessary that the courts be able to identify at a very early stage in the proceedings which appeals will receive truncated treatment. The reasons for this should be easy to see. Little time would be saved if every appeal was argued before a panel of three judges and an opinion written before the decision not to publish was made. In other words, the earlier in the appellate process the opinion can be shifted to the nonpublication track, the more judicial time will be saved. The challenge, therefore, is to develop procedures that perform that task. The judicial establishment has met that challenge only by the adoption of a highly questionable expedient.

The most important development in the push for processing efficiency has been the hiring by the circuit courts of a large number of screeners/decision makers who do their work under the title of "central staff." This development has been critical. In most circuits, appeals are initially channeled through the central staff.[40] They make recommendations concerning how to handle the case—the big decision is whether the court should hear oral argument. That decision, almost always made with only token judicial input, is crucial; an appeal that has not been argued will be shunted on to Track Two and follow truncated decision-making procedures. The decisions in those cases will not be written by the judges or their personal clerks, will not be given precedential status, will not see the pages of the Federal Reporter, and will rarely receive significant attention from either the judge or anyone in her chambers.

It is important to remember that the key decision—the decision not to hear oral argument—is made not by the judges following careful consideration of the briefs and the record but rather by the central staff following *its own truncated review* of the relevant materials. From that recommendation all else flows. Although there is an overlay of judicial involvement in that decision, the numbers clearly show that judges' participation in the triage is a mere token and cannot be taken seriously. The net effect, therefore, is that staff makes most, if not all, of the crucial decisions in most appeals. Thus, effective judicial involvement only occurs *after* the staff releases the case to the judges. That raises a number of questions.

1. How Effective is the Screening?

The first question is: How effective is the screening? In other words, even if we accept the basic premise that most appeals can be properly decided by a truncated

40. The use of central staff and the implications of doing so are discussed in more detail *infra* chapter 8.

process, the regime still depends upon an accurate screening process. It is, of course, impossible to know how well the judges and staff perform that screening task. A more fundamental concern centers on the fact that the circuit courts have been reluctant to reveal anything about screening. How are staff hired? How are they trained, evaluated, promoted, fired? What standards control their recommendations? And so on. We simply lack the data needed to answer these questions. And until the data become available and until there is transparency, we simply cannot analyze the screening process directly. Worse, important questions about persons making important decisions are hidden from public view.

We do know that the system is not perfect. There are certainly a number, a nontrivial number, of unpublished opinions that should have been published. As Judge Danny Boggs and Brian Brooks have written, the unpublished opinion regime assumes that the "easy" cases—those clearly controlled by precedent—can be readily identified, an assumption that is wrong in both fact and theory.[41]

a. Wrong in Fact

There may well be "easy" cases, but that does not mean the courts will always identify them correctly. The Supreme Court, for example, sometimes reverses unpublished decisions, thereby confirming that the circuit court's belief that the case was "easy" was also wrong. The best-known example is *United States v. Edge Broadcasting Company*.[42] There, the Supreme Court reversed an unpublished opinion of the Fourth Circuit that had held a federal statute unconstitutional. Justice White used harsh language to criticize that procedure: "We deem it remarkable and unusual that although the Court of Appeals affirmed a judgment that an Act of Congress was unconstitutional as applied, the court found it appropriate to announce its judgment in an unpublished *per curiam* opinion."[43]

More telling, perhaps is the fact that many commentators have identified cases that on the face of the opinion reveal they involve the public interest, create new law, or otherwise satisfy the criteria for publication set forth by the circuits in their Publication Plans. Unpublished opinions with dissents or concurrences also fall into this category.[44] Judge Wald provides one spectacular insight when she referred to a 1983 study conducted by the District of Columbia Circuit which "concluded that 40 percent of the [unpublished] decisions arguably should have been published under the court's governing criteria."[45] That is a very disturbing statistic. Of course,

41. Boggs & Brooks, *supra* note 37, at 20–21.
42. 509 U.S. 418 (1993).
43. *Id.* at 425 n.3.
44. See Reynolds & Richman, *An Evaluation*, *supra* note 24, at 606–21 for more discussion and examples.
45. *Nat'l Classification Comm'n v. United States*, 974 2d 164, 173 (D.C. Cir. 1985) (Wald, J., concurring).

we cannot know how many decisions fall within the "should have been published" category because the reasoning and factual development in most unpublished opinions is too sketchy to know whether there was enough meat in the appeal to justify a decision to publish.[46]

Other examples abound. In our Federal Judicial Center Study, we identified a number of other unpublished opinions we believe should have been published.[47] In the next chapter, we explore in detail a case whose minimal disposition belied the very strong case for its publication.[48]

b. Wrong in Theory

The early diversion to the nonpublication track assumes that the person sorting opinions can identify at an early stage which cases require the full Learned Hand treatment. In reality, it cannot be known what the precedential possibilities of a decision are until a serious attempt has been made to write the opinion.[49]

2. The Lesson from the War over Citation of Unpublished Opinions

Even before Rule 32.1 was adopted, it was clear to any serious reader of the Federal Reporter that there were many references in its pages to unpublished opinions. Lauren Robel has observed that "many district judges regularly read *all* of the unpublished opinions from circuit courts."[50] Amy Sloan has estimated that, between the beginning of the Federal Appendix series (where unpublished opinions are "published") in 2001 through August of 2007, there were *17,000* citations to unpublished opinions.[51] That's quite a lot of references—and they could not have all been about preclusion (the circuit Plans' major exception to prohibition on citation). It is clear the judges themselves find something interesting in unpublished opinions. What is fascinating about Sloan's research is her finding that very few of those opinions contain a discussion of the precedential status of unpublished opinions.[52] That failure is striking, of course, because the circuits generally deny precedential

46. Most opinions make little effort to respond to all issues raised by the litigants. In order for an outsider to know whether the case presented material that might have led to a publishable decision, therefore, the critic would have to read all of the material available to the judges. That would be a Herculean task, indeed.

47. *See* Reynolds & Richman, *An Evaluation*, *supra* note 24.

48. *See infra* chapter 4.

49. *See infra* chapter 4.

50. Lauren Robel, *The Practice of Precedent: Anastasoff, Noncitation Rules, and the Meaning of Precedent in an Interpretive Community*, 35 IND. L. REV. 399, 407 (2002) (emphasis in original).

51. Amy E. Sloan, *If You Can't Beat 'Em, Join 'Em: A Pragmatic Approach to Nonprecedential Opinions in the Federal Appellate Courts*, 86 NEB. L. REV. 895, 932–33 (2008).

52. *Id.* at 924–25.

status to unpublished opinions. Thus, a panel's citation of an unpublished opinion without at least some discussion of its precedential status is quite odd, yet Sloan finds it routine. The lesson, of course, is that judges, like lawyers, find solace where they can. And because Professor Sloan found little evidence of criticism of the cited unpublished opinions,[53] it is clear that they are generally being used by judges to support their decisions—as precedent, in other words.

a. Wrong in Theory

The notion that reliance on staff (or even judges) to predict which cases are "easy" suffers from theoretical difficulties, as well. Judge Danny Boggs and Brian Brooks point out that "individual panels of judges are only imperfectly able to predict the future events and disputes that will influence the development of the law."[54] We can never know what judges might have done with the case if they had invested some of their own time in an effort to learn what was going on in it.[55]

Everyone knows what it is like to have a change of mind about a problem after working on a solution for a while; there surely is no reason to think that judges are any different. That is why the literature on judging is full of admonitions about how opinions simply "will not write" or about how argument changed the minds of the judges. As Judge Posner wrote: "reasoning that seemed sound 'in the head' may seem half-baked when written down .... Many writers have the experience of not knowing except in a general sense what they are going to write until they start writing. A link is somehow formed between the unconscious and the pen. The link is lost to the judge who does not write."[56] Thus, it certainly seems realistic to expect that some of the appeals shunted off to Track Two would have turned out differently if they had received the Learned Hand treatment.

Of course, we cannot know how extensive the effect is—that is, we do not know how many appeals would have been resolved differently if they had been given full judicial attention. One way to attack the problem might be to examine judicial estimates of how much of their caseload is routine. Judge Harry Edwards, for example, recently estimated that about half of the cases he hears are "easy ... [and] the pertinent legal rules seem unambiguous and their application to the facts

53. *Id.*

54. Boggs & Brooks, *supra* note 37, at 21.

55. The problem is not that the staff who write the opinions are incompetent; rather, the judge brings a different set of experiences and knowledge to the problem.

56. Richard A. Posner, *Judges' Writing Styles (And Do They Matter?)*, 62 U. CHI. L REV. 1421, 1447–48 (1995). *See also* Alvin B. Rubin, Book Review, 130 U. PA. L. REV. 220, 227 (1981) ("We read the briefs, we study the record, we decide that we will affirm or reverse, and we undertake to prepare an opinion stating the decision and its rationale. We find that 'it won't write'—our jargon for saying that we cannot prepare an opinion reaching the desired result in acceptable professional form.").

appears clear."[57] In Judge Edwards's formulation, a case is not easy if either the law is ambiguous or a particular law-application problem is not clear. Thus, it seems fair to take the label "easy cases" as a surrogate for cases that should not be published; the appeal, in other words, is not "easy" if it is either ambiguous or unclear. In either situation, it would appear that the appeal would benefit from oral argument, serious consideration from a judge, and publication of the resolution so others could learn from the precedent. In fact, however, fewer than 20 percent of all opinions are published, suggesting that perhaps another 30 percent of all opinions should have been published but were not.

b. Inconsistency in Publication Decisions

Implicit in the assumptions about limited publication is that the judges (and staff) will follow the criteria for publication set forth in the various Publication Plans. There is ample evidence that they do not do so. First, the Plans are hardly models of clarity and coherence. As David Cleveland's recent summary of the Plans makes clear, there is a wide variety in content among them.[58] That suggests the courts lack a common culture concerning the proper criteria for "publication."

On the other hand, it is not clear that consistency in content would achieve consistent results for there seems to be at best a weak link between a circuit's publication rate and the content of its Publication Plan.[59] Moreover, the disparity in the several circuits' publication rates is so great that it seems clear that the courts (and surely individual judges as well as members of the central staff) have widely divergent views of what constitutes a Track Two case.[60]

F. PREMISE FOUR: FULL PUBLICATION IMPOSES EXCESSIVE COSTS ON LAW'S CONSUMERS

Perhaps the most prominent justification offered in support of unpublished opinions until fairly recently was that it saved time, effort, and money for everyone in the legal system. The cost argument had a number of permutations. Unfortunately, for proponents of the practice of limited publication, technology has seriously eroded although not eliminated those arguments.

57. Harry T. Edwards & Michael A. Livermore, *Pitfalls of Empirical Studies That Attempt to Understand the Factors Affecting Appellate Decision-Making*, 58 Duke L.J. 1895, 1898 (2009).

58. David Cleveland, *supra* note 34, at 53–76.

59. *See* Reynolds & Richman, *An Evaluation*, *supra* note 24, at 587–93.

60. In 2010, the circuit publication rates ranged from 40 percent for the Seventh Circuit to 7 percent for the Fourth Circuit. Admin. Office of U.S. Courts, Judicial Business of the United States Courts: 2010 Annual Report of the Director 46, table S-3 (2010), *available at* http://www.uscourts.gov/uscourts/Statistics/JudicialBusiness/2010/JudicialBusinespdfversion.pdf.

1. Books and Libraries Cost Money

Before the days of the computer and the Internet, it was argued—sometimes strenuously—that serious savings were realized by limiting publication and prohibiting citation of unpublished opinions. Those savings were realized in two areas: fewer opinions meant fewer expensive books had to be bought and stored, and fewer decisions had to be analyzed by lawyers and judges.[61]

There was something to the first of those arguments. Books are expensive, and their storage in libraries and law offices is even more costly. If citation of unpublished opinions was permitted, attorneys would demand access to the opinions so they would be able to monitor legal developments in the circuits; it would be malpractice, of course, not to monitor developments that could be used to advance or undermine a client's case. That demand would ensure that the opinions appeared in print somewhere. Even if the federal courts did not submit their opinions to the Federal Reporter, private reporters would fill the gap.[62] Thus, cost savings related to the purchase and storage of books could be fully realized only by a rule forbidding citation.

Moreover, it was argued that prohibition of citation was needed to prevent unfairness. If unpublished opinions could be cited, wealthy litigants and the government would benefit inordinately; they would collect and maintain their own files of unpublished opinions and use that knowledge to gain an advantage over less wealthy litigants. In addition, wealthy and repeat litigants could manipulate to some extent the publication *vel non* of certain opinions.[63]

Modern technology has seriously eroded, but not eliminated, these arguments. Because all opinions are now available online, storage costs approach zero. Unfortunately, that is not true for access costs. Although all opinions are available (in theory, at least)[64] for free on the official websites of the courts,[65] it is not easy

61. The published/nonpublished dichotomy perhaps has never been rigorously followed in practice. In a study of unpublished opinions we did for the Federal Judicial Center in the late 1970s, we found a number of instances where supposedly unpublished opinions had made their way into the pages of the Federal Reporter. *See* Reynolds & Richman, *An Evaluation*, *supra* note 24, at 582 n.30.

62. The issue is discussed in William L. Reynolds & William M. Richman, *The Non-Precedential Precedent—Limited Publication and Non-Citation Rules in the United States Courts of Appeals*, 78 Colum. L. Rev. 1167, 1186–87 (1978). There are (and were) specialized reporters dealing with subjects ranging from antitrust to tax that regularly report on developments in their fields, including what happened in the world of unpublished opinions.

63. *See* Lauren Robel, *The Myth of the Disposable Opinion*, 85 Mich. L. Rev. 940 (1989) (demonstrating how government attorneys and other repeat players can manipulate the publication process through their access to unpublished opinions).

64. We say "in theory" because finding unpublished opinions online can be somewhat difficult.

65. Some states, such as Maryland, do not make unpublished opinions available in digital form. This can cause enormous difficulties for anyone—lay or attorney—who wishes to find

to run sophisticated searches on those websites. Specialized search engines such as those maintained by Lexis/Nexis and Westlaw are needed to do serious legal research.[66] Those services, of course, cost money and may not be available to the pro se litigant or one with scant resources.[67] The inability to research properly thus could be a serious handicap for those litigants.[68] Nevertheless, the enormous reduction in costs associated with digital opinions means that the cost argument has little merit today.

Digital access to all opinions levels the playing field considerably. It is much more difficult to contend that giving precedential status to all opinions would severely impair the ability of less wealthy litigants to compete. Now resources do not limit a party's *access* to the law, although the amount of resources available can affect the effectiveness of that access. The law has never been a fully level playing field, of course, but equal access to all opinions certainly helps.

Of equal importance, perhaps, giving precedential status to all opinions would mean that more law is available to everyone. The common law, after all, is based on factual analogy; the more fact patterns that can be identified as relevant to a decision, the easier it will be to find precedent.[69] This is particularly important for litigants who lack the ability to conduct sophisticated research; their search will likely focus on factual analogies, so the more cases that are available, the more likely it is a good factual analogy can be found. In other words, although search costs might rise when there are more opinions to sort through, the ability to find law on point would increase. The ability to do so should reduce total research costs because the presence of relevant law makes it easier to predict outcomes. Thus, the presence of more precedent should mean lower costs for everyone.

Finally, we have seen how unpublished opinions are more common in disfavored areas of the law such as immigration and prisoner complaints.[70] Litigants in those areas would benefit the most, therefore, if all opinions were to be precedential.

2. Judges Are Also Consumers

It has always been difficult to take seriously the arguments that judges were interested in saving money for the other players in the legal system. The real cost savings

out what eventually happened in an appeal. *See* Melissa Harris, Closeup, *Keeping it Quiet*, BALTIMORE SUN, Mar. 22, 2009, at 1.

66. Not every unpublished opinion is available on both databases, making research unnecessarily difficult.

67. Of course, research is expensive even to those who have money, and wealthy litigants also will be unhappy with high bills, as anyone who has ever practiced law knows.

68. It is possible, of course, that technological advances will reduce the difficulty of searching opinions online.

69. This point is well developed in Cappalli, *supra* note 21, at 774–84.

70. *See supra* text accompanying note 36.

they envisioned involved themselves. The argument supporting this effort has two parts. The first part is simple: if unpublished opinions can be cited by litigants, then someone responsible has to read them—at least if the judicial job is to be done properly. This cannot be taken too seriously; after all, the judges have mastered the art of outsourcing. Someone will read the cited unpublished opinions, but that person is unlikely to be the judge. It is far more likely the task will be done by law clerks or central staff; judges will not spend time reading opinions they know all too well say nothing at all. To be sure, there are some administrative costs associated with supervising the staffers, but those costs seem to be *de minimis.*

The more sophisticated form of the argument states that if unpublished opinions can be cited, then judges will be forced to spend more time writing them. We might call this the "monster in the closet" argument. It asserts an opinion that can be cited—even if it lacks formal precedential value—inherently tends to be treated as something like a precedent. After all, it will be embarrassing if the court does not deal with contrary decisions, even if they are not "law." Thus judges will have to be more careful in the way they write unpublished opinions and will have to spend more time on developing the facts and the law; ultimately, they will have to work harder to reconcile the result with other decisions in the area. The net effect, of course, is that the time savings sought to be realized by the unpublished opinion regime will be swallowed up by the need to make opinions more presentable. The argument has some force. As we will show in chapter 5, a number of judges expressed those fears in their opposition to a proposal to eliminate the no-citation rule.

There are three problems with that argument, however. The first difficulty is that many unpublished opinions are so lacking in quality that concern over their use as authority is unnecessary. To put it more crudely, the less meat there is in an opinion the less likely anyone else will ever pay attention to it. Of course, this results in a paradox because it creates a powerful incentive to write opinions that provide little or no guidance as to facts, law, reasoning, or anything else—a description that covers the vast majority of unpublished opinions in existence.

The second problem with the monster in the closet argument is that fears about workload are not justified. As we shall show in chapter 5, judges in circuits that permit citation to unpublished opinions state that the practice has had little or no effect on their workload. This is true even in those circuits that had very recently eased up on their ban on citations to unpublished opinions. Judges who dislike citation should be well aware of this fact. Nevertheless, just as the irrational child worries about what's in the closet, the judges worry about the unknown. Thus, the judges fear the extra work that would be created just as little children fear the monster in the closet.

A third response is quite different from the first two. Output efficiency is not the only goal of the federal judiciary. Justice, development of the law, and accountability are also goals of the system. We believe that those goals would be better served by better opinions written through better decision-making processes. Thus, we hope that the end of the citation ban might lead to opinions that a judge would be proud to sign. Alas, that has not happened—at least not yet.

CHAPTER 4
The Counter-Arguments

Even if the validity of the premises underlying the limited publication regime could be accepted, that regime still must survive powerful counter-arguments. There are four such arguments. First, limited publication reduces judicial accountability; second, it lessens judicial responsibility; third, limited publication fundamentally changes the manner in which our decisional law operates; and finally, the burden of limited publication falls most heavily on the poor and disfavored in our society.

A. JUDICIAL ACCOUNTABILITY

Limited publication severely reduces judicial accountability in several important ways. First, an unpublished opinion is rarely signed; apparently, no member of the panel is willing to take individual responsibility for what he (or the staff) has produced. Second, unpublished opinions do not satisfy the basic demands of legal process, for their general quality ranges from merely passable to abysmal. Third, unpublished opinions reduce the possibility that anyone will ever exercise critical review of the decision.

1. *Per Curiam* Decisions

Unpublished opinions are rarely, if ever, signed by an individual judge. Instead, they are issued "*per curiam*," that is, as the opinion "of the court." Although this aspect of unpublished opinions is rarely commented upon, the failure of any of the judges on the panel to take public responsibility for the decision by signing it is one of their most troubling aspects. After all, it has been the practice of American courts since the days of Chief Justice Marshall for an opinion to be *signed* by the judge who wrote it. Thus, virtually every decision of the Supreme Court bears the name of its author and for good reason.[1] By signing the opinion, the author places his reputation on the line. His signature tells the world who is to blame if anything is wrong with the opinion as well as who to praise for whatever good might be in it.[2]

The judicial decision-making process is opaque at best; that is why we demand a reasoned explanation from a court, in order to reassure us that the judges could reach the result through proper decision-making techniques. The fact that an opinion is signed makes it more likely that a judge will wish to protect her reputation by writing one that is cogent and credible. In this way, signing the opinion enhances public confidence in the judiciary.

In a *per curiam* opinion, by contrast, responsibility is necessarily diffused among the members of the panel, and imposing accountability on individual judges becomes more difficult. Because no one knows who Judge *Per Curiam* really is,[3] the shield of anonymity reduces accountability. And there can be little doubt that the American system of jurisprudence believes strongly that reduced accountability often leads to bad decisions.

A four-judge dissent in a Fourth Circuit en banc opinion makes clear that the judges know full well how sloppy they can be in their unpublished opinions. The issue in *Wilson v. Layne*[4] was whether an unpublished opinion could be used to show that a proposition of law had been clearly established for purposes of invoking the doctrine of qualified immunity. The court conceded that although unpublished opinions would be especially useful in establishing the state of the law—after all, they are *supposed* to be used when the law is settled, "it is well known that judges may put considerably less effort into opinions that they do not intend to publish. Because these opinions will not be binding precedent in any court, a judge may be less careful about his legal analysis, *especially when dealing with a novel question of law.*"[5] As David Cleveland observes, this quote starkly reveals that four judges "believed that unpublished opinions were being used to deal with novel issues of law and perhaps carelessly so."[6]

Public accountability through the signed opinion also helps reassure the rest of us that the judges have behaved in accordance with the best standards of judicial

1. The major exceptions in the Supreme Court to this rule are petitions for *certiorari*, which are dismissed for having been improvidently granted, and remands for reconsideration in light of a recent opinion in another case.

2. John Dawson, The Oracles of the Law 406–11 (1986), makes a telling comparison of signed American opinions with the *per curiam* decisions that are the rule in civil law countries. Dawson believes that the American method produces more careful and responsible opinions.

3. Of course, those who understand the world of limited publication know that the opinion should be signed "per staff."

4. 141 F.3d 111, 123–24 n.6 (4th Cir. 1998) (en banc), *aff'd*, 526 U. S. 503 (1999).

5. *Id.* at 124 n.6 (Murnaghan, J., dissenting) (emphasis added).

6. David R. Cleveland, Clear *as Mud: How the Uncertain Precedential Status of Unpublished Opinions Muddles Qualified Immunity Determinations*, 65 U. Miami L. Rev. 45, 66 n.122 (2010).

behavior—that there has been no fear of or favor to a litigant, in other words. Again, the *per curiam* diffuses accountability and provides less reassurance.

2. The Dismal Quality of the Products of Limited Publication

In our study of limited publication thirty years ago, we found that many unpublished opinions failed to satisfy very minimal standards of quality; that is, they failed even to state the issues in the case and give a plausible explanation for the result.[7] Many more opinions had been decided on the basis of the opinion below.[8] Most of the opinions that did meet minimum standards failed to do much more than that: in no circuit were a majority of the opinions longer than three hundred words (about the length of a normal typed page), and in six of the eleven circuits, the majority were fewer than fifty words.[9] Overall, we were astonished at what passed for acceptable in the courts we once revered.

Little has changed in the intervening third of a century. The opinions may read a little better now, thanks to the explosion in central staff, but they rarely satisfy the minimal standards we expect circuit judges to satisfy. Judge Kozinski, an outspoken *supporter* of limited publication, said all that needs to be said a few years ago when he referred to unpublished opinions as "not safe for human consumption."[10]

3. Limited Publication Insulates the Circuit Courts from Criticism

Judges enjoy immense power. That power worries us, and there is much debate about how best to control its exercise. Three powerful control mechanisms are (1) review by other courts, (2) peer pressure, and (3) scholarly criticism. The use of unpublished opinions makes these forms of control less effective—perhaps markedly.

a. Review by Another Court Becomes More Difficult

A decision by a circuit court panel can be overturned only by the Supreme Court or by the circuit judges sitting en banc. The decision not to publish an opinion makes either form of review less likely.

7. See William L. Reynolds & William M. Richman, *An Evaluation of Limited Publication in the United States Courts of Appeals: The Price of Reform*, 48 U. Chi. L. Rev. 573, 600–04 (1981) [hereinafter *An Evaluation*] for data and discussion of the standards we used.

8. *Id.* at 603–04.

9. *Id.* at 606. *See* Eugene Gressman et al., Supreme Court Practice 238–39 (9th ed. 2007).

10. *Quoted in* Stephen R. Barnett, *The Dog that Did Not Bark: No-Citation Rules, Judicial Conference Rulemaking, and Federal Public Defenders*, 62 Wash. & Lee L. Rev. 1491, 1512 n.97 (2005) (public Comments of Judge Kozinski on proposed Fed. R. App. P. 32.1).

(i) The Supreme Court

The Supreme Court hears only about eighty cases every year—about 1 percent of the decisions it is asked to review—and, of course, it is very careful about which ones it chooses to hear. Unpublished opinions are far less likely to be reviewed than opinions that receive the Learned Hand treatment for two reasons. First, it is very difficult to ascertain the reasoning and facts in most unpublished opinions, so it is more difficult for the Court to be sure that an unpublished opinion should be selected for review; and, second, the fact that the opinion is unpublished and, therefore, not "law" means the Court's law declaration function is not needed. In other words, review of an unpublished opinion only involves the error correction function of the Supreme Court, and it is unlikely to take a case solely to correct error. The Court has made this point quite clear: it sees its role as one of law declaration and not error correction.[11] Finally, even if the Court wished to correct for error, it would find that the cursory content of unpublished opinions makes it difficult to do so. Unpublished opinions rarely contain any grist for the judicial mill.

The data confirm that the Supreme Court does not often hear cases involving unpublished opinions. One study found in the quarter century between 1974 and 2000, only fifty-seven unpublished decisions were reviewed—about two per year.[12] The frequency of review seems to be increasing. A later study found that between 2001 and 2005, the Court heard another dozen cases decided by unpublished opinions below, or roughly three a Term.[13] And in the 2007 and 2008 Terms the Court heard another dozen cases.[14] However, there may be less in that number than meets the eye. Most of the unpublished opinions reviewed involved circuit conflicts, where one of the conflicting positions is announced in an unpublished opinion,[15]

11. *Id.* at 606. *See* EUGENE GRESSMAN ET AL., SUPREME COURT PRACTICE 238–39 (9th ed. 2007).

12. Michael Hannon, *A Closer Look at Unpublished Opinions in the United States Courts of Appeals*, 3 J. APP. PRAC. & PROCESS 199, 230–31 (2001).

13. David C. Vladeck & Mitu Gulati, *Judicial Triage: Reflections on the Debate over Unpublished Opinions*, 62 WASH. & LEE L. REV. 1667, 1684, n.61 (2005).

14. There were seven in October Term 2008 and five in October Term 2007: Boyle v. United States, 556 U.S. 938, 129 S. Ct. 2237 (2009); Flore-Figueroa v. United States, 556 U.S. 646, 129 S. Ct. 1886 (2009); Nken v. Holder, 556. U.S. 418, 129 S. Ct. 1749 (2009); Knowles v. Mirzayance, 129 S. Ct. 2426 (2009); Negusie v. Holder, 555 U.S. 511 (2009); Nelson v. United States, 555 U.S. 350, 129 S. Ct.890 (2009); Crawford v. Metro Gov't of Nashville, 555 U.S. 271, 129 S. Ct. 846 (2009); Jimenez v. Quarterman, 555 U.S. 113 (2008); Dada v. Mukasey, 554 U.S. 1 (2008); Ali. v. Fed. Bureau of Prisons, 552 U.S. 214 (2008); Kimbrough v. United States, 552 U.S. 85 (2007); Watson v. United States, 552 U.S. 74 (2007).

15. *See* Scott E. Gant, *Missing the Forest for a Tree: Unpublished Opinions and New Federal Rule of Appellate Procedure 32.1*, 47 B.C. L. REV. 705, 729 (2006) (noting that the Supreme Court "has elected to review dozens of unpublished appeals court opinions ....").

so it may be that the Supreme Court merely has become more alert for opportunities to clarify the law.[16]

The unhappy loser in a case decided by an unpublished opinion has other obstacles in her way, of course. Compared with the loser in a case given the Learned Hand treatment, it is more likely that she will be poor, pro se, and engaged in the type of litigation courts dislike or even disdain. Those facts, when coupled with the inherent disadvantages associated with review of any unpublished opinion, demonstrate the truly difficult road ahead of a litigant seeking to obtain review of such a decision.

(ii) En Banc Review

The other way to review a panel decision is by en banc review within the circuit. That also is far less likely to happen with unpublished opinions, and for the same reasons that Supreme Court review is unlikely: There is no wrong "law" to correct, so there is nothing in the opinion to interest an en banc court. This does not mean it never happens,[17] but it does mean that en banc review is very unlikely.

b. The Reduction in Peer Pressure

Judges write for any number of audiences—lawyers, litigants, the press, academics. Like all of us, no doubt, they wish to be admired, and they hope that their readers will approve of what they have done. The need for that approval is one of the few constraints on professionals who have lifetime jobs. They exercise great power, both over the parties who appear before them and in the development of the law, and yet they work largely free of criticism except from the other members of their panels. Unlike trial judges who receive frequent review of their work from appellate courts, and unlike the Supreme Court whose every act is subject to intense scrutiny, circuit judges rarely receive a critical look from anyone other than the litigants. It is thus unfortunate that the limited publication regime makes it so difficult for outsiders to evaluate what goes on under that regime; it is doubly unfortunate that that regime disproportionately involves the activities of the poor and other disfavored persons in our society.

16. David Cleveland has pointed out that the use of unpublished opinions can mask circuit conflicts even from the gimlet-eyed clerks who scan the *cert* petitions. David R. Cleveland, *Overturning the Last Stone: The Final Step in Returning Precedential Status to All Opinions*, 10 J. App. Prac. & Process 61,114 (2009). That seems very likely, given the vast number of unpublished opinions. Those gimlet-eyed clerks may find some of the conflicts, but they will not find all.

17. An example is the *Ricci* decision, discussed *infra* this chapter at section C.

Judges are subject to criticism from their peers, both implicit and explicit; and the judges also know that they are evaluated by the lawyers, clerks, and other actors in the system. Those forms of criticism and expectations, when coupled with a judge's own sense of professional pride, have certainly been effective in the main; as a group, circuit judges perform at a very high level. Nevertheless, there is always room for improvement as a group. More worrisome are the outliers, those few who do not perform at the high level we expect and whose work can be effectively shielded from public scrutiny by the limited publication system.

Critical evaluation is a necessary component of accountability, but it also is an important element in determining whether the law in an area is adequate—is it clear and faithful to precedent and statutory language? Unfortunately, the truncated nature of most unpublished opinions makes it difficult for critics to address those questions; the text simply fails to provide enough information for an outsider to make even an educated guess as to the state of the law.

B. JUDICIAL RESPONSIBILITY

Part of the work of an appellate judge is to maintain the system of *stare decisis* and to develop the law. The use of unpublished opinions undermines the performance of both jobs.

1. *Stare Decisis*

The common law requires that like cases be decided in like manner. A judge faced with two apparently similar cases must decide them similarly. If not, she is under a duty to explain *why* different results are appropriate. This task is not a mere formality. Rather, *stare decisis* lies at the very heart of the common law. The need to reconcile the case at bar with other decisions helps to reassure us that the court has acted without partiality, and that it has acted competently. The proper use of *stare decisis* also makes the law more predictable, thereby reducing the social and economic costs associated with decision making by clients and lawyers.[18]

A system of *stare decisis* depends, however, on the court's ability to identify those cases that it and lower courts must either follow or distinguish. Yet the limited publication regime discourages the search for similar cases. Once an appeal has been shunted to the unpublished track, we wonder how much effort is devoted to finding it in future "similar" cases. There may be treasure troves of similar appeals in the lists

18. *See generally* William Landis & Richard Posner, *Legal Precedent: A Theoretical and Legal Analysis*, 19 J. LAW & ECON. 249 (1976). Paradoxically, uncertainty about the law may lead to *more* appeals being taken, thereby increasing the workloads of the courts. Alvin B. Rubin, *Views from the Lower Courts*, 23 U.C.L.A. L. REV. 448 (1975).

of unreported decisions, but they will never be found, much less distinguished from the case at bar. No one in the judicial hierarchy has the slightest reason to look for them, of course, for the "similar" cases, by definition, lack precedential value and, as a result, do not have to be dealt with. Moreover, so many unpublished opinions are so substandard that it is impossible in many instances to know whether there is any similarity; in other words, *stare decisis* is impossible unless both facts and reasoning are available.

All of this reinforces the importance of *stare decisis* and the useful discipline it imposes on courts; without it, a panel might be all too tempted to engage in ad hoc decision making. As Judge Alvin Rubin wrote: "The *ad hoc* 'railway ticket' decision—good for this day and station—is a betrayal of the judicial function. Yet some appellate judges favor this kind of opinion because it leaves them elbow room to maneuver in future cases."[19]

2. Maintaining and Developing the Law: Short and Hidden Does Not Do the Trick

The federal appellate courts are primarily responsible for maintaining and developing federal law, both decisional and statutory. They also play an important albeit subsidiary role in the development of state law. Unpublished opinions, because they are by definition nonprecedential, do not satisfy this need.

Even if considered to be precedent, as we discussed earlier, the great majority of unpublished opinions do not satisfy the basic requirements of judicial elaboration.[20] In the words of Judge Kozinski, they are "garbage."[21] The failure of the courts to elaborate and justify properly large numbers of their decisions and to make 85 percent of them nonprecedential is a complete abnegation of this responsibility. This collective failure is made all the worse by the fact that a disproportionate share of the unpublished opinions concern the problems of the poor and other disadvantaged persons in our society.

C. THE NONPRECEDENTIAL PRECEDENT

An old saying tells us, "Taught law is tough law." That helps explain why so many lawyers feel uneasy when they hear that five out of six decisions by the federal circuits do not constitute precedent—by judicial fiat.[22] We were all taught in law

19. *Id.* at 451.
20. *See* Reynolds & Richman, *An Evaluation, supra* note 7, at 600–04.
21. *See supra* chapter 1, text accompanying note 30.
22. We have spoken with many practitioners and professors about limited publication, and the reaction described in the text is typical.

school that a judge rendering a decision must relate that decision to the surrounding web of precedent. We were also taught that it was not acceptable for a judge merely to assert that the relation held; some kind of reasoning was expected. It was drummed into our heads that the explanation was necessary so the decision could serve as a "precedent," that is, something that could guide future judges, lawyers, and members of the public. Finally, we learned that this was behavior expected of all judges, from small claims to the Supreme Court, but our expectations were highest for the aristocracy of the American bench, the appellate judges. Those expectations are profoundly disappointed by the limited publication regime.

The lawyers' instincts about precedent lead to two different concerns about the purported nonprecedential nature of an unpublished opinion. The first is that those opinions may be worth paying attention to, despite what the Publication Plans say. The second concern is that the courts can use the nonprecedential status of unpublished opinions to do some pretty unsavory things.

1. Do Unpublished Opinions Really Lack "Precedential" Value?

One study found that, as of 2001, the federal courts of appeals cited unpublished opinions 4,460 times and that federal district courts had relied on them in 1,967 cases.[23] Many district court judges "regularly read *all* of the unpublished opinions from their circuit courts."[24] As Lauren Robel observed after recounting the data, "it is rational for lawyers to stay apprised of unpublished opinions, for they often explicitly determine outcomes. It is impossible to determine how much more often they influence outcomes more subtly."[25] A pair of lawyers explains why they follow unpublished opinions despite their nominal nonprecedential status:

> First, for many issues, there are few on-point but uncitable appellate decisions, so the time it takes to review those decisions is short .... Second ... [p]ractitioners often review uncitable cases to mine them for new ideas. A prudent lawyer also reviews unpublished cases ... because they indicate how the appellate court has ruled in the past and thus might rule in the future. Moreover, it behooves counsel to review unpublished opinions because they still may influence a court that reads (or remembers deciding) them itself.[26]

The lesson is clear: lawyers ignore unpublished opinions at their peril.

23. Hannon, *supra* note 11, at 235. The total now is certainly much higher.

24. Lauren Robel, *The Practice of Precedent:* Anastasoff, *Noncitation Rules, and the Meaning of Precedent in an Interpretive Community*, 35 IND. L. REV. 399, 407 (2002) (emphasis in original).

25. *Id.*

26. Salem M. Katsh & Alex V. Chachkes, *The Constitutionality of "No Citation" Rules*, 3 J. APP. PRAC. & PROCESS 287, 301–02 (2001).

2. Hiding the Law

Of course, some unpublished opinions do contain sufficient information so that it can be said they develop the law; or they would have done so had they been given precedential value. Circuit Publication Plans generally require that those opinions be published. Why then were they not? There are several possible reasons. First, even the best-intentioned court can make a mistake; it can be difficult to appreciate the full significance of an opinion until after it is written, maybe not until years have gone by.[27] Thus, it is a mistake for a court not to publish *any* elaborated opinion because the issuing court cannot predict in advance what the opinion will come to mean.

Worse, however, is the temptation not to publish an opinion the court knows full well breaks new ground and, therefore, should be published. Two eminent appellate judges provide support for this obvious idea. First, Judge Patricia Wald has written: "I have seen judges purposely compromise on an unpublished opinion incorporating an agreed-upon result in order to avoid a time-consuming public debate about what law controls."[28] Judge Posner has observed that "the unpublished opinion provides a temptation for judges to shove difficult decisions under the rug in cases where a one-liner would be too blatant an evasion of judicial duty."[29] And Judge Richard Arnold observed that judges may use unpublished opinions to resolve appeals where the result may be hard to justify.[30] Although we suspect that there are not too many of those kinds of opinions, there certainly are some, just as there are some of sufficient "public interest" to warrant publication under the criteria in the Publication Plans.[31] Failure to publish either of these types of opinions is disturbing.

Also disturbing would be a decision not to publish an opinion to keep the issue from public view and/or to limit the interest of the Supreme Court in the case.[32] In this category of cases, a court wishing to insulate the decision from further review might issue a short, meaningless, unpublished affirmance, which will effectively hide the case from prying eyes. Appeals involving judicial misconduct might fall into this category,[33] but so do cases where the lower court got the right result (in the

27. Karl Llewellyn famously wrote that we cannot know what a precedent *really* means until it has been elaborated by later courts. KARL LLEWELLYN, THE BRAMBLE BUSH 52 (1960).

28. Patricia M. Wald, *The Rhetoric of Results and the Results of Rhetoric: Judicial Writings*, 62 U. CHI. L. REV. 1371, 1374 (1995).

29. RICHARD POSNER, FEDERAL COURTS: CHALLENGE AND REFORM 165 (1996).

30. Richard S. Arnold, *Unpublished Opinions: A Comment*, 1 J. APP. PRAC. & PROCESS 219, 223 (1999).

31. *See* discussion *infra* chapter 3, note 44 and accompanying text.

32. A related problem could occur if a judge chose not to publish an opinion in order to avoid a controversial issue that could affect his career, such as a possible appointment to the Supreme Court.

33. In Reynolds & Richman, *An Evaluation*, *supra* note 7, at 611, we discuss an example. There, the Tenth Circuit issued an order forbidding the court reporter for Chief Judge Willis

eyes of the circuit court panel), but the circuit court might worry that a published opinion affirming the decision below could excite public interest or encourage either en banc review or a grant of *certiorari* by the Supreme Court. The panel might well conclude discretion is the better part of valor and shunt the appeal to Track Two. Again, that would be wrong. At least Justice Stevens is aware of the problem; he has said: "I tend to grant [*cert*] more on unpublished opinions, on the theory that occasionally judges will use the unpublished opinion as a device to reach a decision that might be a little hard to justify."[34]

3. A (Non) Exemplary Case

An example of a decision that exemplifies the problems just discussed is *Ricci v. DeStefano*.[35] The case was brought by white firefighters in New Haven who alleged they had been denied a promotion because of their race. Their action raised the question "whether a municipality incurs liability when, motivated by a desire to comply with federal anti-discrimination law, it takes race-neutral actions that have racially significant consequences."[36] The case had been the subject of a lengthy opinion by the district court, which rejected the claim brought by the firefighters.[37] That opinion spent ten pages discussing the substantive arguments, concluding that "while the facts of *Hayden* [a Second Circuit precedent] were slightly different than those here, the court finds the holding quite relevant and instructive."[38] Note the district judge did not find the case to be open-and-shut: she spent considerable time discussing the law and found *Hayden* to be "relevant and instructive," but she did not find it controlling. Finally, the case naturally excited public interest, involving as it did claims of reverse discrimination by a city.[39]

On appeal, the proceedings were very strange, as an opinion in the Second Circuit en banc hearing noted

> [T]he parties submitted briefs of eighty-six pages each and a six-volume joint appendix of over 1800 pages; plaintiffs' reply brief was thirty-two pages long. Two *amici* briefs

Ritter of the District of Utah "from carrying out the duties imposed upon him [the reporter] by law." That order was issued at a time when Congress was considering a proposal to hold federal judges accountable short of impeachment, and the problems of Judge Ritter had figured prominently in the debate. The motives of the Tenth Circuit in issuing the order in an unpublished opinion certainly can be questioned.

34. Jeffrey Cole & Elaine E. Bucklo, *A Life Well-Lived: An Interview with Justice John Paul Stevens*, 32 *Litigation* 8, 67 (Spring 2006).

35. 530 F.3d 88 (2d Cir. 2008).

36. *Id.* at 88–89. (Calabresi, J., concurring in the denial of a rehearing en banc).

37. Ricci v. DeStefano, 554 F. Supp. 2d 142 (D. Conn. 2006).

38. *Id.* at 160.

39. *See* Adam Liptak, *Justices to Hear White Firefighters' Bias Claims*, N.Y. Times, Apr. 10, 2009, at A1.

> were filed and oral argument ... lasted over an hour (an unusually long argument in the practice of our Circuit). More than two months [later] ... the panel affirmed ... in a summary order containing a single substantive paragraph.[40]

That "single substantive paragraph" of the "summary order," the Second Circuit's term of art for an unpublished opinion, was nine lines long, contained not a single citation, none at all, and began with this helpful sentence: "We affirm, substantially for the reasons stated in the thorough, thoughtful, and well-reasoned opinion of the court below."[41] The panel did not explain why its agreement with the court below was only "substantial"; that is, it did not explain what part of that opinion it disagreed with. The reader who knows something of the background is left wondering why in the world would the panel dispose of such a case in a conclusory unpublished opinion.

The Second Circuit's rule on unpublished opinions is typically vague: a unanimous panel can decide an appeal through an unpublished opinion only if "each judge of the panel believes that no jurisprudential purpose would be served by an opinion."[42] Was there a "jurisprudential purpose" to be served by publication? Remember the trial judge did not find any precedent controlling, and she went to some trouble to justify her decision. Remember also that the panel only agreed "substantially" with her decision. Finally, remember that the case involved issues of great public moment. Surely, this was an appeal that merited a full opinion, one that would explain not only what "substantially" means, but, of more importance, would give the public the views of well-respected judges on the difficult legal issues. Surely the panel must have realized that the case raised a strong possibility for review by the Supreme Court and that that Court might welcome the considered views of the respected judges on the panel.

Several events confirm this analysis. First, the parties did not treat the case as an easy one—they wrote lengthy briefs in support of their positions, and they were joined by *amici*. Second, the case was *argued*, an unusual occurrence in a case decided by an unpublished opinion,[43] suggesting both the central staff and the judges thought the case worthy of their attention. Third, oral argument was "unusually long," once again suggesting the panel believed the problem was both interesting and not an easy one to resolve. Fourth, and perhaps most telling, on consideration of a suggestion of rehearing en banc, six of the thirteen participating judges voted to hear the case and joined a dissent written by Judge Cabranes, a vote that showed how difficult it was to solve the substantive problem in *Ricci*.

40. *Ricci*, 530 F.3d at 95–96 (Cabranes, J., dissenting).
41. 264 Fed App'x 106 (2d. Cir. 2008)
42. 2d Cir. R. 32.1.
43. *See generally infra* chapter 7.

Why then did the panel issue an unpublished opinion? Only two explanations come to mind. First, the panel may have been unable to reach agreement on how to explain a decision for the City of New Haven. Unwilling to compromise individual views, and knowing that separate opinions would enhance curiosity in the case, the panel[44] might have decided not to publish at all. The other possible reason the panel did not publish is that it may have been trying to hide the case; as we have noted, an unpublished opinion is far less likely to be reviewed by the Supreme Court than is a published opinion.[45] If the panel liked the result but was worried about what the Supreme Court might do, then it might try and keep the case under wraps.

Under either explanation, the decision not to publish was inappropriate. The law obviously was in a state of uncertainty, as the panel's own actions suggest strongly. An opinion clarifying the law would have been of real public importance. A separate opinion would only have enhanced the public interest by stimulating debate. Even without a separate opinion, the debate stirred up by the majority on such an important topic would have helped the Supreme Court when it chose to visit the topic. Thus, the panel's failure to publish was also a failure by the court of its duty to clarify and maintain the law.

The story of *Ricci* was not over, however. Amazingly, there is more to tell. A circuit judge sought a poll on whether the case should be reheard en banc,[46] and that is when things became really interesting. As the Order denying a rehearing stated tersely: "After the poll was concluded … the original, three-judge panel withdrew the summary order and filed a *per curiam* opinion; no subsequent *in banc* poll has been requested."[47] The Second Circuit then voted 7–6 to deny a rehearing, with the minority writing an opinion that explores, without deciding, the correctness of the district court's decision.[48] The end result was the panel "opinion" became precedent for the Second Circuit. It is less clear what that precedent means; remember the panel only agreed "substantially" with the trial court opinion. If the case had not been reviewed by the Supreme Court, the law in the area would have been unsettled.

Eventually, the Supreme Court reversed.[49] The vote was 5–4 (with separate concurrences by Justices Scalia and Alito and a dissent by Justice Ginsburg). That sharply split decision hardly reflects consensus on the issues presented in *Ricci*, and

44. Justice Stevens has suggested that courts may behave that way. *See infra* chapter 6 at note 34 and accompanying text.

45. En banc review was not a concern; the Second Circuit apparently rarely, if ever, grants en banc review. *Ricci*, 530 F.3d at 492 (Jacobs, C. J., dissenting).

46. *Ricci*, 530 F.3d at 88 (order).

47. *Id.* The published panel opinion can be found at 265 Fed. App'x 106 (2d Cir.), *withdrawn by* 530 F.3d 87 (2d Cir. 2008).

48. *Id.* at 93 (Cabranes, J., dissenting). Another dissent countered the arguments offered by the majority that review would be improper because a key issue had been waived by the plaintiffs and that en banc review was generally improper. *Id.* at 92 (Jacobs, C.J., dissenting).

49. Ricci v. DiStefano, 557 U.S. 129 S. Ct. 2658 (2009).

reinforces the conclusion that the law in the area needed further discussion and that the panel's failure to publish was not in the public interest.[50]

D. LIMITED PUBLICATION DISPROPORTIONATELY AFFECTS THE POOR AND DISADVANTAGED

No one will be surprised to learn that appeals with attorneys attached are far more likely to have the result announced in a published opinion than pro se cases. A study by the Federal Judicial Center confirmed this obvious point a few years ago:

> We determined that fully briefed cases are much more likely to be resolved by published opinions than are cases with counseled briefs [that is, briefs submitted by attorneys] filed only on one side. And we also observed that *no case without any counseled brief was resolved by a published opinion in our sample.*[51]

It is easy to explain these stunning data. First, attorneys do earn their keep (at least in most cases). They know how to present facts and arguments so the court can determine whether a case is worth the Learned Hand treatment. Second, the presence of an attorney is also a signal that the appeal is important enough to a client to pay an attorney and, therefore, worth a serious look by the court; the court may also wish to make the attorney look good by giving her appeal Track One status. Perhaps most important, the court realizes the appeal probably will be presented well enough so that it does not have to frustrate itself working through the record and trying to figure out what the arguments are. And a case that has counsel on both sides is even more likely to fit into any or all of the above categories.

It is also not surprising that no appeal without at least one counseled brief ended in a published opinion. It seems likely in any case where the court detected concerns that might lead it to write a published opinion that the court would appoint counsel, thereby removing the case from the no counseled brief category. Unfortunately, we have no idea how many cases fall within that category.[52]

Those explanations of the data compiled by the Federal Judicial Center, however, do not justify the fact that persons without attorneys are far less likely to receive Track One treatment. Once again, the system works in favor of those who have resources and knowledge.

50. The several opinions barely mentioned the panel decision, no doubt because it contained nothing worth mentioning. Normally, one would expect to see a good deal of discussion in an en banc review of what had happened in the court of appeals panel that had decided a case. The absence of any discussion tells us a lot about the quality of the panel decision.

51. Robert Timothy Reagan, *A Snapshot of Briefs, Opinions, and Citations in Federal Appeals*, 8 J. App. Prac. & Process 321, 325 (2006) (emphasis added).

52. One of the authors argued just such a case a few years ago.

On the other side of the ledger, data from the Federal Judicial Center "suggest that a bare majority of fully briefed cases filed in 2002 were resolved by unpublished opinions, and that over a third were resolved by published opinions. In six circuits ..., however, most fully briefed cases were resolved by published opinions."[53] Thus, appeals with attorneys involved are much more likely to receive the Learned Hand treatment, but there is certainly no guarantee.

In our Federal Judicial Center study made in the 1970s, we found that cases involving the poor were disproportionately shunted to Track Two.[54] Now that five out of six federal appellate determinations are unpublished, it seems that even most cases brought by the rich are denied the Learned Hand treatment. Could this deplorable result at least have the benefit of providing more equal treatment to the rich and the poor? Almost certainly not. Comparison of general publication rates with pro se rates shows that, while the circuit courts are assigning more and more cases to Track Two, the odds of an appeal ending up there are greater if the party is poor.

53. Reagan, *supra* note 50, at 326.
54. Reynolds & Richman, *An Evaluation*, *supra* note 7, at 621–26.

CHAPTER 5

The Life and Death of the No-Citation Rules

The common law courts of England had no need for a rule concerning what authorities could be properly used to persuade a court. After all, there were few reports and even fewer treatises. Moreover, at least some of what had been written down was of debatable accuracy; as a result, whether the report of a case represented fairly what had really happened and what the judges had really said was itself something that needed to be discussed in court. Finally, much of the law was contained in the collective memory of the legal profession. It is no wonder, therefore, that anything that might have probative value was fair game for the attorneys.[1]

The situation in the American courts until well into the nineteenth century must have been much the same. There were few reports and commentators were of doubtful authenticity (except of course for the indispensable Blackstone). Again, anything a party thought might have persuasive value must have been grist for the judicial mill.[2] Attorneys were constrained in their use of authority only by their forensic skill and common sense. Finally, because, there were no rules limiting the precedential value of a class of opinions,[3] there was no need to prevent reference to them. Limitations on what could be cited, in other words, was not a topic of discussion. Thus, we are aware of no rules in American courts constraining the use of authority in argument until the development of rules concerning unpublished opinions by the federal courts in the 1960s.[4]

1. In the nineteenth century, British courts developed rules for the citation of nonjudicial authorities. The basic premise was if the author was still alive, he could not be cited.

2. Written submissions from the attorneys must have been unusual and probably were not very helpful; thus, the Supreme Court did not even require briefs from the litigants until 1821. William H. Rehnquist, *From Webster to Word-Processing: The Ascendance of the Appellate Brief*, 1 J. App. Practice & Process 1 (1999).

3. That is not to say that all judicial utterances were thought to be equally persuasive; rather, anything said by judges could be used in argument.

4. The development of those rules is discussed in chapter 3.

That freedom of citation changed with the advent of limited publication. The limited publication and no-citation rules were a package deal. It is easy to see why that was so. After all, what was the point of citing cases that lacked precedential value? If the case could provide no support for a litigant because it had been designated as nonprecedential, there could be no reason for her to refer to it. Why not save everyone—parties, lawyers, and, of course, judges—the precious time devoured by attempts to deal with irrelevant opinions? And so, the circuit courts largely limited or even forbade the citation of unpublished opinions. Prohibitions brought a great benefit: if unpublished opinions could not be cited, they could be written carelessly, even thoughtlessly. Indeed, they need contain little other than the decision itself. The court need not worry about what it had said ever again.

Curiously, the decision to restrict citation seems to have been rather haphazard. Once the circuit courts chose the limited publication route, the decision to restrict severely the citation of unpublished opinions seems to have been reached with little thought. Although the circuits struggled somewhat with the problem of defining what opinions should and should not be published, there was little debate over the decision to limit citation to unpublished opinions.

All of the courts agreed soon after the adoption of limited publication regimes that citation to unpublished opinions was fine in the context of preclusion (issues like *res judicata*, collateral estoppel, and law of the case), and some circuits completely prohibited all other citation to unpublished opinions. Some did not, however, and the issue was apparently thought to be so insignificant that those differences sparked no debate. As a result, by the late 1970s, six circuits had banned the citation of unpublished opinions except in cases where preclusion was an issue.[5] Two circuits had no rules at all on the question, and two more permitted citation under some circumstances.[6] Some circuits even went so far as to attempt to prohibit their unpublished opinions from being cited by other courts.[7]

The no-citation rules of course, were laughable.

> [T]here is nonetheless something unsettling about rules that say to litigants that although their cases were decided correctly, the judges do not want anyone to let their judicial colleagues know what they did; something censorious and upside-down about rules that say to lawyers that although they may cite district court opinions, state court

5. One oddity of the preclusion exception to the no-citation rule is that preclusion often requires a fact-intensive inquiry. Was this issue raised? Was it fully litigated? Because so many of the unpublished opinions lack depth and reasoning, it would be difficult to answer those questions.

6. The practice at that time is discussed in William L. Reynolds & William M. Richman, *The Non-Precedential Precedent—Limited Publication and No-Citation Rules in the United States Courts of Appeals*, 78 COLUM. L. REV. 1167, 1179–81 (1978).

7. Scott E. Gant, *Missing the Forest for a Tree: Unpublished Opinions and New Federal Rule of Appellate Procedure 32.1*, 47 B.C. L. REV. 705, 713–14 (2006), lists the various circuit rules before Rule 32.1 went into effect.

opinions, law review articles, or even non-legal materials in their briefs, those briefs may subject their authors to professional discipline if they refer to certain writings of the very judges who sit on the court hearing the appeal; something confiscatory about rules that say to members of the public that although they have, through their taxes, paid for the production of an opinion, they may not derive any use from that opinion in subsequent disputes; and something arrogant about rules that confer upon judges the power to determine prospectively what cases will provide useful precedential or persuasive authority in cases years down the line, cases that raise issues the judges, for all their experience and collective wisdom, cannot pretend to foresee.[8]

Absurdity made the no-citation rules vulnerable. As discussion about them increased and technology developed, the push for change began. At first slowly, and then in a dramatic development that began in the late 1990s, the non-citation rules promulgated by the individual circuits were replaced at the end of 2006 with Rule 32.1 of the Federal Rules of Appellate Procedure. Today, Rule 32.1 generally forbids any restriction on the citation of any federal decision.

Although the no-citation rules no longer have a direct impact on the decision-making process, they have interest today because of the light they shed on the whole problem of unpublished opinions as well as the mysterious workings of the judicial establishment. This chapter explores the establishment of the non-citation rules, their faults, their eventual demise, and the citation practice in the circuit courts today.[9]

A. THE PROS AND CONS OF THE NO-CITATION RULE

The arguments for and against the no-citation rules track to a large extent the arguments made in connection with the more general practices involving unpublished opinions.[10] It is worth some repetition here, however, to get a full flavor of the effect of the rules prohibiting citation to unpublished opinions. Because those rules, like all of the rules involving unpublished opinions, were adopted with little thought and less legislative history, the arguments in their favor have to be reconstructed largely from guesswork. There seem to be two reasons that support limiting citation: doing

8. David Greenwald & Frederick A. O. Schwartz, Jr., *The Censorial Judiciary*, 35 U.C. Davis L. Rev. 1133, 1174 (2002). Hillel Levin, *Making the Law in the District Courts*, 53 Vill. L. Rev. 783, 984 (2009), describes the non-citation rules as "perfectly ripe, large and low-hanging fruit . . . ."

9. State courts have a variety of rules and practices regarding citation. The practices of the several states are surveyed in Stephen R. Barnett, *No-Citation Rules Under Siege: A Battlefield Report and Analysis*, 5. J. App. Prac. & Process, 473, 485 (2003) (finding that citation to unpublished opinions is permitted in twenty-one states and forbidden in twenty-five; the trend today, however, is in favor of permitting citations).

10. *See* discussion in chapter 3.

so prevents unfairness to litigants and saves judicial resources. Thus, the Hruska Commission in 1975 favored non-citation rules in order to prevent "publication by private publishers," and out of fear that "access to [unpublished] opinions may be unequal, favoring those members of the bar with the resources to monitor, acquire and file them."[11]

1. Unfairness to Litigants

Under this heading comes the notion that not all litigants have equal access to unpublished opinions, as well as the judges' goodhearted concern that it would be too difficult (or expensive) to research the vast number of worthless (by definition) opinions lacking in precedential value to determine what opinions to cite. Whatever might have been said on behalf of those concerns in 1970, today they have been seriously undermined by technology.[12] Unpublished opinions are now available online and can be easily accessed and analyzed there. Although it is easier to perform sophisticated research using specialized (and costly) databases like Westlaw or Lexis/Nexis, the opinions are available and free. In the lengthy debate over Rule 32.1, the cost to litigants of looking for opinions was not even raised.

2. Saving Judicial Resources

The real argument on behalf of the no-citation rules involved the conservation of judicial resources. It is the *judges* who do not want to wade through the morass of their earlier work, and, even more important to them, to worry that something they signed off on without much thought or effort might be used as authority in later cases. Even the fact that the opinion lacks formal precedential value—in other words, the ability to cite it—might have a psychological effect. Better to banish the opinion from history by labeling it unclean. Great blocks of time can be saved if opinions do not have to contain any serious explanation and do not have to be reconciled with one another. This concern became a major obstacle to the adoption of Rule 32.1.

It does not take much reflection to show the shallowness of those worries. First, as things now stand, it will be the law clerks and staff attorneys who will be reviewing the great mass of unpublished opinions that (hypothetically) will be cited. In any event, there is little meat in those opinions. As discussed earlier, the vast majority of

11. Comm'n of Revision of Fed. Court Appellate Sys., Structure and Internal Procedures: Recommendations for Change 114 (1975).

12. Gone also is the related concern about the need to store the many extra volumes of case reporters that would have to be published if there were no "unpublished opinions." Today, of course, volumes of hard copy reporters are rarely consulted by anyone.

those opinions contain little or no substance—instead, they are simply a bare-bones recitation of facts and something purporting to be controlling authority.[13]

That observation provides the cynical answer to the judicial worry about spending more time writing precedent-worthy opinions: all the courts have to do is continue to issue opinions that are so empty of content that litigants will be hard-pressed to find anything that can be used in later cases. Long ago, in other words, judges solved the core work problem posed by citation by making the unpublished opinion useless to anyone other than the parties; litigants simply will not cite cases unless there is some reason to do so.

B. THE ADOPTION OF RULE 32.1[14]

Although little thought went into citation practice when Publication Plans were adopted in the 1970s, the prolonged struggle—internecine warfare might be a better term—over Rule 32.1 changed that. We now have had a long discussion over citation practices, a serious survey of experiences by bench and bar, and a Rule addressing the problem. Rule 32.1, in other words, has taught us a lot.

The rules concerning citation in the several circuits just before the adoption of Rule 32.1 can be easily summarized:

> The federal courts of appeals take three approaches to regulating the citation of unreported opinions. Four "restrictive" circuits—the Second, Seventh, Ninth, and Federal—ban it altogether. Six "discouraging" circuits—the First, Fourth, Sixth, Eighth, Tenth, and Eleventh—permit it in limited circumstances (typically when no published opinion adequately addresses the same issue as the unpublished opinion). Three "permissive" circuits—the Third, Fifth, and D.C.—freely permit it.[15]

13. *See supra* chapter 2.

14. This part draws heavily on the following sources: an excellent study prepared by the staff of the Federal Judicial Center: TIM REAGAN, CITATIONS TO UNPUBLISHED OPINIONS IN THE FEDERAL COURTS OF APPEALS (2005) [hereinafter FJC REPORT]; an article written by the Reporter for the Appellate Rules Committee during the consideration and adoption of Rule 32.1, Patrick J. Schiltz, *Much Ado about Nothing: Explaining the Sturm und Drang over the Citation of Unpublished Opinions*, 62 WASH. & LEE L. REV. 1429 (2005) [hereinafter *Much Ado*]; and a *Symposium* on Rule 32.1 published in vol. 62 of the WASHINGTON & LEE LAW REVIEW. Schiltz, now a federal trial judge, commented further in Patrick J. Schiltz, *The Citation of Unpublished Opinions in the Federal Court of Appeals*, 74 FORD. L. REV. 23 (2005) [hereinafter *Citation*]. Another excellent recent review of the problem is David R. Cleveland, *Overturning the Last Stone: The Final Step in Returning Precedential Status to All Opinions*, 10 J. APP. PRAC. & PROCESS 61 (2009); and Professor Cleveland summarized the outcome in the circuit courts in David R. Cleveland, *Local Rules in the Wake of Federal Rule of Appellate Procedure 32.1*, 11 J. APP. PRAC. & PROCESS 19 (2010).

15. Schiltz, *Much Ado*, *supra* note 14, at 1430–31 (footnotes omitted).

This state of the circuit rules regarding citation prohibition had not changed very much from their promulgation a quarter century earlier.[16] What had changed was the attitude of the bar (and some of the bench) toward the practice.

Practitioners and academics had long been displeased with the limited publication regime, although curiously, the primary target of that criticism has been the rules that limited the citation of unpublished opinions. Exactly why the unhappiness focused on the no-citation practice rather than other pernicious practices associated with limited publication is hard to fathom. No doubt attorneys were unhappy with their inability to cite whatever they wanted to, but what they wanted to cite was not precedent, so why attack the lesser of the two evils? After all, the no-citation practice was the least of the problems generated by the Appellate Triage Regime. We believe that the poor quality of unpublished opinions, the lack of precedential value, and the prominent role of central staff are far more important things to worry about. Patrick Schiltz, the Reporter for the Advisory Committee on the Federal Rules of Appellate Procedure (called in this book the Appellate Rules Committee), agrees that citation prohibition is not much of an issue; the title of his fine article about the adoption of Rule 32.1 begins "Much Ado about Little . . . ." Schiltz also believes that Rule 32.1 will have little impact (it's not "sex or religion," he adds).[17] There can be little doubt, however, that the proposal to adopt Rule 32.1 created intense passions. Before explaining why, some legislative history will be useful.

The federal judicial establishment had noticed "many problems" with non-citation policies as early as 1990,[18] but attempts to address the issue were long delayed in the face of significant opposition, and it was not until 1998 that formal consideration of possible changes in those policies began. The immediate impetus was a memorandum from the Department of Justice to the Appellate Rules Committee. That committee eventually developed three versions of what was to become Rule 32.1.[19] The differences among them involved the question of whether (and how) to recognize unpublished opinions. One version specifically authorized nonprecedential opinions and provided that those opinions could be cited for their "persuasive value." The other two versions did not expressly authorize nonprecedential opinions, but did permit citation of them, although one version stated that such citation was allowed "only in limited circumstances."[20]

The Committee considered and rejected all three versions. In the end, it decided only to deal narrowly with the citation problem, deliberately bypassing the question of what, if any, precedential value should be assigned to unpublished opinions.

16. *See supra* section A. Several circuits had grown more relaxed in their no-citation policies in the interim.

17. Schiltz, *Much Ado, supra* note 14, at 1433.

18. Report of the Federal Courts Study Commission 130 (1990).

19. Federal Rule of Appellate Procedure 32 deals with briefing formalities and has nothing to do with citation practice. It is not altogether clear why Rule 32.1 is located where it is.

20. Schiltz, *Much Ado, supra* note 14, at 1448.

It focused on the prohibition of citation because the Committee did not want to take on the issue of the constitutionality of that practice.[21] Instead, the proposal stated that "[n]o prohibition or restriction may be imposed upon the citation of judicial opinions ... that have been designated as 'unpublished'...."[22]

That proposal sparked a firestorm. Patrick Schiltz wrote that the no-citation problem occupied more of his time as Reporter of the Appellate Advisory Committee than all of the other Committee activities during his tenure—*combined*.[23] Both sides held strongly to their positions.[24] An avalanche of comments from the Ninth Circuit led to suggestions that Chief Judge Alex Kozinski had fomented intense opposition to the proposal[25]—not just among the judges but also among public defenders and law professors. In turn, proponents of the Rule believed the question had become one of principle, as can be seen in the minutes of a meeting of the Appellate Rules Committee:

> Committee members argued that the main problem with no-citation rules—and the main reason to approve Rule 32.1—is that an Article III court should not be able to forbid parties from citing back to it the public actions that the court itself has taken. It is antithetical to American values and to the common law system for a court to forbid a party or an attorney from calling to the court's attention its own prior decisions, from arguing to the court that its prior decisions were not correct, and from arguing that the court should or should not act consistently with those prior decisions in the present case. One member ... said that it was "ludicrous" that an attorney could not cite a court's prior decisions to the court itself, but can cite those decisions to virtually everyone else in the world, including other courts. Yet another member—a judge—said

21. At the time, the constitutional issues discussed *infra* chapter 6 were being actively discussed in judicial and academic circles.

22. Samuel A. Alito Jr., Report of the Advisory Committee on Appellate Rules 28–29 (May 22, 2003). At the time, Justice Alito was a judge in the Third Circuit and the chair of the Appellate Rules Committee. Both Alito and Chief Justice Roberts, who also was on the Appellate Rules Committee, approved of Rule 32.1, as did every appellate judge on the Committee. Schiltz, *Much Ado*, *supra* note 14, at 1452.

23. *Schiltz, Much Ado*, *supra* note 14, at 1461–62.

24. Schiltz notes that the proposal was supported by the American Bar Association, the American Trial Lawyers Association, and the American Academy of Appellate Lawyers—and opposed, bizarrely, by the American Civil Liberties Union. *Id.* at 1460–61.

25. Stephen R. Bartlett, *The Dog that Did Not Bark: No-Citation Rules, Judicial Conference Rulemaking, and Federal Public Defenders*, 62 Wash. & Lee L. Rev. 1491, 1498–1502 (2005). Bartlett notes that the Ninth Circuit commenters on Rule 32.1 were near unanimous in their opposition to it and that in both volume and unanimity of opposition, the Ninth Circuit was a true outlier. For example, thirty-eight of the thirty-nine judges in the Ninth Circuit who commented on the proposed rule opposed it. Professor Bartlett also notes that all sixty-two public defenders in the Ninth Circuit opposed the proposed rule. *See also* Stephen R. Burbank, *The Politics of the Federal Judiciary: Tiered Appellate Decision-Making*, 89 Judicature 20, 22 (2006) (opposition to the rule "had all the markings of an interest group lobbying campaign ... led by Judge Kozinski....").

that judges should not be the only government officials who can shield themselves from being confronted with their past actions.[26]

What explained this passion?[27] Reporter Schiltz considered this question in some detail. Proponents of the new Rule, he suggests, were motivated by a number of concerns.[28] Among them were support for free speech principles, accountability of the judiciary, transparency, equal justice ("like cases should be decided in like fashion"), equality of treatment for litigants regardless of status, freedom to represent clients as the attorney sees fit (including the use of citations), and, finally, frustration with the proliferation of petty local rules. Schiltz added that the bitter debate over no-citation rules masked a more basic anger many practitioners have with the limited publication regime.

All of those reasons make sense, especially the last one. The list tracks arguments that we and many others have made against that system over the years, and unimportant as Rule 32.1 might be in comparison with the other issues we discuss, the fight over it gave opponents of the system a rare chance to strike out against its injustice.

Schiltz believes that practical concerns motivated the opponents.[29] First, he contends, some judges reacted defensively to attacks on something they had established—they do not like being told, for example, that they are violating free speech norms. (We might add, although Schiltz does not, that judges do not appreciate criticism; in this, they are no doubt like all of us; but judges, by virtue of their position, rarely receive open criticism.) Judges also were seriously worried about the future of the judiciary if limited publication were to end; they believed the system could no longer work and disaster would result. That belief, of course, would make one quite forceful in articulating opposition to a prohibition on citation. A third explanation for judicial hostility to Rule 32.1 was fear that citation is the proverbial camel's nose under the tent; today, citation prohibition goes, tomorrow the same happens to nonprecedential value, and the day after that, unpublished opinions. A final factor, he writes, might have been guilt over the whole rotten system.

All of these points make sense, but we believe the crux of the opposition involved Schiltz's third point—that opposition to the proposed rule primarily centered on matters that Rule 32.1 did *not* address: it did not eliminate nonprecedential opinions, and the Advisory Note to the Rule expressly confirms that was the intent of

26. Quoted in Schiltz, *Much Ado*, *supra* note 14, at 1451–52.

27. In addition to the points discussed in the text, passion surely was also inflamed by the controversy over the panel decision in *Anastasoff v. United States*, 223 F.3d 898 (8th Cir.), *vacated as moot*, 235 F. 3d 1054 (8th Cir. 200) (en banc). *See* David R. Cleveland, *Overturning the Last Stone: The Final Step in Returning Precedential Status to All Opinions*, 10 J. App. Prac. & Process 61, 97 (2009). We discuss *Anastasoff infra* chapter 6.

28. Schiltz, *Much Ado*, *supra* note 14, at 1467–75. Schiltz does not mention the strong egos of the participants on both sides as a contributing factor. No doubt he was being diplomatic.

29. The text is based on *id.* at 1475–90.

its adopters. Nevertheless, the fear that the nonprecedential status of unpublished opinions themselves was at risk was not wholly irrational. Judges, or at least some of them, believed that the citation of unpublished opinions would put pressure on them to write more thoughtful opinions and, ultimately, to give precedential effect to more decisions.[30] Some judges, in other words, feared that loosening rules against citation might ultimately lead to according precedential value to unpublished opinions. If that were to happen, the workload would overwhelm them.

The trouble with that fear was that the opposition had ample evidence, gathered by impeccable sources, to reassure them about what would happen if Rule 32.1 were to be adopted. They chose to ignore the evidence. Why they did so is an open question; we do not believe that the other grounds cited by Reporter Schiltz are strong enough to support the intensity of the opposition. Perhaps the only explanation is the monster in the closet; like the child afraid of the monster, the judges also fear the great unknown, ignoring the ample evidence of reality.

C. THE FEDERAL JUDICIAL CENTER STUDY

Were the Ninth Circuit judges and the rest of the opposition right to worry about Rule 32.1? Should more concern have been expressed by the judges in other courts? Fortunately, there is some fairly good evidence that sheds light on that question. In 2005, in the midst of the debate over the proposed change, the Federal Judicial Center issued a landmark report entitled *Citations to Unpublished Opinions in the Federal Courts of Appeals*.[31] The Report describes its methodology in this way:

> We surveyed all 257 sitting circuit judges and asked them how citation rules are likely to affect the time it takes to prepare unpublished opinions, the length of unpublished opinions, and the frequency of unpublished opinions. We also asked judges in circuits whose courts permit citation to unpublished opinions in unrelated cases—the discouraging circuits and the permissive circuits—whether these citations require additional work, are helpful, and are inconsistent with published authority. We asked judges in restrictive circuits whether special characteristics of their circuits would create problems if attorneys were permitted to cite unpublished opinions in unrelated cases. The courts of appeals in both the First and the District of Columbia Circuits changed their local rules recently to relax their restrictions on citations to unpublished opinions, and we asked judges in those circuits about the effects of the rule changes.[32]

30. This point is discussed in Amy E. Sloan, *If You Can't Beat 'Em, Join 'Em: A Pragmatic Approach to Nonprecedential Opinions in the Federal Appellate Courts*, 86 Neb. L. Rev. 895, 897 (2008).
31. FJC Report, *supra note* 14. The report was prepared at the request of the Standing Committee on Practice and Procedure. *Id.* at 1.
32. *Id.*

The authors of the Report also asked a random sample of attorneys involved in appeals for their views on unpublished opinions.[33] Finally, the report collected data on the citation of unpublished opinions from attorneys and judges, and the relative length of published and unpublished opinions.[34] The Report, in short, is an indispensable document for anyone interested in the area. A sampling of the responses to the Federal Judicial Center survey, both pro and con, follows.

1. What the Judges Had to Say

The Federal Judicial Center questionnaire was sent to all active and senior circuit judges. The response rate was excellent: 86 percent.[35] The judges were asked how changes in citation practice would affect the length of unpublished opinions and the time it took to draft them.[36] The results are fascinating.

a. *Question One.* Judges in circuits that *permit* citation were asked what would happen if citations were *prohibited*. Their responses:
   - Length. 82 percent predicted that the length of opinions would not change.
   - Time. 84 percent predicted that there would be no change in drafting time.
   - Summary. The judges believed that prohibiting citation of unpublished opinions would have little effect on either opinion length or drafting time. In other words, judges in circuits with actual experience in using unpublished opinions did not believe that eliminating them would affect the workload of the courts.

b. *Question Two.* Judges in circuits where citation is freely permitted were asked how they would be affected if citations were permitted only when there was no published opinion on point. The judges were asked, in other words, what they thought would be the effect of moving from a *permissive* to a *discouraging* citation position. There was a response rate of 72 percent of the judges.[37]
   - Length. Three-quarters of the respondents did not believe opinion length would change. Most of the remaining judges thought that opinions would become moderately longer.[38]

33. *Id.* at 2. The appeals chosen had been briefed by both sides, and attorneys for both sides were sent the questionnaire. Pro se litigants apparently were not consulted.

34. *Id.*

35. *Id.* at 3.

36. The study does not explain why it asked about opinion length as well as drafting time; it seems reasonable to suppose that opinion length is a rough, somewhat objective surrogate for effort. If so, it was a good surrogate, for the answers to both the length and time parts of the question were very similar.

37. This rate is noticeably lower than the 82 percent rate obtained for Question One. It is hard to think of an explanation for this discrepancy.

38. *Id.* at 5.

- Time. Again, three-quarters of the respondents believed that the suggested change would have little effect on the time spent preparing unpublished opinions.[39]
- Summary. Question Two confirms that judges who are experienced in having unpublished opinions cited to them do not believe that limiting citations would affect their workload.

c. *Question Three*. Finally, the Federal Judicial Center asked judges in those circuits that either prohibited or discouraged citations what they expected would happen if citations to unpublished opinions were freely permitted. Question Three had several subparts; the results can be summarized this way.[40]

- Circuits that Discourage Unpublished Opinions. Eighty percent of the judges who responded did not expect either the number or length of unpublished opinions to increase if citations were freely permitted. A small majority predicted that time spent in opinion preparation would not change.

  Sixty-nine percent of the judges in the discouraging circuits did not believe that opinion length would increase with unrestricted citations.
- Circuits that Prohibit Unpublished Opinions. The responses for the judges in those courts had a different pattern from those in the other circuits.

  A majority (56 percent) said drafting time would increase if citations were freely permitted. More than a third (37 percent) said drafting time would increase either a great deal or a very great deal.

  A large majority (78 percent) of the judges predicted that the length of unpublished opinions would increase if they could be freely cited.

  An interesting difference among the restrictive circuits emerged: although 72 percent of the judges in the Second, Ninth, and Federal Circuits predicted "special problems" with unlimited citations, only 42 percent in the Seventh Circuit thought there would be a problem.

2. The Bottom Line

In short, the experience of the judges who had made the switch from restrictive to permissive citation dramatically confirmed that citation practice had had little or no effect on their work.[41] The judges with actual experience did not believe that permitting citation of unpublished opinions had increased their workload.

39. *Id.* at 6.

40. Each subpart had response rates of at least 79 percent. *Id.* at 6–8.

41. The authors of the Report also asked 384 randomly chosen attorneys about citation practice. Once again, the response rate was high: 84 percent. *Id.* at 15. The attorneys were given two

And yet the Ninth Circuit judges and other opponents of Rule 32.1 ignored this strong evidence from their own colleagues in other circuits, evidence that the same judges surely would have given great credence in other contexts. It is not clear why they did so. Perhaps they feared the unknown, much like a small child afraid of the dark. More likely, of course, is that the judicial opponents saw Rule 32.1 as the first step on a slippery slope, the bottom of which is the end of limited publication.

D. THE NEW CITATION RULE

Despite the somewhat intense opposition it provoked, the proposed Rule 32.1 made it through the various barriers to its adoption, and it became effective on December 1, 2006.

The Rule is simple enough. It provides:

Rule 32.1. Citing Judicial Dispositions

1. Citation Permitted. A court may not prohibit or restrict the citation of federal judicial opinions, orders, judgments, or other written dispositions that have been: (i) designated as "unpublished," "not for publication," "non-precedential," "not precedent," or the like; and (ii) issued on or after January 1, 2007.
2. Copies Required. If a party cites a federal judicial opinion, order, judgment, or other written disposition that is not available in a publicly accessible electronic

questions. One question asked whether they wanted to be able to cite unpublished opinions, and the second asked what they believed would be the impact of a change to a permissive citation regime:

Question One. The lawyers were asked whether, when doing research for this appeal, did they run into unpublished opinion from the circuit hearing the appeal that they wanted to cite but could not due to the circuit's rules. Forty percent said yes.

- The attorneys were asked the same question concerning whether there were unpublished opinions in other circuits that they wished to cite. About a quarter (27 percent) replied yes. *Id.* at 15–16.
- For both subquestions, more attorneys from restrictive circuits said yes than did those from either permissive or discouraging courts. *Id.* at 16.

Question Two. Attorneys were asked whether, if the circuit's rules on citation had been more lenient, they would have cited an unpublished opinion. The results were almost identical with those from Question One.

- Forty-eight percent said they would have liked to cite an unpublished opinion from their own circuit. *Id.* at 16–17.
- Thirty-two percent would have cited an opinion from another circuit. *Id.* at 16–17. Again, the lawyers in the restrictive circuits said yes more often than those in either the permissive or the discouraging circuits. *Id.* at 17.

In short, the attorneys wanted to be able to cite unpublished opinions.

database, the party must file and serve a copy of that opinion, order, judgment, or disposition with the brief or other paper in which it is cited.

In short, a court cannot prevent—or restrict—the citation of *any* federal judicial written disposition issued on or after January 1, 2007.[42] That Rule 32.1 had nothing to do with the precedential status of unpublished opinions was made clear by the Advisory Note, which stated:

> Rule 32.1 is extremely limited. It does not require any court to issue an unpublished opinion or forbid any court from doing so .... It says nothing about what effect a court must give to one of its unpublished opinions or to the unpublished opinions of another court. Rule 32.1 only addresses the citation of federal judicial dispositions that have been designated as "unpublished" or "non-precedential" ....[43]

Amy Sloan has observed that Rule 32.1 is the first recognition of the existence of limited publication by a system-wide Rule that has been adopted by the Supreme Court.[44] Sloan fears that official recognition might lend legitimacy to limited publication. On the other hand, success at eliminating non-citation practice suggests that the whole system of limited publication might be vulnerable.

E. THE NEW RULE IN PRACTICE

Rule 32.1 appears straightforward enough on its face, and the circuits have had little trouble implementing it formally. The key question that needed to be addressed involved whether unpublished opinions issued before the adoption of Rule 32.1 could be cited.[45] Seven circuits permit unlimited citations to their own earlier opinions;[46] two circuits permit citation of earlier unpublished opinions only when there is no relevant published authority;[47] and the last three circuits forbid

42. The term "disposition" is not defined, but it seems intended to be very broad—if the decision is *written*, it is covered. No mention is made in Rule 32.1, however, of citation to *oral* dispositions. Rule 32.1 also fails to deal expressly with citations to dispositions made before its effective date of December 1, 2006. Note that the Rule does not apply to unpublished *state court* opinions.

43. Advisory Note to Rule 32.1.

44. Amy E. Sloan, *If You Can't Beat 'Em, Join 'Em: A Pragmatic Approach to Nonprecedential Opinions in the Federal Appellate Courts*, 86 Neb. L. Rev. 895, 900 (2008).

45. See David R. Cleveland, *Local Rules in the Wake of Federal Rule of Appellate Procedure 32.1*, 11 J. App. Prac. & Process 19–24 (2010), and Robert Timothy Reagan, Fed. Judicial Ctr., Citing Unpublished Federal Appellate Opinions Issued Before 2007 (Mar. 9, 2007) for complete discussions of the problem as well as references to the relevant rules.

46. These are the First, Third, Fifth, Sixth, Tenth, Eleventh, and District of Columbia Circuits—although the last only permits citations to its opinions issued after 2001.

47. The Fourth and Eighth Circuits.

citation to unpublished opinions issued before 2007.[48] All circuits permit citation for preclusion-related purposes. It is amazing after the prolonged struggle to adopt Rule 32.1 that the circuits have forsaken uniformity in putting it into effect. It is equally amazing that once again some circuits have ignored the rich history of those courts that had permitted citation without creating problems.

A nationwide rule permitting citation to pre-2007 opinions would be a sensible course for the law to take. The concept is a familiar one. We learn early in law school that all opinions that are not "controlling" are persuasive, and that a judge must consider all authority in making his decision. In turn, that helps the court ensure that like cases get decided in like fashion, which, after all, is the bedrock of common law adjudication.

F. DID RULE 32.1 ACCOMPLISH ANYTHING?

The bitter battle over Rule 32.1 may have little immediate practical impact. The Federal Judicial Center Report revealed that citations to unpublished opinions in those circuits that had previously permitted it had proven of little value to the courts.[49] Patrick Schiltz wrote, "[t]he argument that Rule 32.1 will provide some practical benefits has always struck me as less than compelling."[50] That surely is correct; there is so little meat in most unpublished opinions, so little in the way of facts or analysis, that it is difficult to see how those decisions are of any use to anyone.

Nevertheless, there are some positives. There are, after all, some unpublished decisions that have some substance, and now they can be fully woven into the tapestry of the common law. Even in the bare-bones opinions, the possibility of citation might impel a bit more care in opinion preparation and writing. It is also important that an attorney can make a claim for consistency by citing any case and that a judge can now cite to the decision on which she is relying; these steps make the system more transparent and, therefore, better. Citation can also convert the unpublished, nonprecedential opinion into something different, something quasi-precedential in character.

Left largely unanswered after the adoption of Rule 32.1 is the question of what, if any, precedential value should be given to unpublished opinions once they have been cited. The leading contender here is "persuasive" precedent. The Local Rules of two circuits expressly use the term "persuasive value" when addressing the question of citation of older unpublished opinions.[51] Commentators like Amy Sloan and

48. The Second, Seventh, and Ninth Circuits.

49. The data are discussed in Schiltz, *Much Ado*, supra note 14, at 1464–65.

50. *Id.* at 1466.

51. *See* David R. Cleveland, *Local Rules in the Wake of Federal Rule of Appellate Procedure 32.1*, 11 J. APP. PRAC. & PROCESS 19, 45–46 (2010).

Steve Barnett have also suggested unpublished opinions be accorded "persuasive" status.[52]

That makes a lot of sense. We have all known since very early in law school what it means for a decision to be "persuasive"; it is everything that is not "controlling." Beyond that, it is not a technical term; rather, it means that the earlier decision can be used in argument (to borrow a phrase) "for what it's worth." A court can consider, among other things, the quality of the reasoning and the apparent thought and effort that went into the cited opinion. It is not worthless, for it still is part of the law, but it is also something that need not be followed if that seems inappropriate under all of the circumstances. In this way, courts can realize the benefits that they see in the limited publication regime while ameliorating some of the costs.

It probably does not matter whether a circuit has adopted a local rule formally embracing the concept of persuasive precedent. Once unpublished opinions can be cited, they will be used. Consider in this regard *Bragg v. Linden Research, Inc.*[53] One of the questions in that case was whether the court could exercise personal jurisdiction over Second Life, the virtual world site; in answering that question, the court relied on an unpublished Third Circuit precedent, *Wellness Publishing*,[54] which it said "provides useful guidance, albeit in a non-precedential opinion."[55] The *Bragg* court proceeded to follow carefully the analysis in the unpublished appellate decision. By doing so, the *Bragg* court pulled off a clever trick: it managed to make both opinions more authoritative. The trial court opinion gained in authority by virtue of its close connection with the appellate opinion, and the latter, although formally unpublished, became harder for the appellate court to change because of the clear reliance on it in other cases.

Even if a number of district court opinions were to do what *Bragg* did, however, *Wellness Publishing* will never achieve the status of a published opinion. That is because *Wellness Publishing* is formally unpublished and, therefore, can be overturned by a panel decision; if it had been given the precedential status that comes with "publication," *Wellness Publishing*, because of the law of the circuit doctrine, could be overturned only on en banc review. In this way, nonprecedential opinions can acquire a form of persuasive authority. A later panel faced with a *Bragg/Wellness Publishing* situation may have the power to overturn the earlier rulings but will find that harder to do than if no other decision had overtly followed the unpublished opinion.

52. See Amy E. Sloan, *If You Can't Beat 'Em, Join 'Em: A Pragmatic Approach to Nonprecedential Opinions in the Federal Appellate Courts*, 86 NEB. L. REV. 895, 923 (2008); Stephen R. Barnett, *No-Citation Rules Under Siege: A Battlefield Report and Analysis*, 5. J. APP. PRAC. & PROCESS, 473, 497 (2003).

53. 487 F. Supp. 2d 593 (E.D. Pa. 2007).

54. Wellness Publ'g v. Barefoot, 128 Fed. App'x 266 (3d Cir. 2005).

55. *Bragg*, 487 F. Supp. 2d at 598.

Bragg may confirm Judge Kozinski's worst fears about Rule 32.1, for it shows how a nonprecedent may still be used as a precedent. The end of citation limits shows that limited publication can be attacked. But of course, we, along with all critics of limited publication schemes, consider that a good thing. The rallying cry might be, "Today citation, tomorrow precedent."

Another way of looking at this is to say that the ability to cite all decisions means each disposition by an appellate court enters the discussion about the future of the law. And that is as it should be. The common law that we learned to love in law school made everything grist for the judicial mill. Maybe we are finally returning to our roots.

CHAPTER 6

The Constitution and Unpublished Opinions

The discussion has so far ignored any possible constitutional challenges to the limited publication regime. Although law professors (and a few judges) have expressed concern with the constitutionality of the practice, not much has come of that unease.

For at least a third of a century, litigants and academics have questioned the constitutionality of limited publication.[1] During most of that time, the arguments have centered on grounds traditionally associated with the assertion of individual rights: due process, equal protection, and free speech. Those arguments have failed. Then, in the year 2000, a highly respected federal judge[2] embraced a different constitutional provision, one addressing institutional concerns, and issued the only opinion holding any aspect of the limited publication regime unconstitutional. In the end, however, that argument also failed.

This section examines the various constitutional arguments involving unpublished opinions and concludes with a brief examination of what individual members of the Supreme Court have said about the issue. The section concludes with an analysis of why pragmatic concerns make it unlikely that any constitutional argument would ever prevail.

1. *See generally* David R. Cleveland, *Draining the Morass: Ending the Jurisprudentially Unsound Unpublication System*, 92 MARQ. L. REV. 685 (2008) (summarizing constitutional arguments against unpublished decisions) [hereinafter *Draining*]; David R. Cleveland, *Overturning the Last Stone: The Final Step in Returning Precedential Status to all Opinions*, 10 J. APP. PRAC. & PROCESS 61 (2009) (reviewing constitutional arguments) [hereinafter *Overturning*].

2. Anastasoff v. United States, 223 F.3d 898 (8th Cir 2000). Judge Richard S. Arnold wrote the opinion.

A. TRADITIONAL RIGHTS-BASED ARGUMENTS

Arguments based on claims of individual rights do not lack appeal. Although courts have easily disposed of those arguments, an examination of their merits helps underline the deep problems created by the current system of unpublished opinions.

1. Due Process

The due process challenge to the use of unpublished opinions is easy to state, especially when the unpublished opinion is written to resolve an appeal of a criminal conviction. Part of an accused's right to fair procedures, so the claim runs, is a reasoned explanation from the appellate panel, one that is available for the world to see. A necessary element of due process, in other words, is something resembling the Learned Hand treatment of appeals. That argument has met with short shrift. The following explanation is typical:

> Litigants are entitled to have all issues fully considered and ruled on by a panel of the Court of Appeals. Appellant, however, seems to equate meaningful review to a full written opinion. In doing so, Appellant fails to distinguish between the review process and the manner in which the Court announces its decision .... In general, decisions regarding publication and the extent to which the Court determines that a written explanation of its decisions is called for is driven by whether a full opinion will benefit bench, bar, or the litigants. These decisions, however, are quite distinct from the meaningfulness of the Court's review.[3]

In other words, the decision and the explanation (if any) of that decision are entirely separate matters. Only the decision need be fair for the process to be constitutional; fairness, however, requires no public explanation of how it was reached. Thus, the reasoning behind the decision (if any) does not have to be set forth unless the court feels like doing so.

Part of the explanation is that there was not even a statutory right to appeal a criminal conviction until 1889, much less a constitutional right to do so.[4] Thus, a reasoned explanation, or, indeed, any explanation by an appellate court, should not be considered "fundamental" for due process purposes. Of course, if the courts were really interested in due process for litigants, they would be troubled by the heavy delegation of effective decision-making authority to nonjudicial personnel and the practice in some circuits of providing no explanation at all in some cases.[5]

3. United States v. Pajooh, 143 F.3d 203, 204 (5th Cir.), *cert. denied*, 525 U.S. 1009 (1998).
4. *Id.* at 204.
5. See the discussion of very short opinions in chapter 3, *supra*.

Judges worried about such things would not have let matters come to where they now are.[6]

2. Equal Protection

The equal protection argument is also readily apparent. Litigants whose cases are resolved by unpublished opinions receive different and, therefore (at least arguably) unconstitutional treatment from the judiciary. This argument is also easily disposed of. Disparate treatment is unconstitutional under well-established equal protection principles only if the treatment has an impact on a fundamental right or involves a protected class. Because unpublished opinions do not themselves involve either category, they do not offend equal protection.

One scholar has argued that a fundamental right/equal protection analysis might be triggered when a litigant, whose losing case was resolved in an unpublished opinion, has been treated differently than a later, similarly situated litigant who won, at least in part, because the earlier, unpublished opinion lacked precedential value. Fundamental right analysis comes into play because persons who are similarly situated (litigants) are being treated unequally.[7] That argument is likely to fail, however, because the constitution does not demand equality of treatment, but only that the process be fair, that the disparity in treatment have a rational basis[8] and not have as its basis something regarded as fundamental, such as race or speech. In short, until courts view the disparate treatment accorded litigants by the limited publication model as denying important rights, the system will easily withstand due process and equal protection analysis. Until that happens, those challenges will be judged on a rational basis standard—almost always a losing proposition.

3. Free Speech

The First Amendment argument centers on the non-citation rules. The argument can be stated simply: a litigant or judge who cannot cite (that is, "speak about") an earlier decision has been denied her free speech rights.[9] Although the decision in

6. Cleveland, *Overturning, supra* note 1, at 155–62, provides a more sympathetic view of the due process argument.

7. *See* Cleveland, *Draining, supra* note 1, at 151.

8. Cleveland, *Overturning, supra* note 1, at 152–55, contends that strict scrutiny is the appropriate standard of review. There is something to that argument, at least in criminal cases, but because the precedential status of an opinion is "procedural," we think that a rational basis test is more likely to be applied.

9. *See, e.g., In re* Rules of the U.S. Court of Appeals for the Tenth Circuit, 955 F.2d 36 (10th Cir. 1992) (Holloway, C.J., dissenting from issuance of rules); David Dunn, *Unreported Decisions in the United States Courts of Appeals*, 63 CORNELL L. REV. 128, 141–45 (1977); Stephen R. Barnett, *"Unpublished" Judicial Opinions in the United States: Law or Not?* 2 EUR. BUS. ORG. L.

Legal Services Corp. v. Velasquez[10] provides support for that argument,[11] it seems to have been mooted by the adoption of Federal Rule of Appellate Procedure 32.1 in 2006. Now, both the litigant and the judge can make any argument they wish and even cite unpublished opinions in support of it. Moreover, the opinions can be read, analyzed, and cited by others. Although the opinions may lack precedential value, there has been no loss of voice by anyone—only a loss of authority.

B. INSTITUTIONAL CONCERNS: WHAT IS THE "JUDICIAL POWER"? THE *ANASTASOFF* QUERY

More controversial has been an argument based on the very nature of a *court*: can judges ever issue an opinion that is *not* precedential? After some uncertainty, that question seems to have received a positive answer from both judges and commentators.

The issue arose when opponents of unpublished opinions won a brief victory in *Anastasoff v. United States*,[12] where a panel of the Eighth Circuit held that Article III of the United States Constitution required that all federal court decisions must serve as precedents. That decision, however, was reversed on other grounds by an en banc court and has since been seriously questioned by judges and scholars alike.

The facts of *Anastasoff* were very simple. A taxpayer had sought a tax refund. The request for the refund was *mailed* by the taxpayer within the three-year statutory period for requesting refunds, but *received* by the government three years and one day after she filed her return. The government denied the request on limitations grounds, and the taxpayer sued to obtain her refund. Unfortunately for her, the suit was brought in Missouri, part of the Eighth Circuit. That circuit court had earlier held, in a very similar case, that such a claim was time-barred; that is, that the limitations period required *receipt* by the government of the refund request within three years of the date the return was filed. Although that earlier decision, *Christie v. United States*,[13] was an unpublished opinion, Eighth Circuit doctrine held that every decision bound later panels; the first decision, in other words, could only be overturned by an en banc court.[14] Thus, the *Anastasoff* court was bound to follow *Christie* and deny the claim. In response, the *Anastasoff* plaintiff argued she could

REV. 429 (2001); Salem M. Katsh & Alex V. Chachkes, *Constitutionality of "No-Citation" Rules*, 3 J. APP. PRAC. & PROCESS 287 (2001).

10. 531 U.S. 533 (2001).

11. The Court struck down a ban on the use of federal funds to argue for a change in welfare law on the ground that it violated the speech rights of litigants and their attorneys. *Id.* at 545.

12. 223 F.3d 898 (8th Cir. 2000).

13. No. 91–2375 MN, 1992 U.S. App. LEXIS 38446 (8th Cir. Mar. 20, 1992) (*per curiam*).

14. The law of the circuit rule is discussed in chapter 3.

not be bound by an unpublished decision; after all, that decision, by definition, was *not* precedential. A panel of the Eighth Circuit rejected her argument.

1. The *Anastasoff* Panel

The unanimous panel opinion by Judge Richard Arnold[15] began by noting that Eighth Circuit Rule 28A(i) expressly denies precedential effect to unpublished opinions. Thus, the unpublished *Christie* decision would not control. If *Christie* did have precedential value, the taxpayer would lose, because its holding could be overturned only by the full circuit court sitting en banc. Thus, the taxpayer would lose unless Rule 28A saved her from the precedential effect of *Christie*.

Judge Arnold saw the issue in constitutional terms: does the practice of denying precedential effect to unpublished opinions "expand the judicial power beyond the bounds of Article III [of the United States Constitution] ...."[16] Judge Arnold turned to history to answer that question. Relying on authorities as hallowed as Blackstone, Hamilton, and Story, he concluded that in 1787, a system of precedent lay at the heart of the job done by judges. The framers understood that the exercise of judicial power by any court, including a federal court established under Article III, imposed a duty to follow precedent; only by doing so could courts avoid acting legislatively. That understanding meant, Arnold wrote, that every decision had to be authority for later cases—that it had to have precedential value. In short, judges had to make law—set a precedent—in every case they decided. Any other result would be "alarming," as Justice Story once put it[17]. For that reason, the concept of a decision lacking in precedential value was foreign to the framers: Article III required *every* decision to have precedential status.

Arnold then noted that lawyers and judges in 1787 considered *all* decisions to be precedent; the law could be found in any decision, even if the "opinion" relied on was only a memory of an oral pronouncement. The *Anastasoff* opinion observed that "judges and lawyers of the day [that is, 1787] recognized the authority of unpublished decisions even when they were established only by memory or by a

15. Arnold was a very well-respected judge. President Clinton had wanted to nominate him to the Supreme Court, but Arnold's health proved too fragile. Jeffrey Toobin, The Nine: Inside the Secret World of the Supreme Court 77 (2007). Judge Arnold died in 2004.Judge Arnold must have been waiting for an opportunity to write an opinion like *Anastasoff*. The issue he discussed had not been raised at all in the literature, and it would have been hard to research it properly in the limited time following argument. Arnold clearly was spoiling for a fight on unpublished opinions; the year before *Anastasoff* was decided, he had expressed concern about the practice of issuing nonprecedential opinions and had questioned whether the practice conformed with Article III. Richard S. Arnold, *Unpublished Opinions: A Comment*, 1 J. App. Prac. & Process 219 (1999).

16. *Anastasoff*, 223 F.3d at 900.

17. Joseph Story, Commentaries on the Constitution of the United States § 377 (1833).

lawyer's unpublished memorandum."[18] Failure to do so, therefore, violated Article III,[19] and the denial of precedential effect to unpublished opinions was unconstitutional. As a result, Local Rule 28A was invalid, and the unpublished decision in *Christie* became a precedent that had to be followed; *Christie,* therefore, controlled *Anastasoff,* and the taxpayer lost.

2. The Reaction Elsewhere

The panel decision in *Anastasoff* was not welcomed by other courts.[20] Judge Kozinski handled the heavy artillery for the opposition, and in *Hart v. Massanari,*[21] he soon provided the establishment's answer. Like Arnold, Kozinski used history extensively to make his point, but he reached a completely different result. Kozinski first argued that Article III's use of the term "Judicial Power ... is more likely descriptive than prescriptive."[22] In other words, the term is meant to refer to what courts do in practice, rather than to what they *must* do (so long as the judges follow other constitutional norms such as due process). If the term "judicial power" is not meant to freeze the 1787 understanding of what courts should do, Kozinski explained, then a change in judicial procedure is not necessarily unconstitutional. After all, he observed, judicial practice has changed considerably since 1787; juries, for example, are no longer judges of law as well as fact, and judges no longer sit on appeals of their own *nisi prius* decisions, as they once did.[23] Such long-accepted developments suggest strongly that Article III should not be read as a straitjacket; and reasonable changes in procedure, such as the system of limited publication, should not be found unconstitutional merely because they were unknown at the time the constitution was adopted.

The *Hart* court buttressed its reasoning with three other arguments. First, it examined the concept of precedent in 1787. Judges back then did not see themselves as "making" law, but rather as merely "finding" it. Thus, a common law court always followed precedent because the law was always there waiting to be found; today, of course, we believe courts consciously create law where it is appropriate to

18. 223 F.3d at 903.

19. *Id.* Arnold also noted that issuing a non-precedential decision conflicts with the legislative powers of Congress[,*id.* at 904, a separation of powers argument.]

20. Nor was it welcome by even the Eighth Circuit. On en banc review, the court dismissed the case as moot, although the en banc court noted that the constitutional issue "remains an open question in this court." Anastasoff v. United States, 235 F.3d 1054, 1056 (8th Cir. 2000) (en banc). Virtually, the only kind judicial word for *Anastasoff* is Judge Young's opinion in *Alshrafi v. American Airlines,* 321 F. Supp. 2d 150, 151 n.9 (D. Mass. 2004) ("[T]his Court considers the reasoning of *Anastasoff* especially compelling ....").

21. 266 F.3d 1155 (9th Cir. 2001).

22. *Id.* at 1161.

23. *Id.* at 1162. The opinion also refers to the decrease in multi-judge panels issuing opinions *seriatim,* rather than as an opinion "of the Court." *Id.* & n.6.

do so. Moreover, a doctrine of strict precedent requires both an equally strict hierarchy of courts and a reliable and accurate system of reporting decisions, both of which we have today, although neither was present two centuries earlier.[24] Finally, Kozinski argued, the limited publication regime is a reasonable and long-accepted method to address the burgeoning caseload problem in the federal circuit courts.

Judge Kozinski's opinion in *Hall* seems to have ended the discussion in the circuit courts. Apparently, and understandably, the judges have little interest in the topic of unpublished opinions and the Constitution.

Academic commentators, although often hostile themselves to limited publication plans, also generally agree with the reasoning in *Hall*.[25] There is much to be said on both sides of the *Anastasoff/Hall* debate. On the one hand, the common law did treat everything as precedent—anything a judge or court did was fodder for an attorney arguing a legal point. To be sure, some precedent was more worthwhile or more reliable than others, but if it was out there, it could be used. On the other hand, Judge Kozinski is surely right that the framers did not intend to freeze the concept of "judicial power" in its meaning in 1787. The framers were notoriously practical persons, and it would be odd for us to conclude that in drafting Article III they meant to end the evolution of the judicial system. That view is supported by a respected historian of American legal development who found that "a firm doctrine of *stare decisis*" did not take hold in this country "until the first half of the nineteenth century."[26]

But there may be a deeper meaning to be found in *Anastasoff*. Lauren Robel has observed that Judge Arnold's opinion

> describes the process of common law decisionmaking in deeply cultural terms .... Common-law understandings of precedent entail more than a practical view that all opinions contain information with predictive value. What makes those opinions predictive is the requirement of justification for deviation from them. The normative commitment to justification is as firmly entrenched in our understandings of precedent as is our belief in the predictive value of case results.[27]

What is important, in other words, is the justification of the decision, something that we have long demanded of those who judge us, something that is absent in so many unpublished opinions. Penelope Pether similarly notes that the "normative

24. *Id.* at 1164–65. The need for each factor should be obvious: without reliable reporting of decisions, it can be difficult to fathom what an opinion actually *means*, and the existence of a judicial hierarchy is needed to tell the world which tribunals must follow what decisions.

25. *See* Cleveland, *Overturning, supra note* 1, at 62 n.5 (listing more than a dozen articles on the topic).

26. Frederick G. Kempin Jr., *Precedent and Stare Decisis: The Critical Years, 1800 to 1850*, 3 Am. J. Legal Hist. 28, 36 (1959).

27. Lauren N. Robel, *The Practice of Precedent:* Anastasoff, *Noncitation Rules, and the Meaning of Precedent in an Interpretive Community*, 35 Ind. L. Rev. 399, 414 (2002).

crux of Judge Arnold's jurisprudence likewise sounds in the arbitrariness of the [limited publication] rules and what they formally justify, their lack of principle, and their authorizing unreasoned decision making."[28] Thus Judge Arnold captured the deep unease about limited publication shared by so many familiar with the practice. Unfortunately, the judges themselves do not seem to share his concern—or, if they do, choose to remain silent.

In any event, the last few years have seen no indication that the judges are at all inclined to build on *Anastasoff*. It seems highly unlikely, therefore, that any court will again issue an opinion using Article III to strike down a regime of limited publication. That does not mean, however, that the controversy over *Anastasoff* has had no impact. It surely played a major role in the effort to eliminate the no-citation rules, an effort that ended in the adoption of Rule 32.1 of the Federal Rules of Appellate procedure in 2006,[29] and Judge Arnold and his panel succeeded in focusing the attention of the legal world on the disaster that we call limited publication.

More generally, *Anastasoff* reflects uneasiness among at least some judges with the system they have established. That concern is shared by many academics and practicing attorneys as well. Is there any chance that the Supreme Court will act on the issue?

C. UNPUBLISHED OPINIONS IN THE SUPREME COURT

The circuit court rules on limited publication are, of course, ultimately subject to the rule-making authority of the Supreme Court. But the Court seems singularly uninterested (or unwilling) to address the constitutional challenges presented by nonpublication regimes. It is not as if the issue has not been presented to the Justices. One scholar has identified at least three dozen petitions for *certiorari* that have raised the question of the constitutionality of limited publication regimes;[30] only once, however, has the Supreme Court granted such a petition. And the decision in the case did not reach the issue of publication.

One of the questions presented by the petitioner in *Browder v. Director, Department of Corrections of Illinois*,[31] was whether a federal circuit court has "the inherent power to withhold any of its opinions from publication and to

28. Penelope Pether, *Constitutional Solipsism: Toward a Thick Doctrine of Article III Duty; Or Why the Federal Circuits' Nonprecedential Rules are (Profoundly) Unconstitutional*, 17 Wm & Mary Bill of Rights J., 955, 1028 (2009) (footnote omitted). Pether calls for the application of the "thick residue of normative constitutional standards" found in Article III of the Constitution. *Id.*

29. *See* discussion in chapter 3.

30. Cleveland, *Draining*, *supra note* 1, at 711 n.172. This article provides a comprehensive review of what the Justices have said and done with respect to unpublished opinions.

31. 434 U.S. 257 (1978).

deprive *a priori* such opinions of precedential value."[32] Although the petitioner was supported on this question by an *amicus* brief filed by the Chicago Council of Lawyers, the Court did not reach the unpublished opinion issue. Instead, the Court held that because it lacked subject matter jurisdiction, the petition must be dismissed;[33] on limited publication, it noted only that "petitioner questioned the validity of the Seventh Circuit's 'unpublished opinion' rule. We leave these questions to another day."[34]

Over the years, however, several Justices in separate opinions have expressed dissatisfaction with the limited publication regime. Thus, in *County of Los Angeles v. Kling*, Justice Stevens wrote that "the Court of Appeals would have been well advised to discuss the record in greater depth .... That decision not to publish the opinion or permit it to be cited—like the decision to promulgate a rule spawning a body of secret law—was plainly wrong."[35] Similarly, a dissent in *Smith v. United States* observed, "[n]onpublication must not be a convenient means to prevent review. An unpublished opinion may have a lingering effect in the Circuit and surely is as important to the parties concerned as is a published opinion."[36] Nevertheless, those expressions of concern have never led a single Justice to examine carefully the widespread acceptance of limited publication.[37] Indeed, those isolated comments are better seen as a reflection of judicial irritation with particular decisions; they do not reflect a concern with the unpublished opinion situation, or at least concern serious enough to warrant paying close attention to. It seems unlikely, therefore, that the Supreme Court will ever address the constitutional issues raised by unpublished opinions. Not only do those questions appear to be of little interest to the Court, but it also will not want to disturb the solution reached over time by the courts who must deal with their own caseload problem.[38]

32. Brief for Petitioner at 7, *Browder*, 434 U.S. 510 (No. 76-5325).

33. 434 U.S. at 258.

34. *Id.* at 258 n.1.

35. *Kling*, 474 U.S. 936, 940 (1985) (Stevens, J., dissenting). Justice Stevens cited two of our articles in note 1 of his dissent from the denial of *certiorari*.

36. *Smith*, 502 U.S. 1017, 1020 n.2 (Blackmun, O'Connor, and Souter, JJ., dissenting).

37. Chief Justice Roberts and Justice Alito have not said anything about unpublished opinions since they joined the Court. They are well aware of the controversy, however, for both were members of the Advisory Committee on the Federal Rules of Appellate Procedure (and then-Judge Alito chaired the Committee) when Rule 32.1, which permitted citation of unpublished opinions, was adopted.

38. In addition, when Justice Alito was a circuit judge, he testified in 2002 before the Judiciary Committee of the House of Representatives on the subject of unpublished opinions. He said: "Opinions dealing with the easy application of established law to specific facts have little use as precedent for other litigants or posterity." *Quoted in* Richard B. Cappalli, *The Common Law's Case Against Non-Precedential Opinions*, 76 S. Cal. L. Rev. 755, 768 n.64. That is hardly the statement of someone bent on radical change of the status quo.

D. PRUDENTIAL CONSIDERATIONS

It seems, therefore, the judiciary is unlikely to hold that the unpublished opinion regime violates the Constitution. That surely is the correct result. A "thought experiment" is useful here to see the position the judges have gotten themselves into. If the Supreme Court were to undo the limited publication regime with a single stroke of the judicial pen, havoc would ensue—at least if the proponents of that regime are to be believed.[39] The argument runs something like this: because all opinions would be precedential, they would have to be thought about and written more carefully and contain more explanation. Moreover, judges would not be able to delegate as much of the decision-making process to central staff; precedential opinions, after all, demand more quality control, especially at the top. These changes and the resultant increase in workload would be too much for the current roster of appellate judges to handle.[40] In chapters 11 through 14, we discuss some possible remedies for the crisis in caseload, such as curtailment of the subject matter jurisdiction of the federal courts or the addition of many new judges. The adoption of those measures would require congressional action, of course, and it is likely that the Supreme Court, even if it wished to address the constitutional issue, would abstain for prudential reasons and wait for Congress to act.

Congress is the only body capable of dealing with the problems that would be created by a finding that the regime of limited publication was unconstitutional; it is safe to predict that the Court will not act on its own.[41] That prediction, however, does not mean that the Justices could not lobby Congress to adopt the necessary alleviative measures. As we shall show in chapters 10–14, however, that is something the judicial establishment has resolutely refused to do.

In the end, the establishment will prevail on the constitutional issues. But what does it say about our federal appellate courts that serious legal scholars—and

39. This would be true even if the Court were to stay its Order finding the regime unconstitutional for some limited time to give Congress a chance to adopt a solution. *See* Northern Pipeline Constr. Co v. Marathon Pipeline Co., 458 U.S. 50 (1982) (delaying for more than three months the effect of a decision holding the nation's bankruptcy courts unconstitutional). As we suggest later, see *infra* chapter 11, significant increases in judges would be necessary to handle the work.

40. See the discussion in chapter 3 of judicial arguments concerning the need for limited publication based on caseload pressures.

41. A secondary concern might be that many states have limited publication regimes that resemble the federal system. A decision by the Supreme Court that limited publication was unconstitutional could have a dramatic impact in those states. If the decision were made on some of the grounds that we have discussed—e.g., equal protection or due process—the states would be directly bound by the decision. Even if the decision were based on Article III grounds, however, some state courts might feel a need to follow the federal lead; after all, states also have separation of power concerns. In any event, a discontinuity between federal and state courts in such an important area would be highly troubling.

judges—have raised fundamental questions about the constitutionality of their basic procedures? Should not the courts strive to avoid those questions being raised at all? It is, after all, a basic premise of constitutional law that statutes should be construed so as to avoid constitutional dilemmas. Should not the courts follow the same precept in running their own show? Or is it enough to assert, as the judges surely would, that the ends—prompt resolution of all cases and serious resolution of important cases—justify the means?

CHAPTER 7

Restricting Oral Argument

A. INTRODUCTION

Oral argument and the common law once were inseparable. The common law was born in England, grew to maturity, and was transplanted to America as a system where the words *spoken* by judges and counsel were of fundamental importance. The common law of England did not develop from the work of legislatures and treatise writers, as happened on the Continent, nor did it develop from the carefully crafted opinions of appellate judges, as has become the custom in the United States. Rather, the common law grew out of the needs of litigation and the many oral exchanges that courts and litigants conducted to try to decide disputes and explain their resolutions. The explanations of the decisions and the facts that underlay those explanations—what we call today the *ratio decidendi*—were spoken, not written. To be sure, those decisions, including the colloquy between court and counsel, eventually emerged in written form in what we call today "Reports," but only as compilations of the reporters' notes and memories of what had actually been said. Thus, the famous Year Books, available from the thirteenth century on, were merely unofficial compilations, sometimes by law students, of what had been said earlier in court.

Oral argument is vital to many of the central myths of the English bar. Their history is replete with great show trials such as those of Sir Thomas More and Queen Catherine, trials where the destiny of the nation turned on the forensic ability of the participants. And perhaps the most dramatic moment in the whole history of the common law occurred when Lord Coke denied the King plenary power over his judges.[1]

1. Coke, under intense pressure from James I, recanted. For an American reader the story is perhaps best told in CATHERINE DRINKER BOWEN, THE LION AND THE THRONE: THE LIFE AND TIMES OF SIR EDWARD COKE 304–06 (1959).

Early American legal history was no different. Great show trials—the seditious libel trial of Peter Zenger, the impeachment of Justice Chase, the treason trial of Aaron Burr—turned on oral argument and are indelibly stamped in our history. As time passed, however, orality lost some of its importance; we remember great cases like *Brown v. Board of Education*[2] or the *Watergate Tapes Case*[3] not so much for what was said (although that remains important), but for what was written in the opinion. Nevertheless, the nation still pays close attention to what is said in important cases.[4]

It is well not to wax too rhapsodic over oral argument in the old days. Writing in 1941, for example, Roscoe Pound deplored "[t]he decadence of oral argument."[5] He attributed that condition to the practice in the last quarter of the nineteenth century of submitting cases for decision on the briefs, that is, without argument. Although Pound blamed that development "to no small extent" on "the volume of work in reviewing courts,"[6] it is certainly possible that submission was also a result of the expense of traveling to a distant court to argue relatively small matters.[7] Nevertheless, oral argument has remained a critical component of the way both the public and the profession imagine the process we call justice.

A generation ago, a law student's first year centered on the crucible of his moot court argument.[8] There were a number of reasons that was so, but a large part involved the profession's collective memory of the great legal orators, from Luther Martin to Daniel Webster to Thurgood Marshall, who had done so much to shape the Republic.[9] What the students of a generation ago did not realize, however, was

2. 347 U.S. 483 (1954).

3. United States v. Nixon, 418 U.S. 683 (1974).

4. The rise of blogs and podcasts of oral argument in the Supreme Court surely have increased attention paid to arguments and hearings there.

5. Roscoe Pound, Appellate Procedure in Civil Cases 369 (1941).

6. *Id.* at 370. Dean Pound did not explain how widespread a phenomenon was submission; he did identify five states in which counsel had to request argument. *Id.* at 369.

7. *Id.* Pound was referring to an era before the introduction of intermediate appellate courts; those courts tend to be dispersed geographically and make attending argument less costly.

8. A good bibliography on oral argument can be found in Eugene Gressman, et al., Supreme Court Practice 748 n.1 (9th ed. 2007). The current edition of Supreme Court Practice, the bible on that topic, devotes fifty-four (very good) pages to oral argument. A fine recent treatise, Mayer Brown LLP, Federal Appellate Practice (2008), has thirty-five pages on oral argument. *Id.* at 437–72.

9. Great orators also played a major role in English legal history, and in most common-law countries argument continues to play an important role. In Britain, for example, argument can still last for days. Peter E. Quint, Civil Disobedience and the German Courts: The Pershing Missile Protests in Comparative Perspective 143 (2008). Argument is less important in the civil law tradition, perhaps because common law judges are "schooled in a more vigorous tradition of advocacy." *Id.* at 144. Professor Quint notes a paradox: because oral argument is so infrequent in the German Federal Constitutional Court, that body "can afford to devote substantial time and attention to it when it does occur." *Id.*

that even as they underwent their trial by terror, the appellate argument was rapidly becoming obsolete. Today, extended oral argument is a rarity in the federal circuit courts; the norm is no argument at all, and most arguments last fifteen minutes or less.[10] This is true even though many judges and practitioners still wax poetic about the value of argument. Chief Justice Hughes, for example, wrote that "The one who decides must hear."[11] Chief Justice Roberts recently called oral argument "terribly, terribly important .... [I]t is the organizing point for the entire judicial process."[12] A survey of federal circuit judges found that seven of eight found oral argument either "very helpful" or "often helpful."[13] The Supreme Court, of course, hears arguments in virtually every case that it decides, making clear that it certainly finds value in the process. Indeed, the Court does not permit counsel to submit a case on the briefs, that is, without oral argument.[14] And minds do change. Judges Jerry Smith, Myron Bright, and Morris Arnold have estimated that oral arguments changed their minds respectively in 10, 17, and 37 percent of the cases they had heard.[15] In order to understand the impact of those changes, it is necessary to consider why there is oral argument and what is lost if it is curtailed.

B. THE VALUE OF ORAL ARGUMENT

Oral argument has at least four benefits. First, it helps the courts reach a more thoroughly informed and considered decision. Second, oral argument helps to legitimize the result and its justification. Third, it permits the parties to show their belief in their cases. And fourth, oral argument helps the court explain its decisions. We examine each of those benefits in the context of the Appellate Triage regime.

1. Informed Decision Making

The greatest benefit of oral argument is that it permits the parties to provide information about the case to the court.[16] Indeed, until fairly recently, oral advocacy was the

10. In many law schools, oral argument no longer is the centerpiece of a student's first year.

11. Morgan v. United States, 298 U.S. 468, 481 (1936).

12. John G. Roberts Jr., *Oral Advocacy and the Re-emergence of a Supreme Court Bar*, 30 J. SUP. CT. HIST. J. 68, 69 (2005). The then newly minted Circuit Judge Roberts gives several other examples of prominent jurists extolling the virtues of oral argument.

13. Lauren K. Robel, *Caseload and Judging: Judicial Adaptations to Caseload*, 1990 BYU L. REV. 3, 54.

14. Franchise Tax Bd. v. Alcan Aluminum, Ltd., 493 U.S. 930, 930 (1989) ("The request of respondents to submit the case on the briefs is denied.").

15. *See* MAYER BROWN LLP, FEDERAL APPELLATE PRACTICE 439 (2008).

16. Of course, there is always the problem of getting the court to listen. Dean Acheson related that when he was a law clerk to Justice Holmes, the latter wrote letters while "he was waiting for counsel to catch up with his understanding of their case. This gave him, he used to say, an undeserved reputation for attention and honesty." DEAN ACHESON, MORNING AND NOON 58 (1965).

only way that the litigants could provide the court with legal and factual arguments. Until the twentieth century, the only written document received by most courts from counsel was a statement of errors allegedly made by the trial judge. Modern communications technology, however, has long since ensured the primacy of the written word over the oral, and today the ironically named "briefs" filed by the parties are used to convey most, if not all, of the necessary information. Moreover, that written submission can easily (and now instantaneously) convey the same information to the other litigants so that they have time to frame their responses and share them with the court and the opposition. In this way, the ascendency of the written word informs debate by suppressing surprise and providing time for measured responses. As a result, the parties can respond intelligently to the arguments of the other side, and the court, prepared as the adversarial system postulates by those responsive arguments, can deliver a measured and reasoned opinion.

Nevertheless, written argument has not eliminated the oral variety. The latter still has a number of virtues even in an age of written communication. First, not all litigants (or their attorneys) can write well or persuasively. Second, judges may have questions raised by the written materials but not answered by them. Third, oral argument brings the judges together to discuss the cases. Fourth, oral argument provides litigants with the opportunity to infuse their arguments with passion.

a. Imperfect Writing Skills Require Oral Argument

The ability of litigants to convey information in writing is limited by their ability to write well. The ability to present a coherent and persuasive written statement of facts and legal argument is not universal, as anyone who has read prisoner petitions (or even student papers) knows all too well. Clear writing is needed to avoid confusion and enhance understanding. Unfortunately, it is not always present. Quality writing can be found, of course. Complicated litigation involving sophisticated counsel (a major securities case, for example) generally generates high-quality writing. That quality is not found in the work product of all attorneys, however. Even less likely is it to be found in the written submissions of pro se litigants. The typical pro se litigant is not likely to be trained either in the law or in the skills of written explication and persuasion. Instead, oral argument, especially from the parties themselves, may be needed if the court is to learn the issues and facts.

Thus, oral argument may be more important in cases where representation either does not exist or is not of the highest quality. This does not mean that oral argument may not be valuable to the court in cases where there has been good representation. The judges, after all, may have views of the problem that have not been addressed in the briefs, and sometimes the parties have tried to disguise critical weak spots in the case. Oral argument thus gives the court an opportunity to pin counsel to a position or to elicit as yet unstated facts.

Although oral argument can be important in cases with good counsel, it is far more important in those appeals where the litigant lacks the needed expository skills. A good panel can then elicit from the party what her grievance really is about. Moreover, because the litigants know the case better than the judges, they can be helpful in clearing up misunderstandings. Judge Posner has written that judges at times are "very badly in need of the advocates' help" at oral argument, both because the attorneys are more familiar with cases and because of the tendency of circuit judges to be generalists.[17]

More generally, American appellate judges are far removed from the grain they grind in their mills. They are presented with sterile paper full of facts and legal theories, filtered through counsel and clerks. Oral argument can help them cut through the clutter and get to the essentials of the case.

b. Influencing the Decision

What is said at oral argument sometimes makes it into the opinion in the case. Concessions by counsel provide a common example; courts frequently note that a party during argument may abandon a particular point. How the opinion would have read if argument had not been heard, of course, cannot be known. An example can be found in *Helicopteros Nacionales de Colombia v. Hall*,[18] a well-known personal jurisdiction case.

Argument also provides the litigants with an opportunity to correct any misconceptions the court might have about the case. Thus, Roscoe Pound, commenting on a reduced role for oral argument, observed that the practice of submitting on the briefs meant that "defects" in the opinion, "which could have been remedied at the hearing are raised for the first time in the opinion."[19] Pound's warning is particularly on point for cases involving pro se litigants who of course have a difficult time making their case.

c. Bringing the Judges Together

Oral argument forces the judges to concentrate on the case both as individuals and as a group. The former benefit is easy to grasp: the parties are before the judge, and, unless she is asleep, she must absorb something about the matter at hand. But the

17. Richard A. Posner, *From the Bench: Convincing a Federal Court of Appeals*, 25 *Litigation* 3 (Winter 1999).

18. 466 U.S. 408, 415 (1984). The concession involved the plaintiff's statement that he was not arguing lack of specific jurisdiction. The concession is discussed in Robert J. Condlin, *"Defendant Veto" or "Totality of the Circumstances?": It's Time for the Supreme Court to Straighten Out the Personal Jurisdiction Standard Once Again*, 54 Cath. U. L. Rev. 53, 99 n.308 (2004). The Court has cautioned, however, about reading too much into "spontaneous responses" made during argument. *Moose Lodge No. 107 v. Irvis*, 407 U.S. 163, 170 (1972).

19. Roscoe Pound, Appellate Procedure in Civil Cases 369 (1941).

judges must also focus as a *panel*. That happens, perhaps informally, when the judges come together before argument. More important is the commonplace occurrence where argument can turn into an exchange of views among the panel members. Also important is the post-argument conference. As one recent law clerk has observed: "While judges can and do discuss cases long after argument through the exchange of memoranda, the undivided focus of a conferencing panel ... has a certain intrinsic value that cannot otherwise be duplicated."[20] Without argument, all of those benefits are lost. That loss is particularly unfortunate when it occurs in cases where central staff attorneys have prepared the dispositive memorandum for it means that the full panel may never get together to discuss the questions presented.

d. Passion

Oral argument also provides an opportunity for a litigant to show her belief in her case. Although lawyers are often taught that passion should be carefully controlled, its display can be important for several reasons. Passion may awaken a bored court and lead it to perform its duty, and it also may serve as a much-needed outlet for a frustrated party. Although any litigant can be passionate about her case, it is likely that it is of far more importance to those who cannot write well.[21] Finally, the passion released at oral argument may help reconcile the losing litigant to her fate. Knowing that she has given it her best shot and lost must have some soothing effect.

And oral argument can also quiet passion. A litigant who has appeared in front of an attentive, respectful, and informed judge who looks her in the eye and explains why she has lost is much more likely to accept the result than one who receives an order in the mail months after she has submitted her attempt to explain her case in writing.

2. Judicial Explanation of the Decision

At one time, judges provided litigants with an explanation for a decision, the *ratio decidendi*, only during or shortly after oral argument.[22] This took the form of an oral opinion, delivered from the bench. These opinions were delivered *seriatim*, a practice that persisted in the Supreme Court until the time of John Marshall. Although

20. Michael Duvall, *When is Oral Argument Important? A Judicial Clerk's View of the Debate*, 9 J. App. Prac. & Process 121, 125 (2007).

21. There are judges, of course, who do not want to hear passionate voices. Although there is much to be said for that point of view, we believe that passion has its place in the judicial process.

22. John H. Langbein, *Chancellor Kent and the History of Legal Education*, 93 Colum. L. Rev. 547, 571–72 (1993). Sometimes the justification for the decision could only be inferred from the argument—there was no judicial explanation in the case report.

oral opinions still exist in England,[23] American appellate judges today rarely, if ever, rely on an oral, as opposed to written, explanation of their decisions.[24] Instead, the precedent is to be extracted from the pages of the Reporter in which it is published, and the written opinion is not supplemented by an official oral explanation.[25] Thus, oral argument no longer plays an official role in explaining the decision of appellate courts.[26]

3. Legitimacy, Proof That the Court Paid Attention

Another important product of oral argument is that the judges can provide visible assurance that they have read and thought about the briefs submitted by the parties, and that they will listen to anything further that the litigants have to say. The argument, in other words, provides legitimacy. As Professor Owen Fiss observed: "Oral argument places the decision-maker face-to-face with the contestants and gives what is often a remote and abstract legal system an important human character."[27] At oral argument, the litigants can listen to the judges' questions and comments and see for themselves that the judges have worked on the case. Again, this exchange of views between court and litigant is more important in low-profile cases. Lawyers and clients involved in major litigation *know* that the court has worked hard on their issues; that effort may not be so apparent to someone who receives an unsigned two-paragraph opinion disposing of her claim.

4. Quality of Decision Making

Oral argument also helps the quality of the decision. Judges at argument are focused on the problem at hand; their questions can start a colloquy not only with counsel but also with the other members of the panel. Judges who did not pay attention to the briefs may find themselves interested by the argument and begin thinking about

23. J.E. Cote, *The Oral Judgment Practice in the Canadian Appellate Courts*, 5 J. App. Prac & Process 435 (2003). Many of these oral judgments were delivered *ex tempore*, although the practice finally seems to have died out. *Id.* at 441.

24. In 2010, no oral opinion was handed down in any Circuit. Admin. Office of U.S. Courts, Judicial Business of the United States Courts: 2010 Annual Report of the Director 46, table S-3 (2010), *available at* http://www.uscourts.gov/uscourts/Statistics/JudicialBusiness/2010/judicialbusinespdfversion.pdf.

25. Nevertheless, oral opinions are sometimes delivered, even by the Supreme Court. Those opinions are almost always followed by a written opinion. The two versions of the opinion have been known to differ markedly from one another, especially in tone. The spoken comments do not, alas, make it into the official United States Reports.

26. Oral explanation by trial judges, of course, still plays a critical role in outlining what they do.

27. Owen M. Fiss, *The Bureaucratization of the Judiciary*, 92 Yale L.J. 1442, 1484 (1983).

the matter before them. The authors of *Supreme Court Practice* observe that "rapid fire questions sometimes reflect a dialogue taking place among the Justices."[28] Justice Scalia has said that "[y]ou hear the questions of others and see how their minds are working and that stimulates your own thinking."[29] Judge Easterbrook wrote memorably that "the brief is counsel's monologue; argument the dialogue ...."[30] That interchange can be especially important on a geographically dispersed court where the panel may not meet in person unless an argument takes place. Finally, as Chief Justice Roberts wrote shortly after becoming a circuit court judge:

> Oral argument matters, but not just because of what the lawyers have to say. It is the organizing point for the whole judicial process. The judges read the briefs, do the research, and talk to their law clerks to prepare for the argument. The voting conference is held right after the oral argument .... And without disputing in any way the dominance of the briefing in the decisional process, it is natural, with the voting coming so closely on the heels of oral argument, that the discussion at conference is going to focus on what took place at argument.[31]

C. ORAL ARGUMENT: THE RULES IN THE CIRCUIT COURTS

The published rules and procedures in the circuit courts concerning oral argument as well as the actual practice today belie its professed importance. More important, oral argument is used *less* in the types of cases—pro se appeals—where it would be most important. That practice is perverse.

The controlling provision, Federal Rule of Appellate Procedure 34, contains little direct guidance to litigants and the circuit courts concerning oral argument. It provides:

(a) In General.
    (1) Party's Statement. Any party may file, or a court may require by local rule a statement explaining why oral argument should, or need not, be permitted.
    (2) Standards. Oral argument must be allowed in every case unless a panel of three judges who have examined the briefs and record unanimously agrees that oral argument is unnecessary for any of the following reasons:
        (A) The appeal is frivolous;
        (B) The dispositive issue or issues have been authoritatively decided; or

28. Eugene Gressman et al., Supreme Court Practice 789 (9th ed. 2007).
29. *Id.* at 791.
30. *Quoted in* Mayer Brown LLP, Federal Appellate Practice 439 (2008).
31. John G. Roberts Jr., *Oral Advocacy and the Re-emergence of a Supreme Court Bar*, 30 J. Sup. Ct. Hist. J. 68,, 70 (2005).

(C) The facts and legal arguments are adequately presented in the briefs and record, and the decisional process would not be significantly aided by oral argument.

In short, Rule 34 provides a strong presumption ("*must* be allowed") in favor of argument. That presumption can only be overcome under the Rule if a unanimous panel of three judges concludes that oral argument would not "significantly" help to decide the case. On the other hand, Rule 34 contains a major loophole. Rule 34(a) states that a circuit's local rules "*may* require" a statement from the parties as to why argument should be allowed. Once that statement is required, as is true in many circuits, obtaining the necessary permission quickly can be turned into a formidable hurdle, especially for a pro se litigant who may not even know of the need to file the required "statement."

The published rules and procedures of the circuit courts add little to the implicit presumption in favor of oral argument found in Rule 34. Most merely repeat its content; some do add an extra fillip or two.[32] Those local rules, however, do suggest the disdain with which the courts now view argument;[33] almost all circuits limit argument to between ten and twenty minutes per side, "although shorter limits are not uncommon."[34]

Worse, the decision to grant oral argument is often made by use of a "screening mechanism" operated by central staff. A treatise prepared by experienced advocates explains:

> Different circuits have adopted different approaches to allowing oral argument. Some allow oral argument—even if brief—as a matter of course when the parties request it. Others use a screening mechanism administered by the court's administrative staff or the panel assigned to the case to select cases suitable for oral argument.[35]

Thus, in some courts, cases with counsel automatically receive favored treatment; in others, the staff decides who gets oral argument.

Taken together, these circuit rules severely restrict the utility of argument. As anyone who has argued a case knows, it is difficult to make a cogent argument of any sort in ten minutes, even for experienced counsel. A pro se litigant, unsure of proper procedure and unskilled in advocacy, will have a far more

32. The Sixth Circuit, for example, instructs counsel not to read from "a prepared text." 6TH CIR. R. 34(h)(1).

33. The Supreme Court has similarly reduced the time available for argument: to two hours in 1849, forty-five to ninety minutes per side in 1911, to the present thirty minutes per side. Michael Duvall, *When is Oral Argument Important? A Judicial Clerk's View of the Debate*, 9 J. APP. PRAC. & PROCESS 121, 122 (2007).

34. MAYER BROWN LLP, FEDERAL APPELLATE PRACTICE 444 (2008).

35. *Id.* at 439–40. The quote comes from a subchapter appropriately entitled *How to Obtain Oral Argument.*

difficult time getting things out. For those litigants, of course, oral argument could prove very helpful, indeed, for the court can extract the argument by a series of questions. Of course, the reality is that the pro se litigant will not even receive her ten minutes; rather, she will be denied the opportunity to argue altogether.[36]

D. THE PRACTICE IN THE CIRCUIT COURTS TODAY

Despite the acclaim given the many virtues of oral argument, it is increasingly an endangered species. This part first examines the data on oral argument today, and then looks at the formal procedures established by the appellate courts to see if those provisions shed light on the data. Finally, alternative explanations for the data are sought.

1. The Data

In Reporting Year 2010, only 26.4 percent of all appeals were terminated following an "oral hearing."[37] That percentage reflects a long-standing trend in favor of reduced argument. In 1985, 56 percent of terminations followed oral argument, a percentage that fell to 45 percent in 1992 and 32 percent in 2001.[38]

Although the trend shows consistency, the data on argument, when broken down among the various circuits, show a surprising *lack* of consistency. The range of frequency of argument among them is vast. The lowest figure in 2010 was for the Fourth Circuit, which only granted oral argument in 13.1 percent of the cases before it, and the highest was 46.7 percent in the Seventh Circuit. That is a pretty dramatic range, and neither the circuits nor the institutional judiciary has attempted to explain it. The question is: can anything be found to explain it?

36. To be sure, if the court believes the case would benefit from argument, it might appoint an attorney to represent the litigant. We do not believe that happens with any frequency.

37. ADMIN. OFFICE OF U.S. COURTS, 2001 ANNUAL REPORT OF THE DIRECTOR 44, table S-1 (2001), *available at* http://www.uscourts.gov/uscourts/Statistics/JudicialBusiness/2010/judicialbusinespdfversion.pdf. The data do not tell us how much time was allotted for each hearing or how much argument there was at each hearing.

38. The 1985 and 1992 figures are from William M. Richman & William L. Reynolds, *Elitism, Expediency, and the New Certiorari: Requiem for the Learned Hand Tradition*, 81 CORNELL L. REV. 273, 279 (1996). The 2001 figure is from JAMES C. DUFF, JUDICIAL BUSINESS OF THE UNITED STATES COURTS: 2010 ANNUAL REPORT OF THE DIRECTOR 47, table S-1 (2001), *available at* www.uscourts.gov/uscourts/Statistics/JudicialBusiness/2001/front/JudicialBusinespdfversion.pdf.

a. Formal Rules

One possibility, of course, is that the Local Appellate Rules and implementing Internal Operating Procedures in some courts lead to a more restrictive attitude toward argument. Unfortunately, there is not a whole lot in the published procedures to go on. No circuit's local rule differs dramatically from any other's or from Rule 34 itself. To be sure, some circuits state presumptive time limits for argument.[39] The times suggested range from ten to twenty minutes, although the Second Circuit, in brutal candor, until recently, told pro se litigants that they would get only five minutes, but if they had an attorney they would "normally" get ten or fifteen minutes (assuming they were lucky enough to get an argument in the first place).[40]

The written rules do have some interesting provisions. The First Circuit discourages the reservation of time for rebuttal,[41] for example, and the Sixth has a presumption against argument if a party has not filed a brief.[42] A panel in the Second Circuit decides whether to allow oral argument; if it says no to argument, the parties are given notice and an opportunity to explain why argument is needed.[43]

More interesting are the provisions concerning screening. Somewhat surprisingly, several circuits deal expressly with the screening procedures they use to determine what cases are assigned oral argument. A couple of the circuit provisions on screening are quite explicit. Thus, the Fifth Circuit Internal Operating Procedure to Rule 34 provides:

> The judges of the court screen cases with assistance from the Staff Attorney. When the last brief is filed, a case is generally sent to the staff attorney for prescreening classification. If the Staff Attorney concludes that the case does not warrant oral argument ... [t]he clerk then routes the case to one of the court's judges .... [44]

If that judge agrees with the staff attorney that oral argument is not needed, "the briefs, *together with a proposed opinion*" are sent to the other two judges on the panel. All three members of the panel must agree that the case does not merit oral argument; although a party may request oral argument, the request will not be granted unless at least one judge agrees.[45]

39. These include the First, Second, Third, Fourth, Fifth, Sixth, and Eighth Circuits.
40. 2D CIR. LOCAL R. 34 (the Rule has since been amended).
41. 1ST CIR. LOCAL R. 34.0.(c)(2).
42. 6TH CIR. R. 34 (h)(3). One might think that this would be the very type of case that argument most benefit the court; on the other hand, permitting argument when no brief has been filed might discourage brief writing.
43. 2D CIR. LOCAL. R. 34 (a).
44. 5TH CIR. I.O.P. 34–3(A).
45. *Id.* (emphasis added).

Noticeable in the Fifth Circuit provision is the transparency given the role of the staff attorney—one of primacy, clearly. Normally, the fiction of judicial control is asserted in circuit procedures, but the Fifth Circuit commendably has made certain litigants know who really is in charge. It may not be appropriate to delegate such an important function to the staff, but if the court makes that choice, surely it should reveal it to the public. A second remarkable feature about that provision is its admission that a draft opinion is prepared before the other members of the panel have seen the case and certainly before argument. Unfortunately, the commendable candor in the Fifth Circuit concerning its procedures is not shared by all other courts.[46]

b. Just More of the Same?

These interesting details about how Rule 34 has been implemented, however, shed little light on why some circuits grant oral argument far more often than others. It seems unlikely that the length (or shortness) of presumed argument time or the details of how the cases are screened have had any significant impact on the percentage of cases that do receive argument. Nor is it likely that caseload differences, either in number or kind, account for the differences. Instead, it seems that in argument, as elsewhere in the complex field of Appellate Triage, the circuits have their own ideas of how to do things. That might be tolerable if experimentation were being carried out and the circuits were reporting on and considering their differences, but that is not the case.[47] Instead, the courts are applying similar formal rules in very different ways for no apparent reason, once again mocking the notion of equal treatment under the law.

46. There are some exceptions, however. The Eighth Circuit, for example, makes clear the difference it accords pro se litigants, but does not discuss how that difference relates to who writes the opinion:

> Upon the filing of the briefs, every attorney-handled case is screened for argument or nonargument submission. If the court determines that argument is not necessary in an attorney-handled case, the clerk notifies counsel and given [sic] them seven days to object to the no-argument classification . . . .

8th Cir. I.O.P. III.J. (internal citation omitted). Several other circuits also discuss screening briefly.

47. We know of no formal effort by the circuits to engage in discussion with each other concerning their experiences under their various forms of Appellate Triage.

CHAPTER 8

Additional Decision Makers: Deciding by Bureaucracy

Another piece of the Appellate Triage regime the circuit courts have adopted for dealing with the expanded caseload is to increase the number of decision makers. Although Congress and the judiciary have been unenthusiastic about efforts to expand the numbers of circuit judgeships,[1] they have been much less reluctant to expand the number of personnel involved in the decision-making process. Such personnel include two types: (1) judges sitting by designation, usually district judges, judges who have taken senior status, and circuit judges from other circuits and (2) para-judicial personnel (personal law clerks, staff attorneys, appellate commissioners).

A. JUDGES SITTING BY DESIGNATION[2]

The days when a panel was made up of three active circuit judges are long gone. By the early 1990s, "panels often include[d] only one active circuit judge; some include[d] none."[3] The gap has been filled with visiting firefighters, senior judges, visiting judges from other circuits, and district judges. The impact of these jurists is rarely commented upon, but it can be dramatic. In 2010, for example, 22 percent of appellate judge time was provided by resident senior judges and 4.5 percent by visiting judges.[4] In at least one circuit (the Ninth), the percentage of participation in

1. *See infra* chapter 11.
2. *See generally* Sara C. Benesh, *The Contribution of "Extra" Judges*, 48 ARIZ. L. REV. 301 (2006).
3. JUDITH A. MCKENNA, FEDERAL JUDICIAL CENTER, STRUCTURAL AND OTHER ALTERNATIVES FOR THE FEDERAL COURTS OF APPEALS 38 (1993).
4. ADMIN. OFFICE OF THE U.S. COURTS, JUDICIAL BUSINESS OF THE UNITED STATES COURTS: 2010 ANNUAL REPORT OF THE DIRECTOR 45, table S-2 (2010), *available at* http://www.uscourts.gov/uscourts/Statistics/JudicialBusiness/2010/JudicialBusinespdfversion.pdf.

terminations by active judges was only 61 percent.[5] Although no data are available on the use of district judges, a glance through the Federal Reporter reveals that they sit quite frequently on the circuit courts.

1. Circuit Judges

The use of resident senior circuit judges is close to unobjectionable under any standard. They are wise in the folkways of the circuit and should not disrupt the court's normal workings.[6] Visiting circuit judges and district judges are a different story. One study found that Eighth Circuit judges "noted more disadvantages than advantages from district judge participation."[7] Three problems deserve special mention. First, resident circuit judges expressed reluctance to let visiting judges shape the development of the law.[8] Second, visiting circuit judges may disturb collegial ways by their ignorance or disregard for the host circuit's individual practices.[9] Finally, judicial pinch-hitters pose problems of predictability for lawyers and instability of the law of the circuit, with which they are less familiar than resident judges.[10]

2. District Judges

Many district court judges sit on circuit court panels by designation. We believe this is a good thing. The trial judges learn how the appellate courts function, and the appellate courts gain a better appreciation of the difficulties of being a trial court judge. Nevertheless, there are significant drawbacks. First, it permits some gaming

5. *Id.* (33 percent by senior judges; 6 percent by visiting judges).

6. *See* Benesh, *supra* note 2, at 307. *But see* Chicago Council of Lawyers, *Evaluation of the United States Court of Appeals for the Seventh Circuit*, 43 DePaul L. Rev. 673, 720 (1994) (suggesting that the chief judge should be more careful in certifying the continued eligibility of senior circuit judges to sit on panels). During the 2005–2006 fiscal year, senior circuit judges constituted 37 percent of all circuit judges and handled about 17 percent of the cases. Frederic Block, *Senior Status: An "Active" Senior Judge Corrects Some Common Misunderstandings*, 92 Cornell L. Rev. 533, 540 (2007). A credible but practically irrelevant argument that senior judges are unconstitutional appears in the same volume. *See* David R. Stras & Ryan W. Scott, *Are Senior Judges Unconstitutional?*, 92 Cornell L. Rev. 453 (2007).

7. Stephen L. Wasby, *Internal Communication in the Eighth Circuit Court of Appeals*, 58 Wash. U. L.Q. 583, 598 (1980). For a discussion of the pros and cons of trial judge participation in the courts of appeals, see *id.* at 597–600.

8. *Id.* at 598.

9. *See* Marvin Schick, Learned Hand's Court 80 (1970).

10. Interestingly, opponents to significant additions of judgeships mention instability of circuit law as a serious problem but do not seem perturbed by the use of visiting judges. Presumably, additional resident judges would be more familiar with circuit precedent than visiting judges.

of the random assignment system.[11] Second, the district judge, for better or worse, has a somewhat different agenda from that of the circuit judges; that uncertainty renders the decisions less predictable and, therefore, increases costs to everyone in the legal system. Finally, one study concluded that "at least to some degree, district judge participation weakens the authoritative status of panel decisions. Such decisions are likely to be the subject of en banc review or of Supreme Court certiorari petitions."[12]

B. PARA-JUDGES—"GHOSTWRITERS"[13]

The most startling development in appellate courts in the past quarter century has been the very marked increase in the role played by nonjudicial personnel, or "para-judges." The number of a circuit judge's personal clerks has grown from one to four.[14] Far more significant, however, has been the exponential growth in the numbers and role of central staff attorneys—a group unheard of three decades ago. This growth is the direct result of caseload pressures: "[T]he caseload per federal judge has risen to the point where very few judges, however able and dedicated, can keep up with the flow without heavy reliance on law clerks, staff attorneys, and sometimes externs too."[15] The judicial system pays a significant price, however, because inappropriate delegation of quintessentially judicial tasks has become the norm.

1. Chambers Clerks

The practice of judges using recent law graduates as assistants is usually traced to Justice Gray of the United States Supreme Court.[16] However it began, the idea caught on, and soon all Supreme Court Justices were supplied with clerks.[17] By the 1930s, court of appeals judges began to employ one clerk each; they received a

11. Attorneys worry about district judges asked to reverse their brethren on the district court. Thus, in circuits where the court sits in multiple locales, attorneys try to get the appeal heard in locations other than where the case was decided. This is not how a random assignment calendar should function.

12. Richard B. Saphire & Michael E. Solimine, *Diluting Justice on Appeal? An Examination of the Use of District Court Judges Sitting by Designation on the United States Courts of Appeals*, 28 U. Mich. J.L. Reform 351, 378 (1995) (footnote omitted).

13. Richard A. Posner, *Judges' Writing Styles (and Do They Matter?)*, 62 U. Chi. L. Rev. 1421, 1423–24 (1995).

14. Judith A. McKenna, Federal Judicial Center, Structural and Other Alternatives for the Federal Courts of Appeals 52 & n.96 (1993).

15. Richard A. Posner, The Federal Courts: Crisis and Reform 103 (1985).

16. Jonathan Matthew Cohen, Inside Appellate Courts 87 (2002), and sources cited therein at n.7.

17. Donald P. Ubell, *Evolution and Role of Appellate Court Central Staff Attorneys*, 2 Cooley L. Rev. 157, 157–58 (1984).

second in 1969, a third in 1979,[18] and today a circuit judge can have as many as four law clerks if she is willing to settle for one secretary instead of two.[19]

a. The Benefits

Before considering the dangers law clerks pose to the appellate process, it is worth reflecting on the benefits they provide. An obvious benefit is that it improves the quantity of judicial output; a single circuit judge could not hope to keep up with today's caseloads without the help of law clerks. There may also be some dividend in terms of the quality of judicial output. Appellate judging is a lonely job; the judges have very few people they can talk to about the substance of the cases they hear. In Judge Mikva's words:

> The way I define the situation, law clerks' input is always appropriate because these are the only people from whom I can get input. I can't call up law professors and ask, "What do you think about this case?" ... I can't talk to lawyers indiscriminately. I have to confine my musings to what I find on the record, what I hear on oral argument and so on. The law clerks are the only legitimate apparatus I can use for idea bouncing.[20]

Moreover, law clerks can bring more current knowledge of recent trends in the development of the law because they are closer to their academic experiences, most judges being many years out of law school. Finally, some of our finest appellate judges are willing to acknowledge that the clerks sometimes are better than the judges. Judge Posner points out:

> Law clerks would be invaluable even if they were not necessary. Because they are picked on a purely meritocratic basis while judges are not, the law clerk system enables judges to hire assistants who in many cases have better legal analytic capabilities, as well as being fresher and more energetic, than the judge ....[21]

And Judge Kozinski concurs:

> I'm not saying any judges are stupid. But while the people who are judicial law clerks tend to be the best law school graduates, judges become judges for a variety of reasons—political connections, ambition, being in the right place at the right time. For example,

18. *Id.*; Thomas E. Baker, Rationing Justice on Appeal 140–41 (1994).
19. Cohen, *supra* note 16, at 88.
20. Abner J. Mikva, *Maintaining Control of the Judiciary: An Interview with Judge Abner Mikva*, 3 Long Term View 9, 9 (1995).
21. Richard Posner, *The Rise of the Law Clerk*, 3 Long Term View 23, 30 (1995).

many judges are very good people and understand the law, but do not have the time or the patience or the sheer ability to write an opinion that is really excellent.[22]

b. The Dangers—Delegation of Preparation

The heavy reliance on law clerks, however, imposes significant dangers to the integrity of the appellate process. After all, Justice Brandeis noted that the bar's and the public's respect for the federal bench persisted because "they do their own work."[23] The quality and magnitude of the dangers posed depends, at least in part, on the tasks the clerks perform. In the words of Judge Rubin, the question is:

> What are these able, intelligent, mostly young people doing? Surely not merely running citations in *Shepard's* and shelving the judge's law books. They are, in many situations, "para-judges." In some instances, it is to be feared, they are indeed invisible judges, for there are appellate judges whose literary style appears to change annually.[24]

Rubin is right; clerks can perform ministerial tasks without any danger of over-delegation or compromise of the appellate process. But he is also right in concluding that today they do much more. There is little quantitative evidence on what the clerks do, but there have been some empirical studies and there is a wealth of anecdotal evidence.

Uniformly, the judges report that they do not delegate decision making to their clerks. Judge Posner, for example, acknowledges that

> the clerks have a recent legal education, they have analytical skills, and they may be smarter than the judges.... So a law clerk's analytical ... and research suggestions ... may be very valuable to the judge. But where judges are making decisions based in part on life experiences ... then of course the law clerks should not be calling the tune.[25]

And Judge Mikva reports that his standard retort when "clerks had taken their best shot and hadn't persuaded me":

> I would point to the commission on the wall and say, "Look, the commission runs to me, not to you. I have gone through a long process to get to this point. I make the decision

22. Alex Kozinski, *Making the Case for Law Clerks*, 3 LONG TERM VIEW 55, 58 (1995). *See also* John Oakley, *Defining the Limits of Delegation*, 3 LONG TERM VIEW 85, 92 (1995).

23. CHARLES E. WYZANSKI JR., WHEREAS—A JUDGE'S PREMISES: ESSAYS IN JUDGMENT, ETHICS, AND THE LAW 61 (1965) (quoting Justice Louis Brandeis).

24. Alvin B. Rubin, *Views From the Lower Court*, 23 UCLA L. REV. 448, 455 (1975).

25. Richard A. Posner, *Working Within the Confines of Our Current Judiciary*, 3 LONG TERM VIEW 32, 32 (1995). *See also* Patricia M. Wald, *Critical Discourse in the Chambers*, 3 LONG TERM VIEW 45 (1995).

that must be made here. You can counsel me, you can talk to me about it, but the decision has to be mine."[26]

So preliminarily, at least, and at least with regard to cases decided in opinions written in chambers,[27] we can take the judges' word that clerks do not decide cases. What tasks do they perform and what delegation dangers lurk in those tasks?

Most circuit judges report using law clerks to prepare a "bench memorandum" to help the judge prepare for oral argument.[28] The memo summarizes the facts, the parties' contentions, and the state of the law and generally provides the judge with a road map of the case.[29] In some chambers, the memo also suggests a result. Undoubtedly, the memo saves the judge time, especially in complex multiparty cases. Yet its use also causes concern. What if the judge skimps on research or on review of the record or the briefs because of reliance on the memo? Hints of that appear in the remarks of some judges:

> I start off each case with their writing a bench memo, and I like to feel that the bench memo is a road map for me. It tells me everyplace they have been and where I need to go. *And it tells me the places I can skip* because they are not important. Lawyers ... tend to be verbose ... and put much more in the record than is necessary.... The clerk is supposed to go over all that ground and then hopefully it spares me the trouble.[30]

The danger of overdelegation here is apparent; every lawyer knows the difference between reading briefs, records, statutes, and cases and reading someone else's summary of those original sources. Further, even if the judge refers to the original documents, she does so having had her view preshaped by the clerk's view. The danger of overdelegation is even greater now than in the past because the ratio of clerks to judges has increased; each clerk, after all, has a caseload that is one-third or one-quarter of the judge's. Thus it is likely that the clerk is more knowledgeable about the details of the case than the judge, and knowledge, even in chambers, is power.

Exacerbating the problem of delegation of preparation is the practice in some courts of the pool bench memo. The idea is efficiency; why have three clerks—one from each member of the panel—prepare a separate bench memo when one clerk

26. Mikva, *supra* note 20, at 9. The judge must have had some very cheeky law clerks; this book's authors clerked on the United States District Court for the District of Maryland for two very different judges, and neither of us can recall arguing with the judge persistently enough to be told who had been appointed by the President and confirmed by the Senate. *See also* Wald, *supra* note 25, at 45. *But see* Kozinski, *supra* note 22, at 56 (in a close case, a clerk might come up with an argument that could change judge's vote).

27. Cases decided in opinions written by central staff attorneys pose more difficult questions. *See* subsection 2, *infra*.

28. Cohen, *supra* note 16, at 91.

29. *Id.*

30. *Id.* (emphasis added).

could prepare one memo to be shared by all three members of the panel? The difficulty, of course, is that pooling multiplies the delegation. Instead of relying on three independent views of the case, the entire panel relies on one. For this reason, some judges do not participate in the pool, and others do so with skepticism. Others participate in the system but have one of their own clerks prepare a "chambers memo," which may be an independent assessment of the case or simply a review and critique of the pool memo.[31]

Some judges clearly see the dangers of delegation of preparation. Judge Posner notes:

> Even research is not fully delegable to law clerks. It is one thing … to rely on a clerk to find the relevant precedents and another to delegate to him the reading of them as well. A judge who relied for his knowledge of cases entirely on what the parties' briefs, and the opinions that his clerks drafted for him, told him about the cases could end up with only a meager knowledge of the law.[32]

So, do the judges overdelegate to their clerks the task of preparing for oral argument, conference, and voting or not? About all the bar and the public can do is trust the judges to know what is delegable and what is not, but it is clear that trust is more warranted in some cases than in others.

c. The Dangers—Delegation of Drafting

Overdelegation to law clerks in the drafting of opinions has produced more controversy than the excessive use of clerks in case preparation. According to the traditional model, judges drafted their opinions and law clerks would edit, cite-check, and proofread them.[33] Today, however, law clerks do most of the drafting. As Professor Oakley reports: "The drafting of opinions by law clerks is prevalent, and increasingly so, to the point where it is seen as something of a quaint idiosyncrasy when a judge attempts to draft his or her own opinions."[34] In Judge Posner's words, "today, a judge-written opinion, at any level of the American judiciary, is rare."[35] Judge Kleinfeld cites as proof of the ubiquity of the practice that "people no longer feel a need to cover it up."[36] And Jonathan Cohen, after conducting extensive interviews with judges and clerks in three circuits, concluded

31. *See id.* at 94–108.
32. Posner, *Rise of the Law Clerk*, *supra* note 21, at 27.
33. Andrew J. Kleinfeld, *Politicization: From the Law Schools to the Courts*, 3 Long Term View 49, 50 (1995).
34. Oakley, *supra* note 22, at 86.
35. Richard A. Posner, *The Material Basis of Jurisprudence*, 69 Ind. L.J. 1, 21 (1993).
36. Kleinfeld, *supra* note 33, at 50. *See* Kozinski, *supra* note 22, 57–58; Mikva, *supra* note 20, 9; Wald, *supra* note 25, at 45–46 (admissions of three of the nation's most distinguished jurists that clerks do a substantial amount of the drafting in their chambers).

that the vast majority of judges assigned their clerks the task of writing first drafts of their opinions.[37]

If there is little controversy over the fact of delegation, there is quite a bit over its propriety. Many judges see no problem with assigning drafting duties to clerks as long as the final product reflects the judge's view of the proper outcome of the case and the reasoning behind the decision.[38] After all, the argument goes, no one expects the President or other political officials to draft their own remarks; ghost-writers are the order of the day. And many of the judges who use their clerks for drafting give them detailed instructions or outlines before they draft and heavily edit their work after.[39]

Nevertheless, there are serious problems with routine delegation of opinion drafting to clerks. For one, the lazy judge can overdo it, failing to give the clerk any more guidance than the desired result. Judges rarely admit such extreme delegation, but some judges suspect their colleagues of it.[40] And clerks and even interns who are still in law school sometimes report huge latitude and little supervision in drafting opinions.[41]

Even if the judge does not abdicate her judicial responsibility completely, and reports of total abdication are rare,[42] there are still problems with clerks bearing the lion's share of the drafting duties in chambers. For one thing, writing a document is not the same thing as editing it; in Judge Posner's words, "whoever does the basic drafting of a document—a judicial opinion or anything else—will have a big impact on the final product."[43] Moreover, reliance on clerks' writing makes the process of judicial appointment less selective. In times past, a second-rate legal talent often did not apply because the candidate knew that if he was unable or unwilling to write his own opinions, he would be exposed to his colleagues and the bar; now, however, any political hack who can select decent clerks, or have them selected by others, can produce passable opinions and thus apply, without fear of exposure. Finally, the craft discipline of writing is one of the few checks on power of the judiciary.[44] The judge is more likely to decide arbitrarily "knowing that there is someone in the back room who can rationalize any decision."[45]

37. COHEN, *supra* note 16, at 113.
38. *See* Wald, *supra* note 25, Kozinski, *supra* note 22, and Mikva, *supra* note 20.
39. COHEN, *supra* note 16, at 112–18.
40. *See* Rubin, *supra* note 24, at 456; Kozinski, *supra* note 22, at 56.
41. COHEN, *supra* note 16, at 117; Kleinfeld, *supra* note 33, at 50.
42. Oakley, *supra* note 22, at 86.
43. POSNER, *supra* note 15, at 360. While many are familiar with the "just won't write" phenomenon, there is very little empirical investigation into the relationship between writing and deciding. And there is even less investigation of the relationship between editing and deciding. Whether the two are the same should be important in any assessment of the benefits and dangers of the proliferation of elbow clerks. Chad M. Oldfather, *Writing, Cognition, and the Nature of the Judicial Function*, 96 GEO. L.J. 1283, 1287 (2008).
44. Mary Ann Glendon, *The New Ball Game*, 3 LONG TERM VIEW 60, 64 (1995).
45. John U. Kester, *The Law Clerk Explosion*, 3 LONG TERM VIEW 14, 15 (1995)

The dangers of the multiplication of law clerks extend beyond the delegation issue; it may be, for instance, that clerk-drafted opinions are simply inferior to those drafted by capable judges. That, at least, is the view of Judge Posner, who finds that clerk-drafted opinions tend to be longer, less candid, over-larded with footnotes and string citations, more timid, and less credible.[46] Moreover, at some point, the judge's supervisory duties will crowd out core judicial functions. Every year, the judge must interview for four clerkship positions, train four clerks, supply recommendations for them, and edit their work. Combine those efforts with hearing oral arguments and conferring with other panel members, ruling on motions, screening less significant cases, attending circuit conferences, and a host of other administrative tasks, and it sounds very much like a full-time job. Where then does the judge get the time to do the quintessential judicial work of reading records and briefs and reasoning toward a decision? Even those who defend the current level of clerk participation in the circuit courts seem to acknowledge that the number of clerks is at or close to its limit.[47]

2. Central Staff Attorneys

Central staff attorneys differ from law clerks in that they work for the court as a whole rather than for a single judge. Typically, they work at the headquarters of the circuit, rather than being scattered around the circuit, as the judges' chambers usually are. Also unlike law clerks, staff attorneys are a relatively recent development; beginning in the sixties, when the Fourth and Fifth Circuits began hiring "habeas clerks"[48] to deal with the explosion of cases brought by state prison inmates seeking habeas corpus relief or relief under the civil rights statutes.[49] Moreover, their caseloads differ from those of law clerks. Clerks work in a broad range of subject matter areas and on cases deemed "important" or "novel." Staff attorneys, by contrast, devote most of their effort to a narrower range of subject matters and to cases deemed to be "routine" or "repetitive."[50] Staff attorneys also differ from law clerks

46. Posner, *supra* note 21, at 25–27.

47. *See* Harry T. Edwards, *The Rising Workload and Perceived "Bureaucracy" of the Federal Courts: A Causation-Based Approach to the Search for Appropriate Remedies*, 68 IOWA L. REV. 871, 889 (1983).

48. The best account of the origin of the central staff and the other expedients the circuit courts have adopted to cope with rising caseloads is found in two articles by Professor Penelope Pether. *See* Penelope Pether, *Sorcerers, Not Apprentices: How Judicial Clerks and Staff Attorneys Impoverish U.S. Law*, 39 ARIZ. ST. L.J. 1 (2007) [hereinafter *Sorcerers*]; Penelope Pether, *Inequitable Injunctions: The Scandal of Private Judging in the U.S. Courts*, 56 STAN. L. REV. 1435 (2004) [hereinafter *Inequitable Injunctions*].

49. *See, e.g.*, 42 U.S.C. § 1983 (2006).

50. *See* text *infra* for a discussion of screening, the method by which the wheat and chaff are separated.

in that hardly anyone is willing to claim that their use produces any benefit other than efficiency. No one maintains that strategy of hiring steadily increasing brigades of staff attorneys produces better justice or provides sounding boards or fresh perspectives to the judges.[51] Pure necessity drives the practice; the judges simply could not keep abreast of the steadily increasing caseload without them.[52] Or put differently, the judges could not devote the time and effort to the relatively few important cases unless the corps of staff attorneys was there to handle the larger, but more prosaic group of cases.

a. Staff Attorneys and "Screening"

It is difficult and probably pointless to consider the role of central staff attorneys without considering it in the context of the entire regime of Appellate Triage. The geometrically rising caseloads of the last forty years have made it impossible for the circuit courts to function as they did in the past. In other words, the courts could not afford each appeal a full argument, a panel conference, and a largely judge-written, precedential published opinion. One path they might have taken is to reduce proportionately the time spent and process afforded to all cases, but they chose otherwise to divide the cases into two groups. With one group they grant oral argument, confer as a panel, and lavish judge and clerk time, preparing opinions of extravagant length and erudition. Judge Kozinski reports going through as many as seventy drafts of such an opinion.[53]

The other group is not scheduled for oral argument; the judges might or might not meet face-to-face to confer on their decision; and the judges and their clerks spend little time on them. Enter the central staff, a group of attorneys assigned to handle the job of researching and writing opinions disposing of the second group of cases. Originally, the proportions heavily favored the first group, which the judges dealt with personally. The second group at first consisted mostly of state prisoner cases handled by a very small group of staff attorneys.[54] Over time, the proportions have changed so that today, only a small minority of cases receives the full traditional appellate process.[55]

The Appellate Triage regime requires, of course, some method for determining which track a particular case belongs on. Practically, the decision is made by placing the case on the "argument" or "non-argument" calendar. The statutory authority to

51. A glowing account of the judge/clerk relationship can be found in Patricia M. Wald, *Selecting Law Clerks*, 89 MICH. L. REV. 152, 153–54 (1990).

52. DONNA STIENSTRA & JOE S. CECIL, THE ROLE OF STAFF ATTORNEYS AND FACE-TO-FACE CONFERENCING IN NON-ARGUMENT DECISIONMAKING 24 (1989).

53. Alex Kozinski, *Making the Case for Law Clerks*, 3 LONG TERM VIEW 55, 58 (1995).

54. *See* Pether, *Sorcerers*, *supra* note 48; Pether, *Inequitable Injunctions*, *supra* note 48.

55. Only about 26 percent of the cases are argued; and only a seventh are terminated in a signed published opinion. ADMIN. OFFICE OF THE U.S. COURTS, *supra* note 4, at 44, table S-1 and 48, table S-3.

deny oral argument comes from Rules 34(a)(1), (2) and 34(f) of the Federal Rules of Appellate Procedure:

(a) In General.
   (1) Party's Statement. Any party may file, or a court may require by local rule a statement explaining why oral argument should, or need not, be permitted.
   (2) Standards. Oral argument must be allowed in every case unless a panel of three judges who have examined the briefs and record unanimously agrees that oral argument is unnecessary for any of the following reasons:
      A) the appeal is frivolous;
      B) the dispositive issue or issues have been authoritatively decided; or
      C) the facts and legal arguments are adequately presented in the briefs and record, and the decisional process would not be significantly aided by oral argument.

   ....

(f) Submission on Briefs. The parties may agree to submit a case for decision on the briefs, but the court may direct that the case be argued.[56]

The rule is clear that oral argument is to be denied only if the panel members determine unanimously that the case meets one of the three criteria of rule 34(a)(2), but it is silent about the process of culling or screening the cases in order to suggest to the panel that a particular case does not warrant argument.

The several circuits differ, at least formally,[57] on this question. In all but one, pro se cases are almost always decided without oral argument.[58] In most, the screening of counseled cases is done by staff attorneys, subject of course to later panel approval.[59] Within the staff-screening model, there are variations. In some circuits, the screening is done by attorneys assigned to the central staff, in others by supervising staff attorneys, and in still others by attorneys assigned to the clerk's office. In some circuits, particular types of cases are not subject to screening at all.

Used in a few circuits, the other main screening model—judge-screening—calls for the judges to play a much larger role in the process. In the Tenth Circuit, the judges are divided into three-judge screening panels, with each judge primarily responsible for one-third of the cases assigned to the panel. In the Third Circuit, judges do the screening, but there are no separate screening panels; rather, regular argument panels determine which cases will be argued and which will not. The

56. Fed. R. App. P. 34.

57. One of the most complete studies of the circuit courts concludes that "[a]s a practical matter ... cases that are screened ... by staff, [are] subject to panel review." Judith A McKenna et al., Case Management Procedures in the Federal Courts of Appeals 8 (2000).

58. *Id.*

59. Arthur D. Hellman, *The View from the Trenches: A Report on the Breakout Sessions at the 2005 National Conference on Appellate Justice*, 8 J. App. Prac. & Process 141, 185 (2006) [hereinafter *The View from the Trenches*]; *see* McKenna et al., *supra* note 57, at 9.

Second Circuit does not screen counseled cases, hearing argument on all cases unless argument is waived or the appellant is a prisoner filing pro se.[60]

Staff-screening is highly problematic. As one commentator has remarked, staff-screening means "the bureaucracy is deciding what the bureaucracy can decide and what needs to be passed on to the judges, which amounts to a self-fulfilling or self-denying prophecy."[61] Moreover, whether a case is assigned to the argument or non-argument docket has an important effect on how it is processed and perhaps how it is ultimately decided. Screened cases, of course, are not argued, and most of the work on them is done by central staff rather than by judges and clerks in chambers. They are decided in short, unpublished, nonprecedential opinions that often give the litigants little or no insight into the court's reasoning.[62] They seldom produce dissents or concurrences, and they affirm rather than reverse the lower courts at very high rates.[63] In argued cases, the parties appear before the panel and learn and can respond to the judges' difficulties with their arguments. The panel members typically confer face-to-face for as long as it takes, and most argued cases are decided in fully precedential published opinions, some of which are long and closely reasoned, and may be the result of hundreds of hours of judge and clerk time.

Given that appellate justice is a societal good apportioned unevenly, assigning a case to one of the two calendars is a high-level allocation of scarce resources to some and not to others. Typically, our government does not assign such highly discretionary and portentous distributive justice calculations to lawyers who may be one or two years out of school. If any piece of case processing requires the wisdom of age and experience and the political investiture of presidential appointment and senatorial confirmation, it is this one. A staff attorney may be able to research a case and write a short conclusory opinion as well as a judge; these are technical skills for which recent law graduates are trained, but they are ill equipped and politically unauthorized to make decisions involving such major allocations of scarce societal resources.

b. Staff Attorneys and the "Screened" Cases

Once the cases are screened into "important" and "routine" categories, it is the staff attorneys' job to dispose of the second group. Exactly how do they go about that task; to whom do they report; and to what extent do the judges review their work?

60. McKenna et al., *supra* note 57, at 10.

61. Thomas E. Baker, *Proposed Intramural Reforms: What the U.S. Courts of Appeals Might Do to Help Themselves*, 25 St. Mary's L.J. 1321, 1336 (1994).

62. William L. Reynolds & William M. Richman, *An Evaluation of Limited Publication in the United States Courts of Appeals: The Price of Reform*, 48 U. Chi. L. Rev. 573, 602 (1981).

63. *See* Lauren K. Robel, *Caseload and Judging: Judicial Adaptations to Caseload*, 1990 BYU L. Rev. 3, 48; *see also* John B. Oakley, *The Screening of Appeals: The Ninth Circuit's Experience in the Eighties and Innovations for the Nineties*, 1991 BYU L. Rev. 859, 922.

While staff attorneys also decide motions, create and maintain issue inventories, and screen cases, the great bulk of their work consists of writing memoranda in the non-argument cases. The memo typically summarizes the facts and relevant legal authorities and suggests a disposition. Often a draft of a proposed opinion accompanies the memo, and almost as often the court adopts the staff attorney's proposed disposition and draft opinion with minor changes.[64]

The staff attorney's memo's fate varies considerably by circuit. In some, the case, accompanied by the memo, goes to each of the three panel judges in series. In other circuits, the memo is distributed to each judge, and then they "confer" in person, by telephone, or by memo. In still others, the memo is not distributed to the panel members at all. The panel meets and hears brief oral presentations by the staff on each case.[65] What all the circuits have in common is that the cases handled by the staff get very little judge time. While some judges insist they read the briefs and relevant record excerpts in all non-argument cases,[66] others candidly admit that they do not.[67]

Moreover, there seems to be little disagreement among the judges on how much time it takes to "confer" on non-argument cases. Some report that a decision can take no more than half a minute, while others might require as much as twenty minutes.[68] In the Ninth Circuit, a non-argument panel can dispose of up to sixty cases in a day, three hundred in a week.[69]

Although some judges have qualms, most judges report considerable satisfaction with the use of staff to screen and handle the substantial portion of the cases deemed "routine."[70] One measure of satisfaction is that the judges often adopt the staff attorney's proposed opinion with little editing. Nevertheless, they are not willing to warrant the work, which explains why almost all circuits deny precedential effect to unpublished opinions[71]—most of which have been prepared by the staff.

Not merely content to deny precedential effect to the opinions, many courts had forbidden their citation. New Rule 32.1 of the Federal Rules of Appellate Procedure now prohibits local rules forbidding citation. It caused an astoundingly contentious

64. Hellman, *The View from the Trenches*, *supra* note 59, at 184–88; Judith A. McKenna et al., *supra* note 57, at 12; Stienstra & Cecil, *supra* note 52, at 28.

65. *Id.*

66. Stienstra & Cecil, *supra* note 52, at 24.

67. *See* Pether, *Sorcerers*, *supra* note 48, at 12–13 (citing Alex Kozinski, *The Appearance of Propriety*, Legal Affairs 19 (Jan.–Feb. 2005)); Hellman, *The View from the Trenches*, *supra* note 59, at 186.

68. Stienstra & Cecil, *supra* note 52, at 27.

69. Hellman, *The View from the Trenches*, *supra* note 59, at 185–86.

70. J. Clifford Wallace, *Improving the Appellate Process Worldwide Through Maximizing Judicial Resources*, 38 Vand. J. Transnat'l L. 187, 189 (2005); Hellman, *The View from the Trenches*, *supra* note 59, at 181.

71. The D.C. Circuit is the only exception. *See* Amy E. Sloan, *If You Can't Beat 'Em, Join 'Em: A Pragmatic Approach to Nonprecedential Opinions in the Federal Appellate Courts*, 86 Neb. L. Rev. 895, 918–22 & nn.159–185 (2007) (containing references to each circuit's local rules on the precedential value of its unpublished opinions).

reaction, given its very limited effect.[72] According to the Reporter for the committee that drafted the rule:

> [The rule] takes no position on whether refusing to treat an "unpublished" opinion as binding precedent is constitutional. It does not require any court to issue an "unpublished" opinion or forbid any court from doing so. It does not dictate the circumstances under which a court may choose to designate an opinion as "unpublished" or specify the procedure that a court must follow in making that decision. It says nothing about what effect a court must give to one of its "unpublished" opinions or to the "unpublished" opinions of another court. The one and only issue addressed by Rule 32.1 is the *citation* of judicial dispositions that have been *designated* as "unpublished."[73]

Given the rule's minimal content, why did it provoke so much opposition? One reason advanced for opposition to the rule was judges' lack of confidence in the quality of many of the unpublished opinions. One commentator has pithily captured the view of some judges:

> [I]n Judge Kozinski's own telling phrase, at least some circuit judges believe that unpublished opinions are metaphorically "not safe for human consumption." That is ... the judges are afraid that they are "*wrong*." They are alleged to have another major shortcoming, too. According to (one of) Judge Kozinski's accounts, unpublished opinions are drafted in "loose, sloppy language" that has the effect of undermining his manifest desire for "binding precedent" ....[74]

To the same effect is the comment of the anonymous circuit judge J9–21 quoted in an attitude study undertaken by the Federal Judicial Center in response to a request from the Appellate Rules Advisory Committee, which was then drafting Rule 32.1:

> [W]e have two kinds of unpublished decisions—those issued in calendared cases before regular panels (not all of which are argued), and those issued in "screening" cases, in which drafts are prepared by central staff and approved by three-judge panels after oral presentations and brief reviews of documents. I would be comfortable having the first group cited, as long as they are not precedential, because a substantial amount of chambers work, by both law clerks and judges, go into them. As to the

72. William M. Richman, *Much Ado about the Tip of an Iceberg*, 62 Wash & Lee L. Rev. 1723, 1724–25 (2005).

73. Comm. on Rules of Practice & Procedure, Judicial Conference of the U.S., Preliminary Draft of Proposed Amendments to the Federal Rules of Appellate, Bankruptcy, Civil, and Criminal Procedure 33–34 (Aug. 2003) (citations omitted).

74. Pether, *Sorcerers*, *supra* note 48, at 9 (footnotes omitted).

second group—screened cases—the dispositions are exceedingly short, and I have much less confidence in whatever reasoning does appear.[75]

Thus it is clear that the attitude of some judges is schizophrenic or at least hypocritical. They are satisfied with the central staff's handling of a large portion of the docket because those cases are routine or trivial; however they are not sufficiently confident in the opinions *that they have supposedly approved* to consider them precedent or even to encourage their citation.

While the judges seem content with the extensive role played by clerks and staff attorneys, the appellate bar is not.[76] The principal problems that lawyers have with the extensive use of central staff are delegation and transparency, concerns that are interrelated. The delegation worry is simple; in the words of an elite ABA committee, practitioners "may ... believe, sometimes correctly, that cases are decided effectively by someone other than an Article III judge."[77] Appellate advocates "find it troubling that judges would not read the briefs and the record in the case, but only a staff memorandum."[78] One prominent attorney has commented that he and his colleagues "regard screening as a device to push the lawyer out of the law entirely. We just don't count anymore."[79] If a senior appellate attorney has spent scores of hours (and thousands of her client's dollars) preparing a brief, it is disconcerting to suspect that the decision in the case and the decision as to what process the case will receive will be made by a lawyer a year or two out of law school, and perhaps one her firm would not consider hiring.[80] And think how much worse it is for the pro se litigant who—if she only knew—has had her appeal effectively rejected by such a person.

The lack of transparency compounds the problem. Professor Hellman emphasizes that the bar is "agnostic" rather than "skeptical" about the role of central staff because attorneys simply do not know what role staff play in the disposition of cases. Although Congress, in response to concern about staff, has required the circuits to publish their "operating procedures,"[81] the results have been vague. The Federal Judicial Center's prediction that "litigants and counsel in an appeal decided

75. Robert Timothy Reagan et al., Federal Judicial Center, Citing Unpublished Opinions in Federal Appeals 73 (2005).

76. Hellman, *The View from the Trenches*, *supra* note 59, at 184–85.

77. Frank A. Kaufman et al., Report of the American Bar Association Standing Committee on Federal Judicial Improvements, The United States Courts of Appeals: Reexamining Structure and Process After a Century of Growth, *reprinted in* 125 F.R.D. 523, 548 (1989) [hereinafter ABA Report].

78. Hellman, *The View from the Trenches*, *supra* note 59, at 186.

79. John P. Frank, Remarks at the Conference on Empirical Research in Judicial Administration (Mar. 4 & 5, 1988), *reprinted in* 21 Ariz. St. L.J. 33, 126 (1989).

80. Elbow clerks, representative of the type of lawyers elite firms seek, typically have much more paradigmatically elite academic qualifications than occupants of staff attorney positions. *See* Pether, *Sorcerers*, *supra* note 48, at 27.

81. 28 U.S.C. § 2077(a) (2006).

without argument seldom [will] know what role, if any, a staff attorney played in the handling of their appeal"[82] surely will remain accurate for a long time to come.[83]

When constructing an argument, it is a lawyer's first instinct to consider the audience. If a staff attorney first must be convinced before the case even gets to a judge,[84] the arguments might well differ from those used if access to the judge were guaranteed.[85] Moreover, lawyers want to know everything a judge considers before making a decision. The idea that there is a secret memo from an unknown bureaucrat that will determine the fate of the case is anathema to most of the bar. Thus the American Bar Association has recommended that a copy of the staff memo be distributed to counsel so any objection by counsel could be responsive to the real premises of the decision.[86] Given the disproportionate judicial response to the relatively minor change wrought by the adoption of Rule 32.1, adoption of a staff-memo-disclosure rule, or even a recommended practice, seems highly unlikely.

There is a delicious irony here. Federal magistrates, a superbly qualified group, must issue a written report disposing of cases assigned by the district court. If a litigant objects to that report, the district court must review the magistrate's report de novo. Moreover, it is grounds for reversal if the district judge simply adopts the magistrate's opinion, as opposed to writing his own.[87] Congress and the appellate courts, in other words, have adopted procedures to assure effective supervision of the work of the magistrates. In contrast, no rule requires any notice to the parties or judicial revision of the drafts suggested by staff. In short, the circuit courts, not surprisingly, are more demanding of the trial courts than they are of themselves.

c. Ominous Developments for Overdelegation: Career Appointments, Specialization, and Proliferation

The first of these three developments was almost inevitable. Originally, staff attorneys, like law clerks, were hired for short terms (one or two years). But if the staff attorney wished to stay and her performance satisfied the court, why not extend the

82. McKenna et al., *supra* note 57, at 51–52.

83. The ABA Report recommended "[f]ormalizing the role of court personnel in such decisions ... to reduce the misapprehensions of parties and counsel about the extent of their power." ABA Report, *supra* note 77, at 549.

84. Patricia M. Wald, *19 Tips from 19 Years on the Appellate Bench*, 1 J. App. Prac. & Process 7–8 (1999).

85. Charles E. Carpenter Jr., *The No-Citation Rule for Unpublished Opinions: Do the Ends of Expediency for Overloaded Appellate Courts Justify the Means of Secrecy?* 50 S.C. L. Rev. 235, 246 (1998).

86. ABA Report, *supra* note 77, at 549. *See also* Baker, *supra* note 18, at 145; Oakley, *supra* note 22, at 902.

87. *E.g.*, Hernandez v. Estelle, 711 F.2d 619 (5th Cir. 1983) (remanding case because of district court's improper reliance on magistrate's report and failure to make independent determination of contested findings).

term? Several benefits accrued immediately. Productivity went up as interviewing, hiring, and training time went down. Moreover, experienced staff attorneys work faster and with more confidence.[88]

From the staff attorney's point of view, the arrangement made good sense. Not every able young lawyer wants to work for a high-pressure firm. Turnover at those places is very high; few associates stay long enough to become partner, and it is not unusual for an "entering class" of associates to total fifty per year. Reasons for turnover vary, but most turnover is voluntary with experienced young lawyers moving to "lifestyle" firms, in-house counsel jobs with clients of the former firm, or government jobs. In that environment, a job as a career staff attorney doesn't look so bad. Not only is the lifestyle (hours and pressure) better than in most firms, but the pay is roughly competitive with other government work; a very senior supervising staff attorney can earn 80 percent of a circuit judge's salary.[89] The job is sufficiently desirable that several staff attorney's offices include attorneys who began their careers as circuit court or district court elbow clerks.

How widespread is the phenomenon? In some circuits, all staff attorneys have career appointments; in others, most are careerists along with a few short-term appointments; in still others, the majority of appointments are limited to relatively short terms (two to five years), with only supervisory staff attorneys having career positions. The trend, however is clear; the percentage of staff attorneys serving in career positions is increasing steadily.

Career appointments increase the risk of overdelegation as judges become more confident in the capabilities of the staff.[90] Moreover, the staff begins to stratify (nearly all circuits have some form of supervisory staff attorney position) and replicate, with staff attorneys interviewing, hiring, training, and supervising other staff attorneys. The judges are less and less familiar with the work of the staff; most "routine" screened cases fall into categories with which the judges have little experience, but more of this in the following paragraphs.

Specialization, the second alarming development, was a feature of the institution of central staff from its inception; after all, the first staff attorneys worked almost exclusively on prisoners' cases.[91] But now, the specialization has spread geographically and topically. In some circuits, staff attorneys do not specialize, except for the de facto specialization that results from their being assigned "routine" and

88. Almost all of the information in this and the next two paragraphs comes from telephone conversations with supervising staff attorneys, human resource officers, and others working for the circuit courts. The informants were not promised confidentiality, and the authors have records of their names and the dates and contents of the conversations, but revealing their names might be troublesome for some, and would not make the information more reliable.

89. The salary for a circuit judge is $184,500. Senior staff attorneys may earn as much as $150,000. *Source*: Telephone conversation with anonymous supervising staff attorney.

90. Donald P. Ubell, *Evolution and Role of Appellate Court Staff Attorneys*, 2 Cooley L. Rev. 157, 163–64 (1984).

91. *See* Pether, *Inequitable Injunctions*, *supra* note 48.

pro se cases. In others, there are multiple divisions devoted to motions, jurisdictional issues, pro se cases, immigration cases, and asylum cases.[92] In an intermediate group, there is no formal specialization, but de facto some staff attorneys acquire a reputation for expertise in a particular area; and cases in that area tend to flow to that attorney.

The benefit of specialization, again, is efficiency, and its danger is, again, overdelegation. The overdelegation problem is perfectly natural from the standpoint of the judge. Most did not have careers devoted to pro se cases, immigration cases, or prisoners' cases. After arriving at the circuit court, they have little exposure to these case types because they are screened for staff treatment. So, imagine yourself a newly minted circuit judge whose prior career concentrated on securities litigation. One of the screened cases that comes before you, in a package with forty others, to be decided in a one-day conference, is an asylum case. Your panel colleague, a veteran of ten years, informs you that the memo and proposed opinion in the asylum case was written by X, a talented, reliable, veteran staff attorney, who has specialized in asylum cases for four years. Given that there are forty other "routine" cases in the group, that there is another set of "important cases" for which you have primary responsibility for preparing a polished published opinion, and that you know you will have little involvement in future asylum cases (which, of course, will be screened out), how much incentive do you have to learn enough asylum law to cast a reasonably informed vote?

The final and most significant of the three ominous developments is the proliferation of staff. Staff attorneys began as groups of two or three recent law school graduates in each of a few circuits. By 1981, Judge McCree complained that "cancerous" growth had increased the total to 136.[93] Today there are about 500 staff attorneys employed in the twelve regional circuit courts of appeals.[94] Compiling a total is no easy matter. Unlike many other judicial statistics published by the Administrative Office of the Courts, the Judicial Conference, and the Federal Judicial Center, there appears to be no readily available public record of the number and distribution of staff attorneys. Moreover, it is not always clear whom to count. Clearly lawyers employed in the Staff Attorney's Office count, but what about those employed in the clerk's office who help the judges rule on dispositive motions? And what about the attorneys who facilitate mediation and settlement of appeals? The total of 500 represents the first two groups, but not the third.

92. The Ninth Circuit is the most specialized with the Second a distant runner up. At the other end of the spectrum, there is little, if any, subject specialization among the staff attorneys in the First Circuit.

93. Wade H. McCree Jr., *Bureaucratic Justice: An Early Warning*, 129 U. Pa. L. Rev. 777, 787 (1981).

94. E-mail message from Gloria Malkin, Attorney Advisor, Appellate Court and Circuit Administration Division, Administrative Office of the U.S. Courts, to William M. Richman (Nov. 21, 2007) (on file with author).

The growth in the numbers of staff has been steady and shows no signs of tapering off; it closely follows the rate of increase in appellate filings and vastly exceeds the growth in the number of authorized judgeships. Illustrative of the trend is a comparison of number of staff attorneys per circuit reported by the Federal Judicial Center in *2000* with the results of telephone inquiries directed to the various circuit courts in *2008*. That comparison reveals that in the interim, central staff has grown in every circuit by percentages ranging from about 10 to nearly 90.[95] If we combine the number of staff attorneys, 500, with the number of elbow clerks, about 630 (approximately 3.5 per judge—of which there are 178), it becomes apparent that for each circuit judge there are more than six helper-attorneys. At that ratio, can the judges still plausibly claim, "we do our own work"? Or have the appellate courts become just another government bureaucracy?

There is a sad irony in reading commentary written ten or fifteen years ago by scholars or judges who offer reassurance about the level of delegation occurring at that time. A very common way to end such a discussion is for the author to opine, "I think on balance that the delegation to clerks and staff and the other appellate shortcuts have not fundamentally damaged the traditional appellate process; but I am sure that if we proceed farther in this direction, they will."[96] Then, of course, we *do* proceed farther and cross the author's line in the sand. How long can we continue to cross those lines, drawn by the best and most responsible thinkers of their time, and still believe we retain anything resembling traditional appellate justice?

d. Hiring, Firing, Training, and Supervision

The work rules in any employment situation have a great deal to do with forming the craft culture of the job. Thus, norms for recruiting, supervision, promotion, and discipline speak volumes about the societal value attached to the job, as well as its prestige, responsibility, and morale. The point seems obvious, but if any confirmation is required, consider the different rules for hiring permanent faculty compared, say, to adjuncts, or the difference in the procedures used to hire line workers versus CEOs.

Given the importance of these considerations, it would be useful to know the facts about the work conditions of the staff. Unfortunately, there are no uniform, settled, and publicized procedures. Thus, we do not know who recruits, interviews, and hires staff attorneys: the judges or other supervisory staff attorneys. Similarly,

95. The Fourth Circuit's corps grew the least—from 32 to 35, and the Ninth Circuit's the most—from 48 to over 85.

96. *See, e.g.*, Hellman, *The View from the Trenches*, *supra* note 59, at 202 (citing comments from several judges in "breakout" sessions); Carpenter, *supra* note 85, at 257; Baker, *Proposed Intramural Reforms*, *supra* note 61, at 1360; A. Leo Levin & Michael E. Kunz, *Thinking About Judgeships*, 44 AM. U. L. REV. 1627, 1653 (1995).

there is no public information concerning their training, supervision, promotion, termination, or discipline.

As is apparent from the preceding sections of this chapter, staff attorneys are public servants who do important work, work that was once performed by judges; and their work arrangements have a substantial effect on how they perform that work. Thus, the continued informality, idiosyncrasy, and nonuniformity of their work rules, as well as the ignorance of the bar and the public concerning those norms, is unacceptable.

CHAPTER 9
The Cumulative Effect of the Appellate Triage Regime

The developments we have discussed have had a profound impact on the work of the federal circuit courts. On the positive side, they have certainly helped the courts process appeals in a timely fashion. Dispositions per judge have increased dramatically over the past thirty years, and the number of pending appeals is small. Limited publication, central staff, and reduced oral argument have done what they were supposed to; the trains do run on time. But that efficiency has come at a significant cost. The costs of the individual appeals expediting strategies have been explored in previous chapters. This chapter takes a more global view and considers the cumulative cost of implementing all the strategies—the cost, in other words, of the entire Appellate Triage regime.

First, and most superficially, the circuit judges and their personnel have a very different look now than they did in Learned Hand's day. The judges on the federal courts of appeals now run something that resembles an office in a large law firm. The judges sit at the apex of a pyramid designed to provide them with layers of support. No longer do the judicial chambers consist of the judge, a secretary, and a couple of law clerks. Life has become much more complicated.

Second, the two-track appellate justice regime has led to the transformation of the federal appellate courts from their traditional and statutory role as *appellate* courts, which must hear and decide all appeals, into what are effectively *discretionary* courts, which get to decide which cases they will hear. They have become, in other words, *certiorari* courts. As a result, the courts are able to decide which appeals merit their full attention. This unilateral change in the circuit courts' function must be seen as judicial activism of the highest order, involving not merely tinkering with some sociopolitical hot-button issue, but rather with the role of the courts themselves. A unilateral change in the function of one of the branches of our tripartite government thus is deeply subversive of the entire constitutional scheme.

Third, appellate justice now runs on two tracks.[1] On Track One are those cases that get the full Learned Hand model; on Track Two are those cases decided by central staff without argument or a formally published, precedential opinion. The percentage of Track Two cases has been increasing steadily for decades, and it is now the overwhelming choice for disposition of disfavored cases. Track Two cases disproportionately involve the claims of the disfavored in our country—prisoners, the poor, immigrants. Circuit judges apparently prefer to deal with other, more "important" matters.

Fourth, not only has the quality of the work produced by the federal courts of appeals suffered in this transformation, but the increase of Track Two cases has also diminished the national capacity for making federal law. The Supreme Court has exacerbated this effect by reducing its own docket, thus transforming the circuit courts, de facto, into courts of last resort for both the error correction and law declaration functions. Moreover, Supreme Court review of unpublished opinions has become extremely unlikely even when the opinion conflicts with other published or unpublished decisions. Finally, those opinions are very unlikely to undergo an en banc review.

Fifth, the limited publication regime has reduced the transparency of the decision-making process of the federal circuit courts[2]. The judges have hidden the growth of central staff and the critical role that staff now plays in judicial decision making; as a result, Congress, the bar, and the public are unaware of the transformation and thus incapable of exerting pressure to curtail it or slow its progress.

Sixth, the Appellate Triage regime has reduced the accountability of the federal circuit judges. By issuing decisions that contain little or no reasoning and that are signed by no one, the judges have drastically reduced their personal involvement in decision making to such an extent that they no longer can be held effectively accountable for most of their decisions.

Finally, the system is deeply at odds with our legal culture. In the past dozen years, the unease about limited publication that is held by so many members of the legal profession has led to two major battles—over the no-citation rules and over the constitutionality of the whole system. The judicial establishment has managed to prevail (so far) in the second of those fights, but there remains a profound unhappiness with the process.

This chapter discusses those unhappy developments—including the possibility that the two-track system may have had some positive side effects.

1. *See supra* Introduction and chapter 1 for a discussion on the two tracks of justice.
2. *See infra* chapter 8.

A. THE OFFICE PYRAMID COMES TO CHAMBERS

Judges once did all of their work themselves, aided only by a couple of (very able) personal law clerks. The work product—the opinions—bore a heavy individual stamp: the opinions were the work of the *judge*. The judge had heard oral argument and had been deeply involved herself in writing an opinion that explained how she had reached the result, an opinion that also would provide guidance to those with similar problems in the future. Today, those long-proven procedures are available only in one of every six appeals heard in the circuit courts.

Federal appellate judges no longer act in splendid isolation. Instead, they act as the commander-in-chief of an intricate enterprise designed to let them formally process as much as possible. The result is that the judges must spend much of their time in nonjudicial tasks, such as administration. The judge's own staff includes four or five law clerks (sometimes known as "elbow" clerks), a couple of assistants/secretaries, and (often) student interns. But there is more, far more: the chief judge is now the manager of a staff (at least in theory) whose primary role is to conserve judicial effort by screening cases and participating significantly in the decision-making process. In other words, the modern federal appellate decision is a team effort. In most cases, the judge's role is minimal, primarily or even exclusively supervisory. Clerks and central staff screen the appeals to determine how much judge time should be allocated to each case. These para-judicial personnel also recommend whether oral argument should be granted and whether a full opinion (or, indeed, any opinion) should be written. Not only is judge time rationed, but also the key decisions allocating judge time are not even made by judges.[3]

The bitter irony, of course, is that the Appellate Triage system was created to conserve judicial time, and it has instead resulted in judges spending *less* time judging and *more* time in administration—that is, running the business. The judge has to devote more time to supervision, leaving less time for performing her basic job—resolving disputes.

This development parallels changes in the practice of law. Many judges come from private practice. Once upon a time, practitioners did their own work, perhaps with the assistance of a small closely knit team. That is no longer true. Today's eminent practitioners often run vast practice groups with teams of junior persons doing everything from document review to depositions to the writing of briefs, memoranda, motions, and pleadings. The practice style is management and not personal input, except in the most important parts of the most important cases. It is not surprising that when those practitioners have ascended to the bench that they have replicated in chambers what made them successful in their earlier lives.

3. *See* chapter 8.

The same can be said of judges who come from an academic life. Scholarship is no longer a task for the solitary scholar alone in the library. Today, many professors generate material from atop their own pyramids of student research assistants, research librarians, junior colleagues, and other helpers.[4] Again, the academics who have become judges must find the judicial decision-making business very comfortable, indeed.

The shift from a very personal office to one where much is delegated not only means that the judges spend more time in administration; it also means that there is more input into the final product from law clerks and staff. In short, much more of the actual work of deciding cases—the research and writing and getting to the bottom line—is done by someone who has not been nominated by the President or confirmed by the Senate. We are sure that these para-judges are very smart and hardworking persons, but there is a very good reason that we require that judges go through a rigorous sifting, nominating, and confirming process. That process, in addition to serving as a political screen (and balance), also looks for attributes like diversity, wisdom, and experience. We believe as a society that those who decide the fate of litigants should be vetted at the highest level. Delegation on a large scale, no matter how diligent the supervision, is not the same.

B. THE NEW *CERTIORARI* COURTS

Every losing litigant has a statutory right to appeal.[5] The expectation has long been that an "appeal" includes a right to have your case reviewed by a panel of judges. Thanks to the decisional shortcuts we have discussed, however, for many years that expectation has been true only in a nominal sense. The circuit court judges today take a personal interest in cases only after a staff attorney recommends personal involvement. Thus, mandatory review has instead come to mean something quite different. Now the trial court's decision is subject to review at the discretion of the judges; in other words, the circuit courts' decision to use discretionary review of appeals has turned the "appellate" courts into *certiorari* courts.[6] Congress, of course, has authorized the Supreme Court to act as a *certiorari* court, but it has not granted that discretionary authority to the courts of appeals. Thus, the transformation of the circuit courts has not only been unwise, but unlawful as well.

4. The practice has become so widespread—acute, one might say—that charges of plagiarism by law school professors can be met with the response that "my student researchers did it, and I did not bother to read what they wrote."

5. 28 U.S.C. § 1291 (2006).

6. The Supreme Court selects cases to review in a manner quite similar to the circuit courts. All Justices other than Justice Alito pool their clerks to review *certiorari* petitions; this pool recommends to the Court which cases to hear.

When we first suggested a generation ago that the circuit courts were acting more and more like *certiorari* courts,[7] perhaps we were indulging in some hyperbole to make the point. Today, however, judges and commentators, even some who approve of the transformation, increasingly are beginning to share our assessment. Thus Judge Kozinski in his opinion in *Hart v. Massanari* put the matter squarely:

> While federal courts of appeals generally lack discretionary review authority, they use their authority to decide cases by unpublished—and non-precedential—dispositions to achieve the same end: They select a manageable number of cases in which to publish precedential opinions, and leave the rest to be decided by unpublished dispositions or judgment orders.[8]

Similarly, Professors Cooper and Berman acknowledge the transformation and applaud it as helpful in that it allows the circuit courts to resolve disputes while still practicing the "passive virtue" of reluctance to make new law.[9] The invocation of Professor Bickel's "passive virtues," of course, merely is a clever way of hiding the fact that the circuit courts are engaged in the lawless resolution of disputes, something that is entirely at odds with the entire history of the common law. It is also at odds with their statutory mandate.

C. TWO-TRACK JUSTICE

The inevitable result of the developments in appellate decision-making procedures in the past half century has been the creation of two completely separate tracks for justice. In chapter 2, we showed that cases involving prisoner rights, social security, criminal convictions, and the like were disproportionately subject to second-class treatment. We also showed that the Appellate Triage system restricts oral argument and that the opinions are the work of central staff with little or no input from a judge or even her personal staff. Finally, the truncated nature of unpublished opinions sharply reduces the transparency of those processes; no one can tell from reading the opinion in most cases why the appeal was decided the way it was or why it was shunted to the nontraditional track. In contrast, a litigant in an "important" antitrust or securities case, one who is represented by serious counsel, will get the full Learned Hand treatment. There will be oral argument, an opinion prepared by the

7. William L. Reynolds & William M. Richman, *An Evaluation of Limited Publication in the United States Courts of Appeals: The Price of Reform*, 48 U. Chi. L. Rev. 573, 625 (1981); the argument had matured by 1996 in William M. Richman & William L. Reynolds, *Elitism, Expediency and the New Certiorari: Requiem for the Learned Hand Tradition*, 81 Cornell L. Rev. 273 (1996).

8. 266 F.3d 1155, 1177 (9th Cir. 2001).

9. Jeffrey O. Cooper & Douglas A. Berman, *Passive Virtues and Casual Vices in the Federal Courts of Appeals*, 66 Brook. L. Rev. 685 (2000).

judge and her staff, and the result will contain a sufficiently detailed explanation so that the whole world can second-guess the result—and have an informed idea as to the state of the law.

Expressed somewhat differently, a litigant on Track One will receive first-class treatment from the courts of appeals. That treatment includes argument in front of a prepared court and an opinion good enough to be inserted into a casebook and that has been thought about sufficiently so that the court is willing to let it guide future cases. Cases on Track One receive the gold standard of judicial involvement; when that standard is used, the circuit courts are very good indeed.

A litigant who is poor, without counsel, and with a boring, repetitive problem, on the other hand, can expect only the second-hand treatment that is available on Track Two. Because Track Two provides so little information to the litigants or to the parties, no one can even guess as to the quality of the justice handed out on that track. We do know, however, that the disfavored will not receive the gold standard in case processing that the favored appeals receive. Certainly the judges believe that the Learned Hand method helps to insure a better product. Thus, it is very likely that the quality of justice given to the poor will not be as good as the quality available to the rich. This disparity does not seem to bother the judges at all. Sworn to provide equal justice to rich and poor alike, the circuit courts are satisfied to provide justice in varying degrees, acting beyond their statutory mandate and taking for themselves a role as arbiters of distributive justice. They decide how the scarce resource of judicial time and effort will be rationed, thus appropriating a power for themselves that the Constitution and the statutes have assigned to the legislative branch.

Of course, this unfortunate result does not come from any deliberate attempt to harm disfavored groups; the federal appellate courts remain, in theory, a bulwark protecting the citizenry. Nevertheless, the harm is there for all to see; judges are simply less likely to devote serious effort and attention to the routine veterans' benefit denial appeal than to the interesting corporate tax case. The discrimination may be ad hoc rather than planned, de facto and not *de jure*, but it is nonetheless real. One of the basic principles behind Anglo-American law is that moral responsibility attaches to harm done with the elbows as well as with the fists. The differential in treatment violates that principle.

D. THERE HAS BEEN A MARKED DIMINUTION IN QUALITY

In addition to the systemic and structural costs exacted by the courts' strategy of reducing appellate process in order to accommodate caseload, there is a significant cost in quality as well. In particular, oral argument has the potential to be of value in many cases where it is not granted, and its denial clearly diminishes the quality of the court's decision making in those cases. Moreover, the poor quality of so many unpublished opinions provides stark evidence that there has been a systemic breakdown in the work product of the circuit courts. Finally, as we have just noted, the absence of the Learned Hand treatment in most cases suggests that it is needed to obtain the highest quality decisions possible.

Initially, representatives of the courts maintained that the truncated appellate process had not reduced the quality of the courts' work.[10] Now, however, there seems to be at least tacit acknowledgment that quality has suffered. Consider the half-hearted defense of contemporary practice offered by the Federal Courts Study Committee:

> [Federal] judges *do much of their own work*, grant oral argument in cases that *need* it, decide cases with *sufficient* thought, and produce opinions in cases of precedential importance with the care *they deserve* . . . .[11]

The cautious wording abandons all pretense that the circuit judges now do all or even most of their own work, or that oral argument is readily available, or that unpublished opinions receive the same care as their published siblings. Thus, one of the leading apologists for the "appellate shortcut" strategy, Judge Kozinski, admits the dismal quality of unpublished opinions and used it as an argument *against* the adoption of Federal Rule of Appellate Procedure 32.1, which permits the citation of unpublished opinions.[12] The judge's appraisal, candidly expressed, is that unpublished opinions should remain uncitable because they are "not fit for human consumption."[13]

There is another problem with inferior quality: not enough law is being made. We believe that every legal discipline could use more opinions making new law, but it is also important that there be more opinions questioning, confirming, and/or modifying existing law. It is hard to believe that in the many thousands of unpublished opinions issued each year the courts have no opportunity to do those things. Merely hardening precedent by reaffirming it or showing how a rule or principle works in a different fact situation would itself be valuable to litigants and lower courts, as well as to the circuit courts themselves. It might even reduce the amount of litigation and thus the number of appeals. Moreover, unpublished opinions occur most often in those fields most likely to involve poor litigants. We suspect that those

10. *See id.* at 707–08 (citing and discussing the work of several defenders of "appellate courts' adaptations to their increased workload").

11. Fed. Courts Study Comm., Judicial Conference of the United States, Report of the Federal Courts Study Committee 109 (1990) (emphasis added).

12. The no-citation issue is discussed in chapter 5, *supra*.

13. Alex Kozinski, *In Opposition to Proposed Federal Rule of Appellate Procedure 32.1*, 51 Fed. Law. 36, 37 (June 2004).

areas are ones where clarification of the law is really needed, but, because of the shortcuts, those areas are the least likely to receive it.

Because the Supreme Court hears only about eighty cases every year, the circuit courts have become by necessity the primary makers of federal law.[14] It is hard to believe that the courts of appeals are doing that job as fully as they should be doing it.

Finally, the problem with quality can extend to the trial courts. Those judges know how appeals in different cases likely will be handled. How careful will even the most conscientious district court judge be if he knows that a prisoner's civil rights case will not receive full review? After all, if most such cases are treated as "chaff," the trial judges are "perfectly rational in choosing to rubber-stamp rather than read"[15] because they do not fear reversal on appeal. It is not surprising, therefore, that the rate of reversal of district court judgments has been cut in half since 1960.[16] Supervision, in other words, must be active to be effective.

E. TRANSPARENCY HAS BEEN DRASTICALLY REDUCED

Central staff attorneys play a critical role in the workings of the courts of appeals. They are the gatekeepers, recommending what cases get heard, and they effectively write dispositive opinions in a great majority of cases. And yet, there is very little formal mention of their work in the various Federal Appellate Rules, Local Rules, or Internal Operating Procedures. We really do not know (except by anecdote) who they are, how they are trained or supervised, how long their careers are, what ethical rules constrain their work, and how much authority they have been given. The personnel who screen the appeals to recommend which track a case should follow and who should write the decisions in the vast majority of cases that are denied the Learned Hand treatment make up the "stealth" component of the federal judiciary. We are continually surprised to find out how little even experienced court watchers, including seasoned practitioners, know of the critical role played by central staff.

It is easy to see why. The public, of course, knows nothing of the situation in the appellate courts, and although the bar generally learned in law school how appellate courts work—they were taught the Learned Hand model—that learning is largely

14. They also make a lot of state law, although, of course, in theory they do no such thing.

15. Mary Lou Stow & Harold J. Spaeth, *Examining an Analogy: Does the Judicial Monster Eat Chaff?*, 75 Judicature 294, 294 (1992).

16. *See* Frank A. Kaufman et al., Report of the American Bar Association Standing Committee on Federal Judicial Improvements, The United States Courts of Appeals: Reexamining Structure and Process After a Century of Growth, *reprinted in* 125 F.R.D. 523, 546 (1989) ("[T]he rate of reversal of district court judgments has gone down, from about 25 percent in 1960 to less than 14 percent in 1987 . . . ."); Admin. Office of U.S. Courts, Judicial Business of the U.S. Courts 2009, at 109, table B-5 (2009) (reversal rate of 9.1 percent in 2009).

irrelevant. The courts have been careful not to let information get out on how the system really functions. They simply do not want the world to know how much power they have delegated to persons who are off everyone's radar. That should not be the case, however. The exercise of secret power is, of course, incompatible with the transparency rightfully demanded in a free society.

This is not to suggest evil motives by the judges or staffers or even to question the competence of those staff who write most of the opinions. Rather, we believe with Justice Brandeis that sunlight is the best disinfectant[17] and that the judiciary should make public and explicit what is done by central staff, how they do it, and why it has been delegated to them.

F. JUDICIAL ACCOUNTABILITY HAS BEEN DRASTICALLY REDUCED

The Appellate Triage regime has drastically reduced judicial accountability. Because we have discussed the reasons earlier, we only summarize here. Central staff takes the lead in "trivial cases," the unwanted stepchildren of the appellate process, by writing initial drafts of opinions which receive only abbreviated review, if that, by the judges themselves. It is difficult to hold any individual responsible for what is in those decisions. Moreover, unpublished opinions are issued unsigned, further diminishing judicial accountability. They are also unlikely to provoke review by the Supreme Court or the circuit court sitting en banc, and they are less likely to provoke commentary from practitioners or scholars. We do not believe that this is the way Congress and the public believe courts should operate.

G. UNPUBLISHED OPINIONS AND THE AMERICAN LEGAL CULTURE ARE FUNDAMENTALLY AT ODDS

Much that we have written in this book reveals a basic disconnect between the system of unpublished opinions that the judicial establishment defends with such vigor and the rest of the American legal world. It is quite clear that many judges, a good chunk of the practicing bar (especially the appellate lawyers and almost all academics who have written on the subject) dislike—detest might not be too strong a word—that system. They believe, as do we, that the system violates the taught norms of our legal culture.

One manifestation of this disconnect is concern over the constitutionality of limited publication, especially the controversy over the *Anastasoff* decision where Judge Richard Arnold held that denying precedential effect to unpublished opinions

17. Louis B. Brandeis, Other People's Money and How the Bankers Use It 92 (1914) ("Sunlight is said to be the best of disinfectants").

violated Article III of the United States Constitution.[18] Although we do not believe that the Supreme Court will ever declare the limited publication system unconstitutional, the discussion that followed *Anastasoff*, as well as other concerns that have been raised about the fundamental fairness of the system, certainly reflect a fundamental unhappiness with both its processes and its outcomes.

Nowhere is this disconnect better captured than in the controversy over the no-citation rules and the adoption of Federal Rule of Appellate Procedure 32.1.[19] Not only was the battle over Rule 32.1 intensely fought, its opponents, led by Chief Judge Kozinski, also ignored—"willfully ignored" is the phrase that comes to mind—compelling evidence from *judicial* sources that eliminating the rules against citation would not have the predicted, adverse consequences. The intensity of the battle revealed how far the establishment has strayed from the basic understanding of our legal culture.

Both episodes—*Anastasoff* and Rule 32.1—reveal how strongly the profession values the traditional common-law method of reaching just results in appellate cases. It also reveals how much the judicial establishment is willing to sacrifice those methods at the altar of expediency. Why they are willing to do so is a question we will explore in chapters 11 through 13.

Is there any hope for change? Remember that the fight over the no-citation rules was bitter and prolonged. The judicial establishment used everything in its bag of tricks to defeat Rule 32.1, even though the no-citation policy that Rule 32.1 addressed was absurd, and, in the words of the man who knew most about it, the whole prolonged struggle was "much ado about little."[20] What will the establishment do when central staff or restrictions on precedent are under attack?

Perhaps of more importance, the senseless opposition to Rule 32.1 highlights the utter indifference of the judicial establishment to opposing views. Thus, there have been no studies in a decade of the effect of Appellate Triage, and there does not appear to be any communication among the courts of the impact of the various ways in which they employ the appeals-expending strategies. Moreover, the numbers and roles of central staff have never been discussed in public, and information about staff is very difficult to get; the importance (or lack) of oral argument seems never to have been discussed in public; and the lack of uniformity in implementing Rule 32.1 all suggest a disregard ("disdain" might be a better word) of the judges for their responsibilities.

18. 223 F.3d 898, 899 (8th Cir.), *vacated as moot*, 235 F.3d 1054 (8th Cir. 2000) (en banc). *Anastasoff* is discussed in chapter 6, *supra*.

19. The no-citation controversy is discussed in chapter 6, *supra*.

20. Patrick Schiltz, *Much Ado about Little: Explaining the* Sturm und Drang *over the Citation of Unpublished Opinions*, 62 WASH. & LEE L. REV. 1429 (2005).

H. THE OTHER SIDE OF THE LEDGER

The cumulative effect of the truncated procedures that we have chronicled has had a devastating impact on the rights of those most in need of judicial protection, those litigants whose claims raise no systemic law-making concerns, but only the claim that they have been denied justice in the trial court. The process has had a corrupting influence on the judiciary, as seen by the degrading fight over Rule 32.1. And it must be demoralizing to many judges to know that they are signing off on decisions that they have not seriously reviewed. The debit side of the ledger is quite bad; are there any benefits to help balance it?

It is difficult to find a silver lining. It is true that appeals have been resolved in a timely fashion for a long time. It is true that the numbers of appellate judges remain relatively small and that the judges have managed to preserve their elite status—for what that may be worth. Beyond that, we can offer as a positive effect of the Appellate Triage regime only that scholars are beginning to devote serious consideration to the decision-making procedures in the circuit courts. When we started writing about unpublished opinions thirty years ago, little attention was paid to those procedures and, indeed, to the work of the circuit courts themselves. Almost no academics were working in the area, and appellate reform was the province of the judges and a few high-minded practitioners. The past decade, however, has seen a steadily growing output of scholarship. That output at first focused on the no-citation problem, but as commentators grew comfortable with the topic, other parts of appellate practice were opened up. As one example, consider the work on the meaning of precedent; able scholars and judges have been thinking and writing about opinion writing and how law is derived from opinions has changed over the past few decades. In this respect, consider renewed interest in the concept of persuasive precedent and the eclectic approach adopted by the D.C. Circuit in its rules.

1. Persuasive Precedent

One hopeful development has been the adoption by six circuits of rules conferring "persuasive" value on their own unpublished opinions, and another circuit has taken no position on whether unpublished opinions are precedential.[21] Seven circuits, in other words, do not strip unpublished opinions of all precedential value. Persuasive

21. Sarah E. Ricks, *A Modest Proposal for Regulating Unpublished, Non-Precedential Federal Appellate Opinions While Courts and Litigants Adapt to Federal Rule of Appellate Procedure 32.1*, 9 J. App. Prac. & Process 17, 22–24 (2007). Professor Ricks explains the development this way:

> To comply with Rule 32.1, twelve of the federal circuits enacted new local rules or procedures concerning citation of unpublished, non-precedential opinions. The Sixth Circuit simply permitted citation of unpublished opinions without speaking to what value

precedent, of course, is a concept known to all first-semester law students. The term describes the weight that a court gives to all decisions of other courts (other than a decision from a higher court in the same judicial system—what we call "controlling precedent"). The term is self-explanatory: the cited opinion does not "control," but it can "persuade." The persuasive value of a precedent depends on many things, but it depends primarily on the explanatory force of the earlier opinion.

All circuit court opinions were "persuasive" before the advent of the law of the circuit rule; that rule made the opinions controlling within the issuing circuit unless and until overruled by the Supreme Court or an en banc panel.[22] As we have earlier discussed, that rule has been used to argue against changing the limited publication regime; judges, it has been said, cannot issue opinions unless they have been so carefully thought out that they should bind all future courts in the circuit.[23] One solution to that perceived problem (apart from writing better opinions) is to treat some opinions as nonbinding, but still useful by treating them as "persuasive" only. A later court that does not like the persuasive precedent can simply state that the unpublished opinion that has been cited to it was not persuasive and move on.

There is a problem here, however, and that is that anyone trained in the common-law tradition cannot accept a mere dismissal of an arguably relevant precedent as not persuasive; we demand an explanation of *why* the precedent does not apply to the facts of the instant case. That, after all, is what the first year of law school teaches us. The reader simply will not accept a conclusory statement that another case is not persuasive. To satisfy its audience, the court is going to have to tell us why the precedent fails to persuade it. Doing so in all cases will take time and energy, negating the time-saving aspects of the Appellate Triage system. In the end, of course, the judges will do what they do now, and that is to write opinions that are so meager in content that they give little comfort to anyone who might wish to cite them. So perhaps treating unpublished opinions as persuasive rather than binding may not be the final answer. But it does have some promise.

> the unpublished opinions will carry. The Second, Fifth, Seventh, and Ninth Circuits adopted local rules expressly stating that unpublished opinions are not precedential, without mentioning potential persuasive value.
>
> By contrast, the First, Eight, Tenth, Eleventh, and Federal Circuits each expressly confer "persuasive" value on the circuit's own non-precedential opinions issued since January 1, 2007. Further, the First and Tenth Circuits give retroactive effect to the rule, according persuasive value to *all* of their non-precedential opinions, regardless of the issue date.
>
> Only the District of Columbia Circuit expressly permits citation of its own current non-precedential opinions *as precedent*.

Id. (footnotes omitted).

22. *See supra* chapter 3.

23. *See supra* chapter 5 (discussing reactions to Fed. R. App. Proc. 32.1). Of course, Supreme Court decisions and opinions from state courts in diversity cases fall outside this description.

2. Precedent for What It's Worth

Perhaps the most interesting approach has been taken by the District of Columbia Circuit, which has adopted the only nonrestrictive rule concerning limited publication: "All unpublished orders or judgments of this court ... entered on or after January 1, 2002, may be cited as precedent."[24] Thus, all opinions from the D.C. Circuit have precedential value, albeit an undefined value. As Sarah Ricks has pointed out, however, the court "cautions"[25] that "a panel's decision to issue an unpublished disposition means that the panel sees no precedential value in that disposition."[26] That caution provides a healthy dose of realism. The judges seem to be well aware that their opinions generally have little that anyone could use as precedent.

In short, the D.C. Circuit has drawn the sting from the unpublished opinion debate by making all opinions formally equal. As the court candidly recognizes, however, some opinions inherently lack persuasive precedential value due to the truncated way in which they are written, a malady that must be addressed in other ways.

Thus there are some hopeful developments in the circuit courts. They do not place the ledger in balance, however. The failure of the courts of appeals to publish satisfactory opinions that can affect future cases has had an unexpected good side: it has generated a good deal of discussion among both judges and academics about the role of the courts, the concept of precedent, and other fundamental concepts not usually talked about after the first year of law school. In this book we cite many articles by authors from all branches of the profession examining those concepts through the lens of the Appellate Triage regime. The number of articles on the subject has increased steadily over time, and it now might well be called a cascade.[27] This is, of course, a good development, for it forces us to consider issues that might otherwise have gone unexamined.[28] Unfortunately, that consideration takes place in the context of an appellate system that denies a full measure of justice to many litigants.

24. D.C. Cir. R. 32.1(b)(1)(B).

25. Ricks, *supra* note 21, at 24.

26. D.C. Cir. R. 36(e)(2).

27. A primary purpose of the estimable *Journal of Appellate Practice and Process* seems to be to publish commentary on the problem of limited publication.

28. Professor Cappalli provides an example of such a development: he contends that part of the perceived problem with judicial workloads is that judges have taken to writing "law review articles" rather than opinions that are limited to a discussion of how the facts of a case relate to law. Richard B. Cappalli, *The Common Law's Case against Non-Precedential Opinions*, 76 S. Cal. L. Rev. 755, 784–91 (2002).

CHAPTER 10

Commissions, Studies, Reports, and Proposals

The previous chapters have exposed the deterioration of the United States Circuit Courts of Appeals over the last forty years. During that same forty-year period, the courts have been the subject of extensive study and investigation by various governmental and nongovernmental bodies. In fact, thirteen separate committees, commissions, study groups, reports, and plans have addressed the circuit courts' problems and have offered an array of solutions.

Those efforts have obvious historical interest; since they coincided with the sea change in the circuit courts, they provide a record of the perceived concerns of the judicial establishment during the transformation. From our point of view, however, not much can be said for the actual product of all that study. For one thing, some of the reports ignored the Hippocratic Oath: "First, do no harm." By recommending different tracks for different appeals, they helped to establish and engrain the Appellate Triage regime. Other aspects of the studies, especially the obsession with "coherence of the law," have not been harmful, but rather needless. The reason is that the available empirical evidence shows that the issues that garnered the most attention in the studies—precedent overload, unresolved conflicts among the circuits, alternate pyramidal structures for the courts—are not problematic. Other issues, which are problematic—the satisfaction of litigants with the Appellate Triage regime, for example—were not studied.

The study groups' perception of the courts' problems reflect the groups' memberships, mostly judges, law professors, and prominent practitioners. Thus, the law-declaration function of the courts receives a great deal of attention while their error correction function receives very little. Concomitantly, the studies devote very little attention to the decision procedures for the large majority of cases, those placed on Track Two by the Appellate Triage system. We conclude that most of the study groups' efforts have ignored the obvious solution to the problem: a substantial increase in the number of federal appellate judgeships. And to the extent that the studies have addressed that solution, their recommendations have been ignored.

This chapter is composed of two sections. The first section simply treats the studies in chronological order; the second abstracts from the several studies certain recurrent diagnoses, recommendations, and proposals and discusses them thematically.

A. THE STUDIES

1. Study of the Division of Jurisdiction between State and Federal Courts: American Law Institute

Prompted initially by a suggestion made by Chief Justice Warren in a speech to the American Law Institute, the A.L.I. formed an Advisory Committee to study and report on the appropriate division of the nation's judicial business between the state and federal courts. The membership of the committee reads like a roster for induction into the federal courts hall of fame. The Chief Reporter, Richard H. Field, was assisted by two Reporters, Paul J. Mishkin and Charles Allen Wright, and an Assistant Reporter, David L. Shapiro. David Cavers served as a Consultant on choice-of-law matters, and the committee's rank and file included such luminaries as Henry J. Friendly, Henry M. Hart, John Minor Wisdom, and Herbert Wechsler. The Committee devoted eight years to the study and produced a final report in 1969.

The objective of the study was to rationalize and modernize federal jurisdiction based on principle so

> [a]ccess to federal courts should not be frozen into a pattern set in 1789 or 1875, whether or not such pattern was right to meet the problems of its time, if it does not make sense in light of the conditions in the last half of the twentieth century.[1]

Guided by the principle that the purpose of diversity jurisdiction is "to assure a high level of justice to the traveler or visitor from another state,"[2] the report recommended a set of narrowly targeted changes to then current law. Most of these narrowed the jurisdiction, but some broadened it, and many have been adopted by Congress over the years. However, the report's most significant recommendation, to bar a plaintiff from bringing a diversity action in a federal court in his own home state, while clearly correct on principle, has not been enacted.

According to the Committee, the basic rationale for federal question jurisdiction is "to preserve uniformity in federal law and to protect litigants ... from the danger

1. A.L.I., Study of the Division of Jurisdiction Between State and Federal Courts 6 (1969).
2. *Id.* at 2.

that state courts will not properly apply that law . . . ."[3] Based on that rationale, the Committee recommended several provisions to broaden the scope of that jurisdiction. The two most radical were to abolish the amount in controversy requirement for federal question cases (adopted by Congress in 1980) and to provide for jurisdiction in removal cases where the defendant relies on a federal defense or counterclaim (not adopted by Congress).

Strictly, the A.L.I. study is beyond the scope of this book since it deals with federal jurisdiction generally, rather than with the jurisdiction, configuration, and operation of the circuit courts of appeals in particular. Nevertheless, it is worth including in this chapter for several reasons. First, it preceded the massive increase in appellate case volume, which was just beginning as the study period ended. Thus it provides a baseline to compare with subsequent studies performed under the threat and then the reality of the increase. Second, its tone differs radically from that of many later studies. Absent are the apocalyptic predictions and defensive, self-serving anecdotes that characterize those later studies; by contrast, the A.L.I. study seems almost academic in tone. Related is the different focus of the A.L.I. study, which concentrates on the principles that determine the nation's need for federal jurisdiction. The later projects focus more on the configuration of the courts of appeals that will best conserve the federal courts' unique character, the consistency of federal law, or the judges' need for collegiality.

2. Accommodating the Workload of the United States Courts of Appeals: American Bar Foundation[4]

Conducted under the auspices of the American Bar Foundation with a grant from the American Bar Endowment, this study was performed by the Project Advisory Committee. Like the A.L.I. study, the project enlisted the efforts of luminary jurists, lawyers, and scholars, among them the Project Director, Paul Carrington, and Project Advisory Committee members, Bernard Segal, Leon Jaworski, David Louisell, Thurgood Marshall, and Paul Mishkin. Unlike the A.L.I. study, it focused more narrowly on the courts of appeals rather than the federal system as a whole.

The kernel of the problem, according to the Committee, appears prominently on the Report's first page:

> In the last decade, the rate of expansion of [the] workload [of the courts of appeals] has accelerated rapidly. The resources provided the Courts . . . to do their work have not . . .

3. *Id.* at 4.

4. Paul D. Carrington, Am. Bar Found., Accommodating the Workload of the United States Courts of Appeals: Report of Recommendations (1968).

increased apace. As a result, there is imbalance between the demands upon the Courts of Appeals as a whole and their ability to respond to them.[5]

The Committee divided its brief Report (only eight pages) into two parts: "Proposals for Immediate Action—Better Use of Resources within the Current Framework" and "Proposals for Reflection—Structural Changes." Many of the recommendations in the first part consisted of "nuts and bolts" suggestions such as increasing the number of elbow clerks, fuller district court opinions that would allow the courts of appeals to affirm on the basis of the opinion below, greater dispatch in presidential appointments to vacancies, and stronger incentives for circuit judges to take senior status.

Other recommendations were more substantive and more controversial. First, the Report recommended that the courts adopt a sorting mechanism, permitting them to allocate time and effort to cases "according to their difficulty and significance." In less important cases there should be limitations on oral argument, greater use of short *per curiam* opinions, and decisions by two-judge panels. The Report did not indicate who should do the screening required to determine which cases warranted only the abbreviated procedures. Nor, of course, could it presage the set of thorny issues such a triage regime would create.

Second, the Report recommended creation of additional circuit judgeships but cautioned that "the expansion of the number of judges on a court, even though gradual in time, changes the nature of the court."[6] Believing enlarging circuits to be wiser than creating new ones, the Committee recommended adding judgeships to existing circuits until the number of judges on a circuit reaches fifteen. Once a circuit exceeds nine judgeships, it should be authorized to split by subject matter into divisions with rotating membership. Innovatively, the Report also recommended establishing a Washington-based "pool" of five or six additional circuit judges who would not be assigned permanently to individual circuits. Rather they would be assigned to duty on particular circuits as temporary needs arose.

The recommended numbers may seem small by today's standards, but the Committee's recommendations were actually quite bold and would have allowed for the possibility of significant growth. At the time, only two circuits had more than nine judgeships (13 in the Fifth and 10 in the Ninth), and no circuit exceeded the 15-judge limit.[7] The circuit courts had a total of 97 judges, and the Committee's recommendations conceivably could have permitted as many as 170. As will become apparent, later studies took a decidedly more conservative view of the possibilities for expansion.[8]

5. *Id.* at 1.
6. *Id.* at 5.
7. 399 F.2d vi–xviii (1969).
8. *See infra* sections 7, 9, 10, and 12.

In the second portion of its report, the Committee's suggestions have proved prescient indeed. The report noted that soon, even the fifteen-judge limit would not suffice to handle the appellate caseload in some circuits, and then there would be a choice between enlarging the circuits to unprecedented size or splitting them. Either way, the Committee foresaw the possibility of more conflicts than the Supreme Court could resolve. It then enumerated several possible solutions including a national court of appeals, nationwide courts with specialized subject matter jurisdiction, and division of the existing circuits into a small number of regional über-circuits. Even more presciently, the Committee saw a fundamental truth subsequent studies have tried to avoid:

> [T]he question is not whether we can preserve all of the present attributes of the existing system, ... but rather in what respects they are to be changed....
>
> ....
>
> There is no way in which adjustment to new workload conditions can be made that will leave intact all the present characteristics of the Courts of Appeals. These courts were an innovation themselves. Since their creation, they have been in constant process of transformation as the amount and kind of their work has changed.[9]

3. The Freund Committee

Charged by the Federal Judicial Center to study the caseload and problems of the Supreme Court, the Freund Committee conducted its work from 1971 to 1972. More formally known as the Study Group on the Caseload of the Supreme Court, the group got its nickname from its chair, Paul Freund of Harvard Law School.[10] Like its predecessors, it was staffed by the "usual suspects": eminent scholars of federal courts and constitutional law and prominent attorneys with experience practicing before the Court. Three of its members had served as law clerks to Justices on the Court.

In addition to studying a wide range of statistical data, the Committee conducted interviews of all of the then serving Justices and three present and former clerks. Its Report begins with a description of the Court's workload, noting that in the previous twenty years, filings had increased from 1,234 to 3,643. The most dramatic growth occurred in *in forma pauperis certiorari* petitions filed by criminal defendants and prisoners seeking post-conviction relief, but there was also substantial growth in the Court's mandatory appellate caseload. The Justices had been able to remain current by relying increasingly on their clerks (by that time increased to

9. Carrington, *supra* note 4, at 6, 8.

10. Fed. Judicial Ctr., Report of the Study Group on the Caseload of the Supreme Court (1972), *reprinted in* 57 F.R.D. 573 (1972).

three per judge), deciding an increasingly smaller percentage of the cases filed, and decreasing the time spent on each case.

In the view of the Committee, the Court was at its saturation point; further caseload increases would compromise its ability to perform its essential function—"to define and vindicate the rights guaranteed by the Constitution, to assure the uniformity of federal law, and to maintain the constitutional distribution of powers in our federal union."[11] The committee was especially concerned that the Court's workload would make it less likely to be able to resolve conflicts among the circuit courts.

In response to these perceived problems, the Committee made several recommendations, but two deserve special discussion. In detail, the Committee reviewed the various contexts in which the Court had mandatory appellate jurisdiction and recommended they be abolished with the Court's remaining jurisdiction comprised almost entirely of *certiorari* cases. Although not immediately, and with fits and starts, Congress eventually enacted this recommendation,[12] and it has been received enthusiastically.[13]

Not so for the Committee's other main recommendation, the establishment of a National Court of Appeals. The recommendation stemmed from the Committee's conclusion that two of the most important consequences of the growth in caseload were the time required to screen a mass of petitions for review and the Court's inability to resolve conflicts between circuits in a timely fashion. Very likely, the Committee had some empirical evidence for the first conclusion, having interviewed several of the justices and their then present and former clerks. The Committee did not offer any empirical evidence of the conflict problem, however; and, indeed it was taken as a given until much later empirical studies cast serious doubt upon it.[14]

After considering and rejecting several other possible configurations, the Committee settled on a National Court of Appeals consisting of seven active circuit judges serving for three-year staggered terms, and selected by a system of automatic rotation. Its jurisdiction would be discretionary and would encompass nearly all of the Supreme Court's appellate and *certiorari* jurisdiction. All such cases would be filed initially by petition in the new court, which could act on them in one of three ways.

One resolution would be denial of review, which would be final and thus cut off access to the Supreme Court. A second possibility would involve the new court's certifying the case to the Supreme Court; it would certify about four hundred cases per year, several times as many as the Supreme Court could be expected to hear.

11. *Id.* at 578.

12. Act of June 27, 1988, Pub. L. No. 100–352, 102 Stat. 662.

13. 16B Charles A. Wright, Arthur R. Miller, & Edward H. Cooper, Federal Practice and Procedure § 4003 (1996).

14. *See, e.g.*, Arthur Hellman, Fed. Judicial Ctr., Unresolved Intercircuit Conflicts: The Nature and Scope of the Problem (1991).

The Supreme Court would have discretion to grant or deny review on the merits or, in cases of intercircuit conflict, remand to the National Court of Appeals with an order to hear and decide the case. The latter category would include those cases of genuine intercircuit conflict that did not pose issues of sufficient comparative importance to warrant Supreme Court review. The third option open to the new court—likely to be exercised in most cases of intercircuit conflict—would be to set the case down for argument and decision on the merits.

The idea behind the Committee's recommendation was to spare the Supreme Court the tedious duty of screening while simultaneously supplying the nation with considerably greater capacity for resolution of intercircuit conflicts. Despite its good intentions, the Committee's recommendation got a chilly reception. Judges and others opposed the new court on the grounds that it diluted the authority of the Supreme Court and denied litigants with worthy claims access to the Court.[15] The resistance prompted one leading commentator to pronounce the court "stillborn,"[16] and another went so far as to suggest that the Committee's recommendation was "goofy."[17]

4. Commission on Revision of the Federal Court Appellate System

Congress established the Commission in 1972[18] in response to the rapid and unprecedented increase in the workload of the circuit courts. Consisting of sixteen members (four members from each house of Congress, four appointed by the President, and four appointed by the Chief Justice), the Commission was known informally by the name of its chair, Senator Roman Hruska. Congress charged the Commission:

> (a) [T]o study the present division of the United States into the several judicial circuits and to report … its recommendations for changes in the geographical boundaries of the circuits ….
>
> (b) [T]o study the structure and internal procedures of the Federal courts of appeal system, and to report … its recommendations for such additional changes … as may be appropriate ….[19]

15. Daniel J. Meador, *The Federal Judiciary—Inflation, Malfunction, and a Proposed Course of Action*, 1981 BYU L. Rev. 617, 627.

16. *Id.*

17. Thomas E. Baker, *A Generation Spent Studying the United States Courts of Appeals: A Chronology*, 34 U.C. Davis L. Rev. 395, 400 (2000). The chronological organization of this chapter follows the one used by Professor Baker in his fine article.

18. Pub. L. No. 92–489, 86 Stat. 807 (1972).

19. *Id.*

a. Phase One

Consistently with its bipartite charge, the Commission held hearings in several cities throughout the country and reported its findings and recommendations in two separate reports published in 1973 and 1975. In its first report,[20] the Commission noted the dramatic increase in the number of appeals, a less dramatic increase in the number of authorized judgeships, and the circuit courts' adoption of a set of appeals-expediting procedures to help cope with the overload. Accordingly, the Commission recommended that Congress create new courts and additional judgeships to respond to the crisis of volume.

Its most important recommendation was a split of the Fifth Circuit into two new courts: the Fifth Circuit, consisting of Georgia, Florida, and Alabama, and the Eleventh, consisting of Texas, Mississippi, and Louisiana. The Commission considered several other configurations including one involving three two-state circuits but found its recommendation superior when judged by the following set of criteria for circuit alignment:

- Circuits should span at least three states.
- No circuit should be created that would require more than nine judges.
- A circuit should contain states with diverse populations, legal business, and socioeconomic interests.
- Realignment should involve the least dislocation possible.
- No circuit should contain noncontiguous states.[21]

Applying the criteria to the Ninth Circuit, the Commission recommended splitting it in two, an arrangement that required dividing California between the Ninth Circuit and the proposed new Twelfth Circuit. Congress accepted the Commission's recommendation to split the Fifth Circuit, but retained the Ninth as a single unit, by far the largest in the system.[22]

b. Phase Two

The best-known recommendation of the Commission was to create a National Court of Appeals. Citing the steadily growing scope of federal regulatory authority and

20. Comm'n on Revision of Fed. Court Appellate Sys., The Geographical Boundaries of the Several Judicial Circuits: Recommendations for Change (1973), *reprinted in* 62 F.R.D. 223 (1974).

21. *Id.* at 231–32.

22. Congress did provide permission to each circuit court with over fifteen judgeships to divide itself into administrative units. *See* Pub. L. No. 95–486, § 6, 92 Stat. 1629, 1633, the relevant portion of which is:

> Sec. 6. Any court of appeals having more than 15 active judges may constitute itself into administrative units complete with such facilities and staff as may be prescribed by the

the steadily diminishing percentage of *certiorari* petitions granted by the Supreme Court, the Commission Report[23] concluded there was "no basis for confidence that the Supreme Court can be expected adequately to satisfy the need for stability and harmony in the national law as the demands continue to increase in the decades ahead."[24]

The Commission's remedy, a new National Court of Appeals, differed substantially from the Freund Committee's conception of such a court. First, instead of a rotating membership, it would be staffed by seven *permanent* Article III judges appointed by the President.[25] Second it would not screen cases for the Supreme Court. Rather, it would have "reference" and "transfer" jurisdiction. The first would consist of cases filed with the Supreme Court that it, in the exercise of discretion, referred to the new court for hearing and decision. The second group of cases would be those transferred from one of the circuit courts because of the perceived need for national law making; the new court then would have discretion to hear the case or decline to accept the transfer.[26] The proposal was largely ignored by Congress but received substantial attention from federal court scholars.[27]

More interesting, from our point of view, was the Commission's recognition that the internal operating procedures of the circuit courts had changed with an increasingly large percentage of their cases being handled without oral argument or a published precedential opinion and with the heavy involvement of staff attorneys.[28] In response, the Commission recommended an amendment to the Federal Rules of Appellate Procedure mandating in most cases oral argument and at least some record, available to the public,[29] of the reasons for the court's decision. The Commission took no position on the citation or precedential value of such abbreviated opinions, a problem which would wait more than thirty years for a partial solution.[30] It did however take a strong stand on the role of staff attorneys, which should not include drafting opinions or screening cases.[31] The circuit courts could have accomplished that change without the aid of legislation or federal rule making,

Administrative Office of the United States Courts, and may perform its en banc function by such number of members of its en banc courts as may be prescribed by rule of the court of appeals.

23. Comm'n on Revision of Fed. Court Appellate Sys., Structural and Internal Procedures: Recommendations for Change (1975), *reprinted in* 67 F.R.D. 195 (1975) [hereinafter Phase Two Report].

24. *Id.* at 212.

25. *Id.* at 237.

26. *Id.* at 238–46.

27. *See* Meador, *supra* note 15, at 626–28.

28. Phase Two Report, *supra* note 23, at 247–48, 260–62.

29. *Id.* at 258.

30. The solution to the citation portion of the problem is Fed. R. App. P. 32.1 (effective in 2006), which prohibits the circuit courts from forbidding citation to their unpublished opinions. The question of precedential value remains unresolved.

31. Phase Two Report, *supra* note 23, at 261.

but so far they have not and in fact have steadily increased the number and responsibilities of the staff attorneys.

5. Advisory Council for Appellate Justice

Created in 1970 and jointly sponsored by the National Center for State Courts and the Federal Judicial Center, the Council was chaired by Professor Maurice Rosenberg and composed of thirty judges, scholars, and practitioners.[32] It conducted a four-year study of the federal appellate courts, compiled a four-volume set of reading materials, and presented its recommendations to the Hruska Commission and at the National Conference on Appellate Justice held in 1975 in San Diego.[33]

Like the Hruska Commission, the Council recommended that Congress create a National Court of Appeals staffed by United States circuit judges assigned to the new court for a substantial term of years and capable of issuing decisions having nationwide precedential effect. Jurisdiction would lie in appeals referred to it by the Supreme Court and would include appeals of state court criminal convictions and cases involving conflicts among the circuits. Upon reaching a decision, the court would forward it to the Supreme Court, and it would become final after the lapse of a specified time if the Supreme Court took no further action.[34]

The Conference on Appellate Justice was attended by 360 judges, lawyers, and scholars and was, in the words of one of its prime movers, a "smashing critical success," but the Council's recommendations "resulted in scant reform."[35]

6. ABA Action Commission

The American Bar Association Board of Governors approved the creation of the Action Commission to Reduce Court Costs and Delay in 1978 and directed it "to

32. Meador, *supra* note 15, at 628. The membership included some genuine federal courts luminaries: inter alia "Seth (LA) and Shirley Hufstedler (9th Cir at the time), Harold Leventhal (D.C. Cir), John Frank (Phoenix), Murray Schwartz (UCLA), Griffin Bell (11th Cir.), John Minor Wisdom (5th Cir.), Al Tate (then Supreme Court of Louisiana), Roger Cramton (then an Assistant Attorney General), and Erwin Griswold (Solicitor General at the time)." PAUL CARRINGTON, APPEALS AND FEDERAL POLITICS, *available at* http://paulcarrington.com/Appeals%20and%20Politics.htm (last visited Mar. 14, 2011) [hereinafter APPEALS AND POLITICS].

33. CARRINGTON, APPEALS AND POLITICS, *supra* note 32; *see* 4 ADVISORY COUNCIL FOR APPELLATE JUSTICE, APPELLATE JUSTICE: 1975, at 163–64 (Paul D. Carrington ed., 1975), *available at* http://contentdm.ncsconline.org/cgi-bin/showfile.exe?CISOROOT=/appellate&CISOPTR=44.

34. ADVISORY COUNCIL FOR APPELLATE JUSTICE, *Recommendation for Improving the Federal Intermediate Appellate System, in* 4 APPELLATE JUSTICE: 1975, *supra* note 33, at 163–64.

35. APPEALS AND POLITICS, *supra* note 32.

test new ideas in actual court experiments"[36] and "to encourage lawyers and bar associations to improve litigation effectiveness."[37] Funded by the Law Enforcement Assistance Administration, the Ford Foundation, and the A.B.A., the Commission was composed of lawyers and leaders of the bar, consumer advocates, judges, academics, and representatives of organizations interested in improving the judicial system. The Commission began its work in 1979 and issued its first progress report a year later. The report contained a host of recommendations, but those of greatest interest here are the ones directed toward the problem of overload in appellate courts.

The so-called "Appellate Package" contained a series of recommendations, some of which had been tried separately but had not yet been instituted in a combined and coordinated program. The parts of the package included: (1) expediting the transmission of the trial record to the circuit court; (2) substituting an abbreviated (perhaps no more than ten pages) memorandum of points and authorities for the traditional appellate brief; (3) exchanging traditional oral argument for a conference type of argument with the judges actively participating; and (4) replacing the written opinion with an oral opinion from the bench at the close of the arguments or within a few days.[38]

Not all cases would receive the abbreviated process; the report advised the courts to "treat different cases differently" and recommended an early triage to determine which cases belonged on the abbreviated track and which would receive the traditional appellate process.[39]

Many of the Commission's recommendations have been implemented by the courts, not necessarily to the advantage of the litigants and the justice system. Thus, the triage system has become fully entrenched, probably beyond the wildest expectations of the members of the Action Commission, with 80 to 90 percent of the caseload receiving some or all of the abbreviated process.[40] The Commission's report did not specify who was to perform the screening, and it might come as a bit of a shock to the members that today, many (and in some circuits all) of the triage decisions are delegated to staff attorneys.[41] Some circuits make extensive use of oral rulings from the bench; and in some, a conference-style argument occurs, but the participants (beside the judges) are court-employed staff attorneys rather than the parties' advocates.[42]

36. Seth Hufstedler & Paul Nejelski, *A.B.A. Action Commission Challenges Litigation Cost and Delay*, 66 A.B.A. J. 965, 965 (1980) (discussing the founding of the Commission and a list of its recommendations); *see also* Joseph R. Weisberger, *Appellate Courts: The Challenge of Inundation*, 31 Am. U. L. Rev. 237 (1982).

37. Hufstedler & Nejelski, *supra* note 36, at 965.

38. *Id.* at 967.

39. *Id.* at 966–67.

40. *See* chapter 9, *supra*.

41. *See* chapter 8, *supra*.

42. *See id.*

It is easy to see why Commission members thought their suggestions might help appellate courts deal with the caseload glut, but the iron law of unintended consequences applies to efforts at court reform just as relentlessly as to other projects. In this case, the courts' implementation of the Commission's recommendations led to a bipartite system of appellate justice where large percentages of the caseload receive scant if any attention from Article III judges, while a small select group of cases enjoys the lion's share of the courts' resources. The Commission members may not have intended it, but the implementation of some of their recommendations has resulted in the rich getting richer while a majority of appellate litigants appear to have lost most of what used to constitute an appeal of right.

7. Two Initiatives from the Justice Department (1977)

In 1977, two separate groups within the Justice Department performed studies of the problems of the federal courts:

a. Department of Justice Committee on Revision of the Federal Judicial System

After a speech to the Sixth Circuit Judicial Conference about the problems facing the federal courts, President Ford directed Attorney General Edward H. Levi to create a Committee on Revision of the Federal Judicial System within the Department of Justice. Chaired by Solicitor General Robert H. Bork, the committee conducted numerous studies, discussed various proposals, and issued a report.[43]

The Report began by noting the threat to the judicial system posed by the alarming increase in filings and the expedients the courts had adopted to deal with it. The Report found decreased oral argument, reduction in written opinions, and increased use of administrative helpers to be the most troublesome of the time-saving devices.

> The American legal tradition has insisted upon practices such as oral argument and written opinions for very good reason. Judges, who must be independent and are properly not subject to any other discipline, are required by our tradition to confront the claims and the arguments of the litigants. They must demonstrate to the public that they are not acting out of whim, caprice, or mere personal preference. Our tradition requires that judges explain their decisions and thereby demonstrate to the public that those decisions are supported by law and reason. Continued erosion of traditional practices could cause a corresponding erosion of the integrity of the law and of the public's confidence in law.[44]

43. U.S. Dep't of Justice Comm. on Revision of Fed. Judicial Sys., The Needs of the Federal Courts, at iv (1977) [hereinafter DOJ Report]. The Committee consisted of eleven members, one of whom was then Assistant Attorney General Antonin Scalia.
44. *Id.* at 3–4.

To deal with such serious threats, the Report proposed solutions "broad in concept and effect" because smaller scope remedies are "simply not adequate to meet a problem of broad scale."[45]

(1) More Judgeships. The Report is somewhat ambivalent on the creation of additional Article III judgeships. While recommending an increase of unspecified size, it warned against wholesale increases, which would, in its view, damage collegiality and diminish personal interaction throughout the judiciary. Moreover, large increases would diminish the prestige of the office, making it more difficult to attract the best and brightest.[46] As we argue in a later chapter, there is no empirical evidence that prestige is a zero-sum game; and even if it is, restricting judicial supply to protect it reflects a seriously flawed value preference.[47]

A far better recommendation is to end the "senatorial courtesy" system of selecting judges in favor of a system of selection by a newly created Commission on the Judicial Appointments Process.[48] This recommendation makes eminent good sense and not only because it promises an improvement in the quality of the bench. By making the selection process less political, the recommendation could reduce the delay in filling open judgeships and thus functionally increase the capacity of the judicial system.

(2) Article I Administrative Courts. Considerably less controversial is the Report's recommendation to create a system of Article I courts to deal with cases arising from the many federal welfare and regulatory programs. While avoiding the pitfalls of an overly specialized court, a set of administrative courts could substantially relieve the burden on the federal courts by adjudicating a host of cases involving "repetitious factual disputes" that seldom give rise to "important legal questions."[49] Despite the lurking classism in this proposal, it has the virtue of improving the quality of justice for the large category of cases that currently receive such short shrift from the circuit courts. For those cases, adjudication by professional and *accountable* Article I courts is vastly preferable to the current system that consigns the bulk of the work on them to anonymous and publicly unaccountable central staff attorneys, with titular but only cursory review by actual appellate judges.[50]

(3) Jurisdictional Reform. Jurisdictional reform is a standard nostrum for the ills of the federal court system, but mostly it is a pipe dream with no chance for congressional implementation.[51] To some extent, the Report participates in this empty ritual by recommending the abolition of diversity jurisdiction. By contrast, however, the Report also includes recommendations which deserve and, in some

45. *Id.* at 4.
46. *Id.* at 6–7.
47. *See infra* chapters 11–14.
48. DOJ Report, *supra* note 43, at 6.
49. *Id.* at 9.
50. We believe some system of specialized courts should play a large part in the solution of the problems of caseload glut and two-track justice in the circuit courts. *See infra* chapter 12.
51. *See infra* chapter 13.

cases, have received congressional approval, such as the abolition of the Supreme Court's mandatory appellate jurisdiction[52] and an exhaustion-of-state-remedies requirement for prisoners' petitions.

b. The Office for the Improvements in the Administration of Justice

Although the Office functioned for only four years, its importance is disproportional to its longevity. With the beginning of President Carter's term, Griffin Bell became Attorney General of the United States. Having served for fifteen years as a judge on the Fifth Circuit, and having been involved in several studies of the courts, it is not surprising that Bell acted quickly on his long-standing interest in the administration of justice. Thus in 1977 he created the Office for the Improvement of Justice within the Justice Department[53] and placed it under the leadership of then Assistant Attorney General Daniel Meador, one of the nation's leading authorities on appellate justice. Its function was the study and improvement of the administration of justice in the nation's judicial and quasi-judicial dispute-resolving tribunals.[54]

The signature achievement of the Office was to conceive of the United States Court of Appeals for the Federal Circuit and to shepherd its implementing legislation through Congress.[55] The court, essentially a merger of the Court of Claims and the Court of Customs and Patent Appeals,[56] is unique among the circuit courts in that its jurisdiction is determined by subject matter, not geography.

Some of the reasons for its successful creation stem from lessons learned from prior attempts at judicial reform. Unlike the courts proposed by the Freund Committee and the Hruska Commission, it does not restrain access to the Supreme Court or create a four-tiered appellate structure; an additional tier would tax the resources of the litigants as well as the status and prestige of the circuit judges. Finally, the creation of the Federal Circuit helps to achieve one of the stated goals of many prior studies—national uniformity on questions of federal law.

It also sets some interesting precedents. Unlike the old Commerce Court, the Federal Circuit provides a *successful* example of an appellate court of specialized nationwide jurisdiction.[57] Further, unlike other proposed tribunals, it is staffed by a

52. DOJ Report, *supra* note 43, at 11–12; Pub. L. No. 100–352, 102 Stat 662 (1988).

53. 42 Fed. Reg. 8140 (Feb. 3, 1977).

54. *Id.* at 8140–41. *See* Meador, *supra* note 15, at 631–34 (giving an account of the inception of the Office).

55. *See* Daniel J. Meador, *Origin of the Federal Circuit: A Personal Account*, 41 Am. U. L. Rev. 581 (1992) (giving a fascinating "blow-by-blow" account of the court's birth pangs).

56. *Id.* at 592. Besides the caseload of those two courts, the Federal Circuit has some additional jurisdiction.

57. It thus poses the question whether other subject matter areas can be carved out of the circuit courts' workload. *See* Robert E. Rains, *A Specialized Court For Social Security? A Critique of Recent Proposals*, 15 Fla. St. U. L. Rev. 1 (1987).

permanent bench, not a rotation of judges from other circuits.[58] Finally, it is fully an Article III court and thus shows that courts of specialized subject matter jurisdiction need not be Article I courts and thus a part of the nation's regulatory, administrative apparatus.[59] Its success suggests that at least some portion of the problem posed by caseload increases and their perceived threat to the coherence of the law can be solved by specialized tribunals with nationwide jurisdiction.[60] They handle cases faster because their judges are experts, and they do away with the problems posed by intercircuit conflicts.

8. The N.Y.U. Study

In 1983, Chief Justice Burger proposed yet another version of a nationwide appellate court, the Intercircuit Tribunal (ICT), as a partial solution to what he perceived as an overwhelming increase in the volume and complexity of the Court's workload.[61] The ICT would have a lifespan limited to five years and consist of twenty-six circuit judges, two from each of the circuits. It would sit in panels of seven to nine judges for periods of six to twelve months and hear intercircuit conflicts and a limited set of statutory interpretation cases.[62] The arguments for and against the new body paralleled those that followed the national courts proposed by the Freund Committee and the Hruska Commission,[63] but the underlying assumption that the Supreme Court was overworked was mostly unquestioned.

The N.Y.U. Project[64] was an ambitious empirical effort to test that fundamental postulate. Conducted by two N.Y.U. law professors, Samuel Estreicher and John Sexton, and about two dozen student members of the *New York University Law Review,* its goal was to determine empirically whether in fact the Supreme Court was overworked. After examining the Court's entire docket (including the cases denied review), its controversial conclusion was that the overload resulted from the Court's choosing to hear cases that did not merit its attention, which constituted about 25 percent of the total.[65]

58. For example, the National Court of Appeals proposed by the Freund Committee. *See supra* section 3.

59. Contrast DOJ REPORT, discussed in section 7, *supra.*

60. See *infra* chapter 13, section A for an argument for such a solution and for citations to commentary pro and con.

61. Warren E. Burger, *Annual Report on the State of the Judiciary,* 69 A.B.A. J. 442, 447 (1983).

62. *Id.*

63. *See supra* sections 3 and 4.

64. *See* Samuel Estreicher & John E. Sexton, *A Managerial Theory of the Supreme Court's Responsibilities: An Empirical Study,* 59 N.Y.U. L. REV. 681 (1984).

65. *Id.* at 758.

The Study concluded that the cause of both the Supreme Court's overloading itself and the general frustration with the Court's inability to satisfy the nation's needs was a misconception of the Court's proper role. The Court should not act as an ultimate check on error in the system, but rather as "the manager of the federal judicial system, overseeing the work of the federal and state courts, and intervening only when necessary to resolve fundamental interbranch or federal–state clashes or to render a final resolution of a question that has ripened for decision after percolation in the lower courts."[66] Then, helpfully, if somewhat presumptuously, the authors proceed to instruct the Court quite specifically on the kinds of cases it should hear and those that do not require its attention.[67]

At this point, a fair question would be: What does this ambitious study of the Supreme Court's workload have to do with the thesis of this book? That there should be large increases in the number of circuit judgeships? The answer lies in the Study's thoughtful discussion of inter-court conflicts.[68] The Study begins with the concept of "square" conflicts, which occur "only when courts in a given jurisdiction—federal circuit or state—are bound to follow a legal rule contrary to the rule that must be followed in another jurisdiction."[69] Note this definition eliminates any conflicts that do not involve federal circuits or states' highest courts, and more significantly, it eliminates conflicts where one court's pronouncement is dictum or an alternative holding. Finally, it puts to the side cases in which courts purport to follow the same legal standard but appear to reach contrary conclusions, in other words, cases where factual discrepancies may account for disparate outcomes.[70]

The authors of the Study did not believe that all "square" conflicts are "intolerable." A conflict is intolerable only if (1) litigants can exploit it through forum shopping, (2) it prohibits multijurisdiction actors from adjusting their affairs to divergent commands, or (3) at least three courts have passed on the question. Using this definition on a pool of 1,860 petitions, the Study found only five petitions involving intolerable conflicts that were improperly denied review.

And yet again, what does this have to do with proper staffing of the circuit courts? One of the persistent arguments against creating enough circuit judgeships to permit the courts to afford traditional appellate process to all cases is that so many judges will proliferate intercircuit conflicts and generally render the law incoherent. The Study findings do not entirely refute this argument; however, by carefully parsing the concept of "a conflict," they give reason to doubt that an adequately sized corps of judges would produce so many intolerable conflicts that the Supreme Court would be unable to keep pace. That finding, confirmed by other more recent studies, is a crucial part of the refutation of the anti-expansionist argument. If

66. *Id.* at 812.
67. *Id.* at 720–40.
68. *Id.* at 722–31.
69. *Id.* at 722.
70. *Id.* at 726.

radical increases in the number of circuit judgeships will not cause an unmanageable increase in intolerable conflicts, the "incoherence of the law" argument suffers seriously. But that argument is a crucial part of the case for a small federal appellate judiciary. Without the threat of legal incoherency, using a truncated process for the majority of federal appeals looks like an unnecessary sacrifice undertaken to avoid a noncredible threat.[71]

9. Report of the ABA Standing Committee on Federal Judicial Improvements[72]

At the outset, the Committee noted its study was a follow-up to the American Bar Foundation's 1968 study of the appellate courts.[73] In the intervening twenty years, the Committee noted that numerous other studies of the federal courts system had occurred, but that most had addressed federal jurisdiction or the need for a national appellate court; few had proffered specific solutions to the problems faced by the courts of appeals.

The principal problem was then, and remains today, massive increases in caseload, but the obvious solution—proportionate increases in judgeships—seemed problematic to the Committee. Adding circuits would increase the likelihood of intercircuit conflict and result in nontraditional alignments (splitting states, one-state circuits, circuits composed of noncontiguous states). Increasing the size of the existing circuits posed another set of concerns, intracircuit conflicts, and unwieldy en banc procedures. Moreover, an increase in judgeships by either means would diminish the prestige of the position.

The Committee noted that the courts, left to their own devices, had devised a strategy for dealing with the problem, the system of Appellate Triage that is the major focus of this book. But that remedy, according to the Committee, threatened the fundamental function the circuit courts were created to serve: relieve the pressure on the Supreme Court; supervise and correct the errors of the district courts; and develop a body of coherent federal law.[74]

The Committee thus saw its function as advancing proposals designed to remedy the problems of the circuit courts while preserving their essential character and function. Thus, it took as its motto the admonition of Lord Macauly: "Reform, that you may preserve."[75] That sentiment parallels perfectly the theme of the earlier

71. See *infra* chapter 12 for a more complete version of this argument.

72. ABA Standing Comm. on Fed. Judicial Improvements, The United States Courts of Appeals: Reexamining Structure and Process After a Century of Change 3–10 (1989) [hereinafter ABA Report: Reexamining].

73. *See supra* section A.2.

74. ABA Report: Reexamining, *supra* note 72, at 8–10.

75. *Id.* at ii.

report of the Project Advisory Committee of the American Bar Foundation.[76] Both seem to acknowledge that change is inevitable and that the central question is: which of the many features of the circuit courts are most central to their mission.

In an attempt to begin that setting of priorities, the committee recommended four specific steps:

(1) to study intercircuit conflict and determine whether a set of nonregional subject-matter-specialized courts would help to solve it;
(2) to consider nationwide adoption of the limited en banc procedure;
(3) to reduce intracircuit inconsistency by assigning a part of the docket to subject-matter-specialized panels; and
(4) to study the use of the Appellate Triage devices in order to preserve the role of Article III judges in deciding appeals.[77]

The most constructive of the four steps are the two that suggest subject-matter-specialized courts and panels; these promise the advantages of expertise, efficiency, and consistency.[78] Experts in a particular subject matter area can be expected to render better decisions; outside of the judicial branch, this proposition seems to be a postulate, for there does not seem to be much sentiment for assigning labor law cases to the Nuclear Regulatory Commission.

Expert judges can work more efficiently because judges working in a particular area of the law learn that area well and can supply expert interpretation of the relevant statutes, case law, administrative regulations, and the policies that underlie them. Specialized judges decide more quickly because they do not need to learn the elementary principles of an unfamiliar subject for each new case on the docket. It is simply wasted effort to have a generalist judge become a "quick study" of admiralty law when the case could be decided by a judge who "makes her living" as an admiralty specialist. Finally, specialization can reduce inconsistency; if opponents of large increases in the circuit judiciary are right that adding more judges multiplies the possibility of legal inconsistency, then specialization helps by reducing the number of actors deciding cases in a particular area. The judges of many courts seem to have understood this truism because they engage in de facto specialization to a remarkable extent.[79]

76. *See supra* section A.2.

> The question is not whether we can preserve all of the present attributes of the existing system, ... but rather in what respects they are to be changed.... .
>
> There is no way in which adjustment to new workload conditions can be made that will leave intact all the present characteristics of the Courts of Appeals.

CARRINGTON, *supra* note 4, at 6, 8.

77. ABA REPORT: REEXAMINING, *supra* note 72, at 41.

78. See *infra* chapter 12 for more complete treatment of this theme.

79. *See infra* chapter 12.C.5.c. (citing Edward K. Cheng, *The Myth of the Generalist Judge*, 61 STAN. L. REV. 519 (2008)).

As benign as this recommendation seems, it nevertheless proved quite controversial as there is a prejudice in our system for "generalist" judges. Indeed that sentiment caused three of the nine Committee members to take the unusual step of writing a Dissenting Statement.[80] Their dissent contains the standard set of arguments against judicial specialization: concentration of power, capture by special interests, and political controversy surrounding appointments.

There are responses to these arguments,[81] but the important point here is that any change in the circuit courts will provoke spirited opposition, yet change is inevitable. Indeed it has already happened and is continuing to happen. The change, of course, is in the internal case-processing system used by the circuit courts; i.e., the abandonment of the traditional model of appellate justice and its replacement by the Appellate Triage model we have already described. The question that remains is this: should we be satisfied with this de facto change in the courts chosen by the judges to reflect their own views on distributive justice? If not, then what—and whose—set of value preferences will inform and control alternative changes in the courts? If the virtues of the traditional model of appellate justice are sufficiently valuable, then other changes—perhaps, specialization—will have to occur, and Lord Macauly's maxim, "Reform that you may preserve," becomes most apt.

10. Report of the Federal Courts Study Committee

Congress established the Federal Courts Study Committee within the Judicial Conference of the United States in 1988[82] and directed the Chief Justice to select the Committee's fifteen members "in such a manner as to be representative of the various interests, needs and concerns which may be affected by the jurisdiction of the Federal Courts."[83] Accordingly, the Chief Justice appointed four members of Congress (two from each house), three circuit judges, two district court judges, one state court judge, four practitioners (two from government practice—one state and one federal—and two from private practice), and a university president. The Committee's charge was to "make a complete study of the courts of the United States and of the several states and transmit a report to the President, the Chief Justice ..., the Congress, the Judicial Conference ... and [various state groups]"[84] Over fifteen months, the Committee, in its own words "conducted the most comprehensive

80. ABA REPORT: REEXAMINING, *supra* note 72, at 43 (dissenting statement by Frank A. Kaufman, James E. Noland, and Mary M. Schroeder).

81. *See* note 79, *supra*.

82. 102 Stat. 4642 (1988).

83. *Id.*

84. FED. COURTS STUDY COMM., JUDICIAL CONFERENCE OF THE UNITED STATES, REPORT OF THE FEDERAL COURTS STUDY COMMITTEE (1990) [hereinafter REPORT OF THE FEDERAL COURTS STUDY COMMITTEE].

examination of the federal court system in the last half century."[85] That examination, which included a survey of federal judges, numerous public hearings, and solicitations of opinions from attorneys, advocacy groups, academics, and other stakeholders in the federal courts,[86] resulted in a final report published in 1990.

Part I of the Report provided an overview of the Committee's perception of the crisis facing the federal courts, citing the usual alarming statistics. But the Report went on to state as fact some controversial and empirically baseless assumptions directly relevant to the theme of this book. Central among them is that the federal courts cannot meet the crisis by proportionate increases in judgeships because (1) the process of nomination and confirmation of judges would become pro forma, (2) a sufficient number of highly qualified candidates could not be found, (3) large increases in judgeships would lead judges to approach their jobs less responsibly, (4) appeal rates would increase, and (5) intra- and intercircuit conflicts would multiply. Based on these assumptions, the report concluded that any growth in the system must be limited and incremental.[87] Later on we will examine these assumptions in considerable detail; here we mention them simply to show the degree of group-think that permeates many of the studies considered in this chapter.[88]

Part I of the Report also offers a set of jurisdictional proposals, which, because they reduce the work of the federal court system generally, would help the circuit courts. Some are the usual suspects: abolition of diversity jurisdiction, at least where the plaintiff is a resident of the forum; and an exhaustion-of-remedies requirement for § 1983 cases. But the report emphasizes diversion more than its predecessors did. Its sensible recommendation is the diversion of Social Security claims, bankruptcy proceedings, Jones Act and FELA claims, and tax litigation to specialized Article III or Article I courts or administrative agencies. These recommendations have some appeal because they not only reduce the burden on the federal court system but also promise expert and expeditious treatment of discrete categories of cases. Nevertheless, by the Committee's own reckoning, they would reduce the circuit courts' caseload by only 17 percent,[89] a reduction easily made up by a few years' "normal" growth.

Chapter 6 of the Report is concerned specifically with the problems of circuit court overload. To its credit, the Committee is honest, reporting that, according to the Judicial Conference's workload standard,[90] the circuit judiciary required at the time a 30 percent increase in judgeships and within ten years likely would need to double the number. Less candid is its assessment of the effect of the Appellate

85. *Id.* at 3.

86. *Id.* at 32–33. *See also* Thomas E. Baker, Rationing Justice on Appeal 408 (1994). Professor Baker was an Associate Reporter for the Committee.

87. Report of the Federal Courts Study Committee, *supra* note 84, at 7–8.

88. *See infra* chapter 12.

89. Report of the Federal Courts Study Committee, *supra* note 84, at 27.

90. See *infra* chapter 11 for discussion of the formula.

Triage system on the quality of the courts' work: "But the appellate courts have avoided major deterioration only by pushing productivity to maximum levels and by adopting truncated procedures that probably have reached the limits of their utility without compromising the quality of the process."[91]

The passage is worth quoting in full because it is typical of the assessments found in many federal court studies. A study will conclude that Appellate Triage has reached a maximum acceptable limit; nevertheless, that limit will be exceeded in only a few years, and the next study will conclude again that the new level of truncation is the maximum allowable. Clearly the target is moving, and the study committees' views of the maximum allowable use of triage seem to coincide with the level prevalent at the time of the study. The problem here is not dishonesty but a gradual desensitizing, a shift in expectations of federal court observers and the tendency to find acceptable whatever conditions currently prevail. Unfortunately the all-too-obvious result is that the circuit courts use the truncated appellate process in a steadily increasing percentage of their cases, eventually transforming the circuit courts into courts of discretionary jurisdiction contrary to their statutory mandate.

One of the forces that has helped to keep the courts too small to handle their workload is concern that greater size will make the courts unwieldy and the law incoherent. Accordingly, the writers of the Report spend a good deal of effort laying out alternative possible configurations for the courts that will enable them to accommodate more judges:[92]

a. *Eliminate the current circuits and redraw new circuit boundaries,* which would themselves be redrawn as conditions require. Consistency could be maintained by requiring all courts to follow precedents established by panels of other courts. These precedents would stand until the Supreme Court spoke on the issue. If the Supreme Court proved unable to handle the volume of decisions requiring correction, intercircuit panels could be established to handle the overload.
b. *Create a four-tiered appellate system* by dividing the nation into as many as thirty regional appellate courts whose decisions would be reviewed by a few higher-level courts fitting between the regional courts and the Supreme Court.
c. *Create national subject-matter appellate courts* to handle tax, admiralty, criminal, civil rights, labor, administrative, and other specialized cases. These would take enough of the circuit courts' load to permit retention of the current circuit alignment.

91. Report of the Federal Courts Study Committee, *supra* note 84, at 110. Our studies have concluded that the use of the truncating devices had already passed the limit of compromised quality.

92. *Id.* at 118–22.

d. *Merge the circuits into a single unified national court of appeals.* This system exists in some states but would raise serious management issues if used in such a large system.
e. *Consolidate the current circuits into a few jumbo circuits,* each as large as or larger than the Ninth Circuit currently is. This alternative would reduce intercircuit conflict but would require significant tinkering with the en banc mechanism to avoid intracircuit conflicts.

The Report's treatment of alternative structure prompts two observations. First, a four-tier system should not be an option. The other configurations might entail additional work and inconvenience for the judges and other court personnel, but a four-tiered system would massively increase the burden on the litigants. In a significant portion of the cases, another level would require another round of briefs, another round of oral argument, and additional delay, thus increasing significantly the total societal investment in appellate justice.

Second, imagining alternative structures is a good thing, but it should not delay large increases in the number of judgeships. The problem of inadequate capacity is *actual and current*; the need to rearrange structure to accommodate problems that the increase in capacity *might* entail is *hypothetical and inchoate*. Waiting to add judgeships until a new structure is in place is a little like waiting to put out the fire until we can decide how to cope with the water damage.

11. The Federal Judicial Center Report

In its Report, the Federal Courts Study Committee did not endorse any of the various alternative structures for the courts of appeals; rather, it recommended that Congress, the courts, bar associations, and scholars give careful attention to and further study of the future of the federal appellate system.[93] Congress responded in § 302(c) of the Federal Courts Study Committee Implementation Act of 1990, which requested the Board of the Federal Judicial Center "to study the full range of structural alternatives for the Federal Courts of Appeals and submit a report on the study to the Congress and the Judicial Conference of the United States" within two years.[94]

The Board wisely handed over the study to three first-rate researchers[95] from the staff of the Center. Relying heavily on the files of the Study Committee and the

93. *Id.* at 116–17.
94. Pub. L. No. 101–650, § 302(c), 104 Stat. 5104, 5104.
95. Those researchers were Judith McKenna, Project Director, Donna Stienstra, and Joe Cecil.

work of prominent scholars in the area,[96] they produced a report and submitted it in 1993 to Congress and the Judicial Conference of the United States.[97]

The resulting study was thorough, undertaking both statistical analyses and attitudinal surveys. It considered each of the Federal Courts Study Commission's five structural alternatives[98] and developed them in greater detail. It considered the plusses and minuses of each alternative structure and indicated for each a "litigation path" to illustrate how the structural change would alter the route of an appeal through the federal appellate process.[99]

The Report also considered a series of "triage" proposals, which, although not technically "structural," involve change that might be considered equally radical:[100]

a. *Leave to Appeal.* This proposal would require disappointed district court litigants to obtain leave to appeal before they could present claims of error to the circuit courts. The Report then focused on three central questions that would determine the contours of any leave-to-appeal system: (1) what types of cases would require leave to appeal, (2) who would decide that preliminary screening question, and (3) what criteria would guide the choice. While a leave-to-appeal system would be a major statutory or *de jure* departure from the current appeal-of-right regime, it is, as we have pointed out elsewhere,[101] functionally the very same system that now prevails. Making that system the law as well as the practice would have the virtue of bringing it out of the shadows and into the light, thus subjecting it to the scrutiny of the bar and the public.
b. *Differentiated Appeal Management.* This system would involve dividing up the appeals into two or more classes of cases that would receive different types of appellate review. Its virtue is that it stretches appellate resources by concentrating them on the problematic cases, leaving the simple, routine cases to some lesser process involving Appellate Commissioners or Appellate Magistrate Judges. If this sounds familiar, it should. It is the system the circuit courts have already adopted de facto, with central staff attorneys[102] now performing the functions that Commissioners or Magistrates would under the proposal. Once again, the formal change would have the virtue of bringing the triage decision, essentially a question of distributive justice, to the attention of the bar and the public.

96. Notable among those scholars were Thomas Baker, then of Texas Tech School of Law, and Arthur Hellman of the University of Pittsburgh School of Law.

97. JUDITH A. MCKENNA, FED. JUDICIAL CTR., STRUCTURAL AND OTHER ALTERNATIVES FOR THE FEDERAL COURTS OF APPEALS (1993).

98. *See supra* section 10.

99. MCKENNA, *supra* note 97, at 105–21.

100. *Id.* at 123–38.

101. William M. Richman & William L. Reynolds, *Elitism, Expediency, and the New Certiorari: Requiem for the Learned Hand Tradition*, 81 CORNELL L. REV. 273 (1996).

102. *See supra* chapter 8.

c. *District Court Review for Error.* The idea here is to separate the functions of appeal into error correction and law declaration. Appeals that require only the former would be decided by special panels at the district court level. Decisions would be nonprecedential and could be appealed to the circuit level only by leave. The panels might consist of three district judges or two district judges and a circuit judge. The district judges could be from the same or a different district, and the trial judge might or might not be a panel member. Cases assigned for district level appeal could be chosen by case type, by standard of review, or by the need for oral argument, and the decision could be made by circuit court panels that would retain some cases and send others to the district level, or by party option.

The proposal has the virtue of assuring every appellant a full review by Article III judges, but it suffers from two difficulties. First, it would entail a significant increase in the workload of the district courts, in turn requiring many new district court judgeships. There is no reason to believe such an increase would be less controversial than an increase in circuit court judgeships, which could solve the appellate overload problem without creation of a new route for appeal. Second, the proposal is really just a four-tier system in disguise, and adding tiers produces huge increases in expense for the litigants, as already noted in the preceding discussion of the four-tier proposal by the Federal Courts Study Committee.

A final word on the tone and the conclusions of the Report. It is not as alarmist as many other studies, characterizing the situation of the circuit courts as "under stress" rather than "in crisis." At the outset, the Report posed the question whether that stress had produced three threats: unjust outcomes, diminished quality of the appellate process, and inconsistent interpretations of federal law.[103] The Report could not conclude the caseload crunch had resulted in a higher incidence of unjust outcomes but warned that day was likely to come soon.[104] It was less confident on the threat to the quality of the appellate process, especially its visibility and accountability; however, it correctly concluded that a return to the traditional appellate process would require a massive increase in judgeships. Finally, relying on a comprehensive empirical study by Professor Arthur Hellman,[105] it concluded that the glut of appeals had not yet produced an increase in intolerable, persistent inter-circuit conflicts sufficient to threaten the consistency and coherence of federal law.

12. Long-Range Plan for the Federal Courts

In an effort to generate a "more systematic capacity to anticipate broader societal changes and plan for more distant horizons," the Report of the Federal Courts

103. McKenna, *supra* note 97, at 13.
104. See the text accompanying note 91, *supra*, for a similar "not-yet-but-soon" conclusion.
105. Hellman, *supra* note 14, at iii.

Study Committee recommended that the Judicial Conference of the United States engage in long-range planning.[106] In response, the Judicial Conference created the Committee on Long Range Planning in 1990, staffed it with four appellate judges, three district judges, a bankruptcy judge, and a magistrate judge, and charged it to prepare a long-range plan for Judicial Conference approval. The Committee's preparatory activities[107] included: reviewing prior study reports; commissioning numerous research projects by its own staff, the Federal Judicial Center, and several independent federal courts scholars; conducting retreats at which invited judges, lawyers, and academics offered suggestions; preparing and circulating a draft report;[108] and holding three public hearings on the draft.

The process culminated in a proposed draft, which was then referred to the Judicial Conference. Individual Conference members were authorized to request additional study of any recommendation resulting in about half of the total 101 recommendations being referred to appropriate Judicial Conference committees, with the remainder being adopted as proposed. The purpose of this phase was to achieve consensus within the Conference on the more controversial recommendations of the Long Range Plan. The resulting Committee studies and reports produced substantial change in or deletion of about a dozen recommendations and resulted in the adoption of the remainder by the Judicial Conference.[109]

After assessing the current state of the judiciary, the Report lays out two opposing apocalyptic visions of the future of the federal courts in 2020. In one vision, Congress has continued to heap business on the federal courts and authorized court growth to accommodate the increase. There are more than one thousand circuit judges split into at least twenty circuits arranged in two tiers. Because of these numbers, the appointment and confirmation process takes up to three years, and judges resign often because of the alienation caused by being "only a small cog in … a vast wheel of justice." The Federal Reporter is now in its seventh series, and federal law has become "vaster and more incoherent than ever."[110]

Equally hysterical is an opposite vision. Funding for staff, salaries, and courthouses has dried up because of overall pressures on the federal budget, yet Congress has continued heaping work on a federal judiciary capped at one thousand judges. Dockets lengthen to the point that litigants seek justice from private providers, and fewer and fewer qualified lawyers are willing to serve on the federal bench under such austere conditions.[111]

106. Judicial Conference of the United States, Long Range Plan for the Federal Courts, appendix B, at 165 (1995) [hereinafter Long Range Plan].

107. *Id.* at 165–74.

108. Judicial Conference of U.S,, Comm. on Long Range Planning, Proposed Long Range Plan for the Federal Courts (1994).

109. Long Range Plan, *supra* note 106, at appendix B, 171–74.

110. *Id.* at 17.

111. *Id.* at 20.

Those frightening visions of a besieged federal judiciary and the consensus-seeking, judge-dominated planning process combined to produce a document that emphasized the needs of the judges, as opposed to other stakeholders. This tendency is apparent in the Plan's jurisdictional recommendations, some of which called for the legislative and executive branches of government to change their habits for the benefit of the courts. Thus the Plan deplored the increased burden on the courts resulting from the growing "federalization" of state crimes, caused by Congress's fear that state judicial and prosecutorial resources were inadequate.[112] And the Plan had recommendations for the executive branch as well, suggesting to the Justice Department that "the potential for harder federal sentencing ... and the greater capacity in the federal prisons would be insufficient ... to warrant prosecution under a federal, rather than a state, criminal statute."[113]

On the civil side, the key recommendations stressed sensible reductions in diversity jurisdiction and an array of diversion paths (mostly to Article I courts and administrative agencies) for cases believed to bog down the federal courts in low-dollar-amount, fact-intensive cases unlikely to implicate the courts' law-making function.[114] Additionally, absent a showing of state court inadequacy, Congress should be hesitant to enact new legislation enforceable in federal courts. These jurisdictional restraint measures would allow a "carefully controlled" growth of the Article III judiciary "so that the creation of new judgeships, while not subject to a numerical ceiling, is limited to that number necessary to exercise federal jurisdiction."[115]

It is not hyperbole to suggest that recommendations like those reveal inappropriate judicial hubris. Presumably, Congress chooses to "federalize" a crime and the Justice Department chooses to prosecute crimes in federal court in response to their perceptions of the needs of the nation for increased security from criminal activity. Similarly, Congress creates new civil remedies in response to its perceptions of other societal needs. As they should, those perceptions reflect political pressures placed on the legislative and executive branches by their constituents, and it is narcissistic to suggest those political pressures should yield to the judges' desires for retaining a compact federal judiciary charged with handling only a limited uniquely federal docket. The federal courts are a tool for accomplishing the nation's goals, and the size of the job should control the size of the tool rather than vice versa.

While the plan had ambitious recommendations for changes in the legislative and executive branches, it is conservative with respect to the courts of appeals. Thus the Plan was "premised on the belief that the present structure of the federal courts is by-and-large appropriate for carrying out their functions" and recommended "no

112. *Id.* at 26 (comment following Recommendation 4).
113. *Id.* at 27 (Recommendation 5(b)).
114. *Id.* at 28–33.
115. *Id.* at 38 (Recommendation 15).

major structural changes in the near term."[116] Thus, it approved of preserving the generalist regional circuit courts, retaining the Supreme Court as the only arbiter of circuit conflicts, and slow measured growth in the number of judgeships.[117]

The Plan's choice of its initial premise of adequacy is curious and probably disingenuous. On the one hand, the Plan acknowledged that there have been "streamlining" changes in appellate procedure, such as screening programs, elimination of oral argument in some cases, abandonment of fully articulated opinions, and increased reliance on staff.[118] Nevertheless, the Plan assumed the traditional hallmarks of the federal appellate system including "oral argument heard in all appropriate matters, cases decided with sufficient thought, [and] opinions carefully produced after collegial deliberation in all cases of precedential importance" could be preserved in the current structure.[119] Given the counterfactual premise and the blithe assumption that all will be well provided only that the *nonjudicial branches* come to their senses, it is hard to see how the Plan added much to a realistic discussion of the future of the circuit courts.

13. The White Commission

a. Origin and Composition

Congress established the Commission on Structural Alternatives for the Federal Courts of Appeals by statute passed in 1997[120] and charged it to:

(i) study the present division of the United states into the several judicial circuits;
(ii) study the structure and alignment of the federal court of appeals system, with particular reference to the Ninth Circuit; and
(iii) report to the President and the Congress its recommendations for such changes in circuit boundaries or structure as may be appropriate for the expeditious and effective disposition of the caseload of the federal courts of appeals, consistent with fundamental concepts of fairness and due process.[121]

116. *Id.* at 41.
117. *Id.* at 43–47, Recommendations 16, 17, and 19.
118. *Id.* at 42.
119. *Id.*
120. Pub. L. No. 105–119, § 305, 111 Stat. 2440, 2491.
121. Commission on Structural Alternatives for the Federal Courts of Appeals, Final Report (1998) [hereinafter Final Report]. This and the following two paragraphs are culled from the Report, at 1–4.

Pursuant to statutory directive, the Chief Justice appointed a five-member commission consisting of retired Justice Byron R. White, two circuit judges, a district judge, and one attorney (the past president of the American Bar Association). The Commission members elected Justice White as its chair and thus has been known informally as the "White Commission."[122]

The Commission reviewed the work of previous studies as well as workload data and statistics supplied by the Federal Judicial Center and the Administrative Office.[123] Its outreach was extensive, including six public hearings at which eighty-nine witnesses testified. It also solicited written statements (ninety-two were received), and the entire Commission or its representatives met with representatives of the Justice Department, the White House Counsel's Office, the judges of the Federal and District of Columbia Circuits (because there was no hearing in the District), and a few law professors (who briefed the Commission on the published research on the federal appellate system).[124] At the Commission's request, the Federal Judicial Center conducted separate opinion surveys of circuit judges, district judges, and a large sample of attorneys who had handled appeals in the circuit courts in the preceding twelve months.[125] In October 1998, the Commission published a draft report for public comment; it received seventy-six comments and submitted its final report before the end of the year.

b. The Ninth Circuit

The Commission owed its existence to the controversy in Congress and elsewhere over the possibility of splitting the Ninth Circuit, just as the old Fifth Circuit had been split in 1981. After several years of on-again, off-again discussion, the House and Senate split on the question and settled on the formation of the Commission as a compromise.[126] The Commission came down on the side of the opponents of a split, rejecting several possible solutions because they would "deprive the west coast of a mechanism for obtaining a consistent body of ... law."[127] Moreover, any possible split—the Commission examined and rejected over a dozen[128]—would produce an inequitable workload division as well as violating one or more of the traditional circuit alignment conventions: each circuit must consist of at least three contiguous states and no state can be split between two circuits.

After rejecting a split of the Ninth Circuit, the Commission recommended instead a "divisional" arrangement of the circuit. While retaining the central

122. *Id.* at 1.
123. *Id.* at 5.
124. *Id.* at 2–3.
125. *Id.* at 4.
126. *Id.* at 34.
127. *Id.* at 52.
128. Four possible configurations are examined by the Commission in greater detail. *Id.* at 54–56.

administration of the circuit, the Report recommended the circuit be restructured into three regionally based *adjudicative* divisions plus a central "Circuit Division." Each regional division would have at least seven active circuit judges and would function as a semi-autonomous decisional unit, with its own en banc process. Decisions of the regional panels would constitute precedent in that region and could be overruled only by a regional en banc process; they would not be binding in other regions. Interregional conflicts would be settled by the Circuit Division, exercising discretionary jurisdiction over conflict-generating cases after review or denial of review by the regional en banc process. Mere error would not be sufficient for Circuit Division jurisdiction; an interregional conflict would be necessary. Regional panel errors that did not implicate interregional conflicts would be settled only by the regional en banc process. The chief judge of the circuit would serve on the Circuit Division, as would twelve active circuit judges, chosen by lot, equally from each division; service on the Circuit Division would be for a term of three years, with terms staggered to assure continuity and gradual rotation.[129]

The Report based its divisional arrangement recommendation in part on the belief that the Ninth Circuit was too big to ensure coherent and consistent interpretation of federal law. There were simply too many decisions for each judge to monitor. Another reason advanced by the Report was dissatisfaction with the then existing en banc process in the Ninth Circuit. The divisional arrangement would permit more frequent and more efficient en banc hearings, smaller en banc panels, and less judge-time involved in each hearing. More frequent en banc hearings would in turn contribute to greater consistency of circuit law. Finally, the divisional arrangement would respect "the unique character of the West," while guarding against parochialism by requiring that some of the judges on each regional division come from outside the region.[130]

One of the reasons cited for not splitting the Ninth Circuit deserves special attention as an excellent example of a particular type of argument that appears too often in the appellate justice planning context: the makeweight arguments used to advocate a conclusion already reached for other reasons (good or bad). At several places in the Report, the Commission notes the value of having a single coherent interpretation of federal law for the "West."[131] Surely this is a makeweight. It seems to suggest the "West" is a more defined, distinct, or cohesive unit than any other section of the country, citing the location of some of its states on the Pacific Rim and the particular legal issues that circumstance generates. But how is the "West" any more *legally* distinctive, unique, insular, or cohesive than the East Coast (separated into the First, Second, Third, Fourth, and Eleventh Circuits) or the South (separated into the Fourth, Fifth, and Eleventh Circuits) or the Canadian border region (separated into the First, Second, Sixth, Seventh, Eighth, and Ninth Circuits)? And

129. *Id.* at 43–47.
130. The Commission lists its reasons. *Id.* at 47–49.
131. *See id.* at 36, 49, 52.

why do Nevada, Arizona, and Montana need a distinct "Western" law but Utah, New Mexico, and Wyoming do not?

We have no view on whether the Ninth Circuit should or should not be split, but we do care about the quality of the arguments used to justify any particular arrangement or allocation (geographic or by social class) of the nation's appellate resources. Having made a decision, it is useless and harmful (it degrades the debate) to add makeweight arguments to support it.

c. Structural Options for the Courts of Appeals

The Report made the customary recitation that the courts of appeals were then (1998) managing their geometrically increasing caseloads without unacceptably compromising the quality of the appellate justice they dispensed. They had accomplished that feat by streamlining the appellate process with the help of the Appellate Triage devices (reduced oral argument, nonpublication of opinions, and reliance on staff attorneys). The second half of the usual recitation is that the process could not be streamlined any *further* "without unacceptably compromising their essential function."[132] Of course, the rest of the story is that the following twelve years witnessed exactly the additional streamlining the Report warned against. In that time period, the oral argument rate dropped from 40 percent to 26 percent;[133] the percentage of unpublished opinions increased from 75 percent to 84 percent of the total;[134] and the size and responsibilities of central staff attorneys increased significantly.[135] The most appropriate metaphor seems to be the urban myth of the boiling frog.[136]

The subsequent progressively increasing rationing of appellate justice cannot be attributed to the fault of the White Commission. Its Final Report contained a full list of recommendations that might have helped avert the slow motion deterioration of the circuit courts. But whether the Report's cures are any better than the disease is an open question.

The Report recommended a three-pronged statutory approach that would allow the circuits to experiment with (1) the divisional concept recommended for the Ninth Circuit, (2) the use of two-judge appellate panels, and (3) district court appellate panels.[137] The divisional approach would involve a statute that permitted

132. *Id.* at 25.

133. *Compare* ADMIN. OFFICE OF U.S. COURTS, JUDICIAL BUSINESS OF THE UNITED STATES COURTS, table S-1 (1998), *with* ADMIN. OFFICE OF U.S. COURTS, JUDICIAL BUSINESS OF THE UNITED STATES COURTS, table S-1 (2010).

134. *Compare* ADMIN. OFFICE OF U.S. COURTS, JUDICIAL BUSINESS OF THE UNITED STATES COURTS, table S-3 (1998), *with* ADMIN. OFFICE OF U.S. COURTS, JUDICIAL BUSINESS OF THE UNITED STATES COURTS, table S-3 (2010).

135. *See supra* chapter 8.

136. *See* Wikipedia, *Boiling Frog*, http://en.wikipedia.org/wiki/Boiling_frog.

137. FINAL REPORT, *supra* note 121, at 60.

any circuit with more than fifteen judgeships to reorganize itself into divisions. The Commission preferred the divisional arrangement to circuit splitting because only two circuits could be split into smaller units that comprised at least three states, a key circuit alignment convention.[138] Both the recommendation and the reason are highly problematic. The divisional arrangement envisioned in the report is a four-tier system, which, in our view, is the least desirable alternative structure for the circuit courts.

First, the premise behind a four-tier system is that the current three-tier system is inadequate to maintain the coherence of the national law, i.e., that the Supreme Court's docket is too small to settle all the pressing intercircuit conflicts and that the existing circuits are so large that intracircuit conflicts are too numerous.

The problem is that there is no empirical evidence for either proposition; indeed, the only available empirical studies suggest that neither type of conflict is currently a serious problem.[139] Moreover, from the point of view of society as a whole, a fourth tier is by far the most expensive way to "solve" the non-problem. At first blush, that might not seem so; after all, adding more judges to a three-tier system is not much cheaper than a four-tier setup. The problem with that view is that it measures only the governmental cost of a four-tier system. A vastly larger portion of the total *societal* cost will be that paid by the litigants. In a four-tier system, each case of any importance will involve another set of briefs, another set of arguments, another set of attorneys fees, and the immeasurable but very real cost of additional delay before a binding resolution. All that cost will be incurred because it has been traditional (except when it's not—e.g., the D.C. Circuit and the Federal Circuit) to draw circuits that contain at least three states.[140] When the divisions are created, each will perforce not consist of three states. Will that be problematic? If not, why incur so much expense to make sure each circuit does?

The Commission's second recommendation was that Congress amend 28 U.S.C. § 46[141] to permit a circuit court by rule to provide for disposition of appeals by panels of two judges of the circuit. The two-judge panels would decide the cases now shunted to the truncated appellate process, and three-judge panels would be convened to decide cases of greater importance or precedential value. If the two judges were unable to agree, they could enlist a third judge or refer the case to a three-judge panel.

This proposal has some potential if the two-judge panel hears oral argument and disposes of the case by a hands-on precedential decision. Real attention from two Article III judges is better than processing by staff attorneys with cursory review by a three-judge panel. However, it is not completely clear the Commission intended the

138. *Id.* at 61.
139. *See infra* chapter 12.
140. *See supra* section A.4.a.
141. Final Report, *supra* note 121, at 62.

two-judge panel procedure to work that way. Indeed, the likely intent was that the two-judge panel would treat the Track Two cases in much the same way three-judge panels do now (no oral argument, minimal conference, desultory opinion drafted by staff attorneys).[142] If that is the proposal, it is unlikely to save much time because judges currently spend so little time on such cases. Alternatively, if the proposal is that the two-judge panel provide the traditional appellate process to the less important cases, then the arrangement would not save judicial time but would rather do the opposite; hands-on review by two judges costs more judge-hours than the currently prevalent cursory review by three. Another issue raised by the proposal is that it leaves the crucial question—who decides which cases get which treatment—up in the air.

The Commission's third proposal was that Congress authorize the circuits to experiment with District Court Appellate Panels (DCAP). The Judicial Conference would provide by local rule for the convening of three-judge panels consisting of one circuit judge and two district judges. Review of a DCAP decision would be in the circuit court but only by leave of that court. The Report suggested likely candidates for DCAP treatment would be diversity appeals, sentencing appeals, and, generally, any cases that require only application of well-settled law to varying facts. If the case presented an unanticipated significant issue, the DCAP could refer it to the circuit court, which would be required to take it.[143] The Report did not ultimately endorse the concept of DCAPs, but recommended experimentation, after which a more informed judgment would follow.

This proposal is not troublesome intrinsically; again, actual review of a case by two district judges and a circuit judge is better than virtual review by a three-judge panel that merely endorses a proposed disposition drafted by the central staff. There are, however, some potential issues. First, the proposal requires triage, and, again, the crucial question is who will decide if the case goes to a DCAP or to the circuit court: the DCAP, the central staff? Second, the proposal adds value only to the extent that it involves actual judicial attention to the screened cases. If instead most of the work, as now, is done by staff attorneys with DCAP ratification, it is difficult to see the value added. Finally, the proposal would require additional district court judgeships to handle the added work, and it is worth asking why creating additional district judgeships is any less problematic than, more simply, creating enough circuit judgeships to provide the traditional appellate process to all appeals.

d. Discretionary Review

The Report discussed but ultimately rejected a proposal to change the jurisdiction of the courts of appeals from mandatory to discretionary. Like the Supreme Court

142. *Id.* at 63.
143. *Id.* at 64–65.

and the high courts in many states, the circuit courts, under the proposal, would be able to choose the cases they decide, thus removing the right to at least one appeal currently afforded federal court litigants.

Although the idea was rejected, the Report's discussion speaks volumes about what any fair-minded observer would conclude from the last forty years of appellate reform. Initially, the Report noted the traditional distinction between *certiorari* and appeal of right and then continued to describe how the clear distinction had changed in the preceding thirty years (1970–1998).

> Up until three decades ago this right to appeal was assumed to include an opportunity to file briefs, to present oral argument to the court, and to receive from the court a written opinion explaining the decision. That conception of an appeal, however, has undergone modification as the appellate courts have adopted screening and tracking procedures through which a large proportion of appeals are decided by the court without oral argument and by judgment orders or unelaborated opinions.
>
> This development has blurred the distinction between obligatory and discretionary review. Under either type of jurisdiction, litigants file papers with the court containing arguments, facts, and legal authority, and the court considers those papers.... In other words, whether the court's jurisdiction is labeled obligatory or discretionary, litigants obtain a judicial examination of their contentions either through an abbreviated process [Track Two in the circuit courts and *certiorari* denial in the Supreme Court] or what is considered the traditional appellate process.[144]

Although the Report went on to consider but reject a hybrid intermediate process for most cases, it again conceded that the circuit courts already were exercising a form of de facto discretionary jurisdiction.

> In [some state appellate] courts, a denial of leave [to appeal] is in functional effect like a decision in a federal court of appeals to send a case through to decision without oral argument and dispose of it without a full opinion. The similarity is especially marked if the court issues only a one-line affirmance.[145]

These passages are truly remarkable; they show the judicial establishment had finally realized what some critics had been arguing for many years: the circuit courts were transforming themselves, without statutory authorization, from courts of mandatory jurisdiction into *certiorari* courts. Remarkably, the Report made this observation in a matter-of-fact fashion, with no apparent indignation or even disapproval.

144. *Id.* at 70–71.
145. *Id.* at 71.

B. SOME OBSERVATIONS ABOUT THE STUDIES

After reviewing a generation's worth of studies and proposals for reforming the federal appellate court system, it is possible to make some observations and draw some conclusions.

1. Alarmism: How Serious Is the Problem?

The studies reveal varying amounts of alarm for the future of the federal appellate courts, with the Long Range Plan leading the league with its two contrasting but equally apocalyptic potential futures for the courts. The amount of alarm is one question, but its target is another. The most extreme rhetoric seems to be directed at the possibility that the federal appellate system will become too large and "bureaucratic." Equally troubling to many of the study groups is the possibility of burgeoning and increasingly incoherent federal law. As a serious concern, this worry has been significantly discounted by empirical studies that demonstrate that incoherence and inconsistency are not currently dangers that face the federal appellate system.[146] Moreover, many of these empirical studies were carried out before the "information revolution" of the past twenty years, which has made dealing with large bodies of digitized data much less unwieldy.

Another cause for alarm that appears in the studies is the possibility that the circuit courts have so transformed their internal processes that some very large proportion of the docket receives scant demonstrable attention of the judges. Several points about this concern are worth noting. First, earlier studies tend to show more of this alarm than do later ones. Second, successive studies have warned that the circuit courts, as of the study date, had reached the limit of their ability to trim the appellate process without serious jeopardy to its central values. A few years later, with a larger portion of the docket committed to the truncated process, another commission will state the same conclusion. Taken together, these two points show that "intolerable damage to the circuit court's central mission" is a moving target. The further away the judges get from a time when the traditional process was the rule rather than the exception, the more tolerant they become of the Track Two process. The Appellate Triage regime began by using a truncated procedure on a small portion of the docket composed largely of pro se prisoner cases; today it accounts for the vast majority of the docket. We have said it before, but the metaphor of the boiling frog is so apt that it bears repeating; as long as the year-to-year change is gradual, the judges appear willing to concentrate their full attention on a

146. *See infra* chapter 12.

steadily decreasing fraction of the docket. Their willingness to tolerate the progressive restriction of the full appellate process to a smaller and smaller portion of the docket appears, so far, to be limitless.

2. Error Correction versus Law Declaration: For Richer, For Poorer

There is a strong consensus that the two functions of an appellate court are error correction and law declaration. The relative importance of the two and the amount of judge-time allocable to each are subject to greater controversy. For better or worse, the circuit judges have made their priorities clear, concentrating the vast majority of their time on the Track One cases, the very few that they (or the central staff attorneys) believe call for law declaration, at the expense of the large portion of the docket that requires only error correction.

By and large, the various studies reveal the same bias. The possibility of a National Court of Appeals, for instance, or some other alternative pyramidal structure is interesting only to the extent that the focus is on the courts' law declaration function. Such a court would not help the courts' error correction mission; its selling point is that it provides a method for coordinating the precedents of the several circuits. Similarly, the various four-tier proposals, the specialized court models, and the consideration of alternative configurations of the federal appellate system are all designed to enhance consistency and coherence of circuit and national law, but again that matters mostly for the "law declaration" cases. Likewise, the many discussions of appropriate circuit size routinely consider the maximum number of judges that could participate in an en banc hearing, a procedure rarely if ever used for Track Two cases.

Two observations about the various study groups' preoccupation with the law declaration function are useful. First, it seems to involve placing the cart before the horse; there is no evidence that law-declaration coherence is currently a problem within or among circuits. *The available empirical studies suggest otherwise.* The notion that doctrinal incoherence will necessarily accompany an increase in judgeships sufficient to accord traditional appellate process to the entire docket is treated as an unquestionable postulate.

The result is a highly suspect cost-benefit analysis: the *actual and current* problem of inadequate capacity is trumped by the future and hypothetical problem of doctrinal incoherence. In other words, the situation is this: today there is woefully insufficient capacity within the federal appellate system, but adding capacity may create problems of law-declaration coherence at some unspecified time in the future. A similar argument might encourage firefighters to allow the building to burn because putting out the fire *might* result in substantial expense required to repair water damage.

The second observation is that the studies' focus on law declaration at the expense of error correction is inherently classist. For most small, one-time litigants, error correction is all that matters; by contrast, rich and powerful governmental and business entities, whose activities may spread across the country or around the world, care a great deal about consistent law declaration. For them, uncertainty is a needless expense. No doubt the composition of the study groups contributed much to this biased focus. With few exceptions, the study groups were made up of circuit and district judges, elected and appointed officials, and distinguished practitioners; there were few places at the table for public service attorneys and none at all for pro se litigants. Ironically, as the percentage of cases afforded full appellate process progressively dwindles, the number of "have-not" litigants has grown to include some with wealth and power, so perhaps the steadily increasing use of Appellate Triage may be self-limiting.

3. The Issues Not Studied

The study groups' focus on law declaration and the "big case" had a great deal to do with the issues they chose to study. But it also controlled the topics they tended to ignore, nearly all of which concern the treatment of the "less important" cases. With a fresh look at the problem, that seems like an odd set of choices. The law-declaration case or Track One case, about 15 to 20 percent of the docket, gets the full traditional appellate procedure, and there really is no dissatisfaction with that. By contrast, the error correction or Track Two case, the vast majority of the docket, gets the very truncated procedure, which many argue is inadequate. Why focus study efforts on the small slice that is satisfactory at the expense of the large slice that is problematic?

What questions did the study groups ignore by focusing so little attention on the mere "error correction" cases? The answer, it turns out, is a vast array of issues that might have made the truncated process more adequate. For instance, the studies include a substantial number of opinion surveys, but not one involving the comparative satisfaction of losing litigants in Track One versus Track Two cases. There are also no opinion surveys of pro se litigants, the vast majority of whom are screened away from the traditional process. There are ample surveys of judges, who do more of the work on the law declaration cases, but no surveys of the staff attorneys, who do nearly all the work on the less favored portion of the docket.

Apart from opinion surveys, it would help to know the racial and income breakdown of litigants in the Track One and Track Two cases. The answer to that question would help decide whether there is equal justice done to "rich and poor alike." There have been scholarly studies of intra- and intercircuit consistency in the law declaration, but not a single "second look" study to determine if some of the Track Two cases have been mischaracterized or even wrongly decided. We know a great deal about the coherence of the law that controls the big cases, but very little about the consistency, coherence, and need for development in the law governing Track Two cases.

The process for deciding Track Two cases also received scant attention. It is widely known that central staff do much of the work on Track Two cases, but the uses of central staff vary widely among the circuits. Where is the study and discussion of which circuit models are better and which are worse?[147] How should staff attorneys be hired and what qualifications should they have? Should they be interviewed by the judges or only the supervising staff attorneys? Should they work always at the circuits' headquarters or might they be spread around the circuit? Is it wise to let them specialize in particular types of cases, or should they all be generalists? Should their jobs be career positions, or should there be a fixed relatively short term (like law clerks)? Most of these questions have not been posed, much less studied by the succession of study groups.

A final overlooked question may be the most important of all: who should decide whether a case belongs on Track One or Two? As is clear by now, that decision controls not only the type of process the case will receive, but also has a potential effect on its outcome because reversal rates are so different for the two groups. There are several possibilities: a special panel of judges, a single judge (with responsibility for screening divided proportionately among the judges), or the staff attorneys? If it is to be the staff, should each attorney bear some portion of the responsibility, with freshly minted law graduates making triage decisions in their first week on the job? Alternatively, should only staff supervisors screen? In small circuits, there is likely to be only one supervisor; should one nonjudicial official have that much say about which cases are useful for law making?

These are all questions that would have profited from additional attention, but the approach of the several study groups in the main was to ignore them and devote more and more attention to a steadily dwindling portion of the docket. Like the two-track system itself, the differential focus of the study groups represents a curious set of policy choices. This observation supports the strong inference that study groups, largely made up of members and friends of the judicial establishment, will not address the real problems that face today's federal circuit courts. Rather, the focus has been on methods of preserving the status of the circuit judges (hence, the various efforts to shift work to the district courts). It is that focus, and the price society pays for maintaining that status, that we find so objectionable.

147. Scholars have paid some attention to these issues; see the sources cited in chapter 8, *supra*. Moreover, there are excellent papers written by the staff of the Federal Judicial Center. *See* Judith A. McKenna, Laurel L. Hooper & Mary Clark, Case Management Procedures in the Federal Courts of Appeals 8 (2000); Donna Stienstra & Joe Cecil, The Role of Staff Attorneys and Face-to-Face Conferencing in Non-Argument Decisionmaking (1989); Federal Judicial Center, Central Legal Staffs in the United States Courts of Appeals: A Survey of Internal Operating Procedures (1978). The reports of the blue ribbon panels, commissions, and study groups pay little attention to these resources. That lacuna should not surprise anyone who has read this far.

CHAPTER 11

The Obvious Solution and the Judicial Opposition

A. THE OBVIOUS SOLUTION: MORE JUDGES

> It is time to face the real problem. If we are not to abandon the tradition of "one appeal as of right," and if we are to make this a true appeal in the traditional sense—one to be heard and decided by judges—we need both more judges and more circuits.[1]
>
> —Judge Alvin B. Rubin

As we have shown in chapters 2 through 8, the United States Circuit Courts of Appeals have responded to the caseload flood, described in chapter 1, with the system of Appellate Triage, a series of appellate process truncating devices. These devices, used to dispose of the less interesting portion of the circuit courts' caseloads, have helped the courts keep current with their dockets, but at a significant cost. The result is that courts today bear little resemblance to the circuit courts of only a generation ago.

What is most remarkable about Judge Rubin's diagnosis is its date—1976. In the intervening thirty-six years, caseload and bureaucratization have both increased radically. Conditions Rubin thought were becoming intolerable are now orders of magnitude worse. When Rubin wrote, the circuit courts were only beginning their decline into courts of discretionary appellate jurisdiction. Today that transformation is all but complete.

The standard justification for the dramatic transformation of the courts of appeals is that the caseload is overwhelming and that conscientious judges working strenuously cannot keep up without using the shortcuts. Thus the judicial establishment views the circuit courts as an enormously overstressed institution in the hands of selfless judges engaged in heroic and creative judicial triage. Certainly the

1. Alvin B. Rubin, *Views From the Lower Court*, 23 UCLA L. Rev. 448, 459 (1976).

caseload is staggering and the courts lack sufficient judges. The staffing model used by the Administrative Office reveals that 179 judges are doing the work of 219 (or just over 300, according to the judicial-workload formula used until 1996). And the judges are keeping current. The average time from the filing of the last brief until hearing or submission was 4.4 months, and from hearing to final disposition, 2.1 months, time periods not drastically longer than they were 40 years ago.[2] They manage to keep up with the steadily increasing volume of filings by using every reasonable time-saving appellate shortcut and by working long, and in some cases, inhuman hours. Thus, in response to an opinion survey undertaken by the Federal Courts Study Committee, 81 percent of the current judges reported that the workload was "heavy" or "overwhelming."[3] Several of the judges' anonymous responses to the survey reinforce the point:

> Done properly, the work is overwhelming. The only way that I can do my work properly is to work nights and weekends. As long as one has the vigor, stamina and good health, it can be done. Eventually, this schedule is bound to take its toll.
>
> ....
>
> My work hours have increased to occupy substantially all of my available time. I would not today accept an appointment to this court if I knew the workload—but I have too much invested to get out.
>
> ....
>
> My typical day begins at 5:30 a.m. including weekends when I get most of my writing done. I feel I am becoming narrowly focused and less of a generally knowledgeable individual, and consequently in many ways less competent as a judge. I try to keep up friendships and have done so only because my friends are tolerant of my neglect. There is so little time for the pleasures of family and outside activities. I feel guilty when I do take any time off—like Sunday afternoon.
>
> ....
>
> I calculated I spent 299 days on judicial work last year. Since I took about two and one-half weeks of vacation, it will be seen that I worked on Saturdays more than half the time and on at least 15 or 16 Sundays. This is entirely too much for me and it is especially difficult for the younger judges who have the responsibility of families with small children. This known factor has caused one very able trial judge to indicate he no longer wished to seek the vacancy that will occur when I seek senior status.[4]

2. Admin. Office of U.S. Courts, Judicial Business of the United States 104, table B4 (2010), *available at*http://www.uscourts.gov/Statistics/JudicialBusiness/JudicialBusiness.

3. *See* Lauren Robel, *Caseload and Judging: Judicial Adaptations to Caseload*, 1990 BYU L. Rev. 38.

4. *Id.* at 39–40.

Like physicians in a mass disaster, the circuit judges work themselves mercilessly and reluctantly have resorted to a triage regime. That system apportions their attention to those cases where they believe it is most needed and can do the most good. That system is the set of appellate shortcuts described in the foregoing chapters. Thus, from the point of view of the judicial establishment, the system is not ideal, but at least the judges are not at fault. Under difficult conditions, they have done everything in their power to produce the maximum result with the inadequate resources Congress and society have apportioned the problem of federal appellate justice.

B. JUDICIAL OPPOSITION

This heroic picture leaves out one crucial and surprising fact. The judicial establishment has consistently acted and lobbied against the single most obvious solution to the caseload glut—the creation of additional judgeships. Ironically, the judiciary has opposed this solution vigorously. To continue the medical analogy, it would be as though the busy surgeon, rushing from one important case to the next while "screening" out the unworthy cases, rejected the help of additional doctors to improve the situation. As odd as it sounds, the judiciary has done just that.

1. The Mechanisms for Restricting Judicial Supply

a. Lobbying

One method the judges have used to keep their numbers small is lobbying. Individual judges have written and spoken passionately against the creation of enough judgeships to handle the load.[5] Individual circuits—the Fifth and the Eleventh are the best examples—have requested too few additional judgeships to meet the actual need or have passed resolutions urging Congress not to create new judgeships.[6] The powerful Judicial Conference routinely requests only a small percentage of the judgeships required to satisfy staffing models. In 2010, for example,

5. *See, e.g.*, Jon O. Newman, *1,000 Judges—The Limit for an Effective Federal Judiciary*, 76 JUDICATURE 187 (1993); Richard A. Posner, *Will the Federal Courts of Appeals Survive until 1984? An Essay on Delegation and Specialization of the Judicial Function*, 56 S. CAL. L. REV. 761 (1983); Gerald B. Tjoflat, *More Judges, Less Justice*, 79 A.B.A. J. 70 (July 1993); Justice Antonin Scalia, *Remarks before the Fellows of the American Bar Foundation and the National Conference of Bar Presidents* (Feb. 15, 1987), *in* WILLIAM W. SCHWARZER & RUSSELL R. WHEELER, FED. JUDICIAL CTR., ON THE FEDERALIZATION OF THE ADMINISTRATION OF CIVIL AND CRIMINAL JUSTICE 44 (Long-Range Planning Series, Paper No. 2, 1994).

6. *See infra* section B.1.b.(2). The resolution of the Eleventh Circuit Judicial Council in 1989 is reported in THOMAS E. BAKER, RATIONING JUSTICE ON APPEAL 203 (1994).

it requested that Congress create nine additional circuit judgeships when its own inadequate and arbitrary[7] staffing model called for forty.[8] National judicial planning and study groups also have inveighed against substantial increases. Thus, the Judicial Conference Committee on Courts Administration and Case Management recommended that federal judgeships (district and circuit) be limited to one thousand, a number that would permanently assure inadequate capacity in the court of appeals.[9] Similarly, the Judicial Conference Committee on Long Range Planning, while rejecting a numerical ceiling, favored "controlled" growth in judgeships "only after other appropriate alternatives have been exhausted."[10]

b. Controlling the Process

Lobbying has not been the only method that the judges have used to restrict their number; even more effective has been their successful control of the process for requesting new judgeships. The judiciary has used that control to adopt three strategies to keep a lid on growth: (1) upward adjustment of the staffing model to mirror the increasing ratio of filings to judgeships; (2) the grant to each circuit court of a power to veto new judgeship requests for that court even when the *revised* staffing model indicates the need for them; and (3) a process for deciding on judgeship requests that is quiet and intramural and that gives other stakeholders negligible opportunity for input or oversight. Here is how those strategies work in practice.

(1) Adjusting the Staffing Formula

The Judicial Conference of the United States periodically submits proposals to Congress requesting the authorization of new judgeships. In order to determine how many to request, the Conference relies on surveys of the circuits and on a

7. Had it used the formula, which seemed adequate until changed in 1996, the number requested should have been well over one hundred. The Government Accounting Office stated publicly that there was no empirical basis for the 1996 change. See the discussion in section B.1.b.(1), *infra*.

8. Additional Judgeships or Conversion of Existing Judgeships Recommended by the Judicial Conference 2010, http://www.uscourts.gov/uscourts/JudgesJudgeships/docs/2011JudgeshipRecommendations. The Conference's recommendation for 2009 again was well short of the need. *See* Recommendation of the Judicial Conference of the United States http://www.uscourts.gov/FederalCourts/JudicialConference/JudgeshipRecommendations (recommending only nine new permanent and three new temporary judgeships. Past practice has been similar). Reports of the Proceedings of the Judicial Conference of the United States 69–70 (Sept. 1992) (requesting nine new judgeships when its own formula would have called for more than five times that many).

9. Report of the Judicial Conference Committee on Court Administration and Case Management to the Judicial Conference Committee on Long Range Planning 3 (Feb. 16, 1993).

10. The Long Range Plan is discussed in chapter 10.

formula that determines the appropriate workload for an appellate judge—typically, so many merits terminations per judge, or so many "participations" per judge, or so many filings per judge. The most recent ratio, adopted by the Conference in 1996, is five hundred adjusted filings per three-judge panel. The Conference defines "adjusted filings" as the result of subtracting from total filings all reinstated cases and of counting pro se cases as one-third of a counseled case.[11]

According to a 2003 study by the General Accounting Office, however, there is no empirical basis for the formula, such as time studies, nor is there consensus on what the formula should be.[12] In other words, the Conference's formula is arbitrary and might just as well have been 400 or 600 adjusted filings per panel.[13] (The Conference used 320 adjusted filings before the upward adjustment of 1996.) Rather than relying on time studies, the Conference assesses the need for judgeships based on the recent past performance of the judges. Unfortunately, that measure takes as a given the procedural shortcuts adopted since 1970 to deal with the caseload glut; it thus assures that the courts will never have enough judges to be able to return to the traditional, Learned Hand model of appellate justice, which served the courts and the country so well for the first eighty years of the courts' history.[14]

The history of the adjustment of the staffing formula reinforces the GAO's conclusion that the measure is arbitrary. Until 1996, the staffing formula used the ratio of 255 "merits disposition" per authorized judgeship.[15] That number of merits dispositions corresponds to about 320 adjusted filings per panel; thus the 1996 change in formulas resulted in increasing the maximum number of adjusted filings per panel from 320 to 500 (about a 60 percent increase in workload). Why the increase?[16]

We cannot be sure, but the following figures are suggestive. The number of circuit judgeships remained constant before and after 1996: 179; the volume of appeals, however, increased annually. Using the pre-1996 formula, there were 25,840 merits

11. U.S. Gov't Accountability Office, GAO-03–788R, Federal Judgeships: The General Accuracy of the Case-Related Workload Measures Used to Assess the Need for Additional District Court and Court of Appeals Judgeships (2003) [hereinafter GAO Report].

12. *Id. See also* Thomas Baker, *Applied Freakonomics: Explaining the "Crisis of Volume,"* 8 J. App. Prac. & Process 101 (2006).

13. Arthur D. Hellman, *Assessing Judgeship Needs in the Federal Courts of Appeals: Policy Choices and Process Concerns*, 5 J. App. Prac. & Process 239, 247 (2003).

14. *Id.*

15. Gordon Bermant et al., Fed. Judicial Ctr., Imposing a Moratorium on the Number of Federal Judges: Analysis of Arguments and Implications 9 (1993), *available at* http://purl.access.gpo.gov/GPO/LPS53494.

16. *Compare* Judicial Business of the United States Courts, tables B1 & S9 (52,319 cases commenced minus 1,231 reinstatements also minus 67 percent of 21,747 pro se cases equals 36,590 adjusted filings) *with* table B1 (25,840 merits terminations). The table in note 21 *infra* summarizes the effect of the change in the formula (1997), *available at* http://www.uscourts.gov/Statistics/JudicialBusiness/JudicialBusiness1997.aspx.

terminations in 1997[17] (requiring 77,520 judge participations). Dividing 77,520 by 255 yields 304 circuit judgeships. Thus, the pre-1996 formula suggested that the Judicial Conference should have asked Congress for 125 new slots. But requesting 125 new judgeships from Congress was incompatible with the circuit judiciary's desire to remain small. The solution was to change the formula.

The Conference did just that, and the gimmick worked. There were 52,319 filings in 1997;[18] reduce that number by 1,231 reinstated appeals[19] and by two-thirds of the pro se appeals (14,498)[20] and you end up with 36,590 adjusted filings. Dividing the adjusted filings by 500 (according to the *new* formula) resulted in a need for 73 panels or 219 judgeships, an increase of only 40. If we allow for the contribution of senior circuit judges and district judges sitting by designation (about 20 percent of all participations), the adjusted filings figure of 36,590 can be reduced to 29,272, which, divided by 500, yields a need for 58.5 panels of three or 176 judgeships, a figure conveniently close to the actual number of circuit judgeships, i.e. the status quo, which much of the circuit judiciary wanted to preserve.[21]

Lest we be accused of being too cynical, consider the GAO's evaluation of the new standard.

> At the time the current measure was developed and approved, using the new benchmark of 500 adjusted case filings resulted in judgeship numbers that closely approximated the judgeship needs of the majority of the courts of appeals [i.e. current judgeships plus a very few requested additional positions], as the judges of each court of appeals perceived

17. *Id.* table B1.
18. *Id.*
19. *Id.*
20. *Id.*, table B9.
21. See *id.*, table S2, for the number of participations by senior and visiting judges. Allowing for their participations, the old formula would have required 91 panels, i.e., a corps of 274 circuit judges.The numbers and the differing formulas can be confusing, so the following chart is useful to show the situation (updated to 2010 statistics).

	Current judgeships	Adjusted filings	Number of panels required	Number of judgeships required	Judgeships required, reduced by 20% (allowing for 20% participations by visiting and senior judges)
Old formula: *320* adjusted filings per judgeship	179	36,553	114	342	274
New formula: *500* adjusted filings per judgeship	179	36,553	73	219	175

them. However, on the basis of the documentation we reviewed, there is no empirical basis on which to assess the accuracy of adjusted filings as a measure of case-related workload for courts of appeals judges.[22]

(2) The Circuit Veto

There is further evidence that the judges' desires, rather than the needs of society, control the judiciary's requests for additional judgeships. Even when the current workload formula justifies the creation of new judgeships, the Judicial Conference will not request them for a circuit unless a majority of its active judges concur in the request. As a result, the current complement of circuit judges is seriously inadequate even as measured by the Conference's own adjusted formula. In 2010, a total of 55,992 appeals were filed. Discounting pro se cases (27,209) by two-thirds and eliminating reinstated cases (1,399) yields a total of 36,533 "adjusted filings."[23] That figure, by the Conference's formula, would justify a circuit bench of 219 active judges. In order to reach that number, the Conference would have had to request 40 new judgeships in its 2011 report to Congress. Instead, in part because of vetoes by majorities on several circuits, it requested only 9.[24]

Those vetoes raise the question of the adequacy of judge-power in the reluctant circuits. A quick look reveals that judgeship inadequacy, while pervasive, is not evenly distributed, with the Fifth and the Eleventh Circuits clearly standing out. With 17 judgeships and 4,741 adjusted filings in 2010, the Fifth Circuit's staffing ratio—836 adjusted filings per panel—is 167 percent of the Conference model.[25] The Eleventh Circuit is worse yet; 3,910 adjusted filings divided among 12 judgeships yields a ratio of 977 adjusted filings per panel—almost twice the accepted model.[26] The reason for the anomalies is that the majorities of judges on those circuits want their courts to remain small and have exercised their peremptory vetoes.[27] Under the current system, their preferences control regardless of the Judicial Conference formula, the desires of the minority of judges on the two courts, and the perceived needs of the circuit's bar and the litigants.

22. GAO Report, *supra* note 11.
23. Admin. Office of U.S. Courts, Judicial Business of the United States Courts, tables B1 & B9 (2009).
24. *See* http://www.uscourts.gov/uscourts/JudgesJudgeships/docs/2011JudgeshipRecommendations.pdf.
25. Judicial Business 2009, tables B2 & B9 and our own calculations.
26. Judicial Business 2009, tables B2 & B9 and our own calculations.
27. Hellman, *supra* note 13, at 255.

(3) An Invisible Process

The chronic, system-wide judgeship shortage and the remarkable outlier ratios in some circuits raise questions about the Judicial Conference's process for arriving at the proper number of judgeship requests. If the courts are significantly understaffed and, as a result, litigants and advocates get short shrift in a large percentage of the cases, why is there so little outcry from those groups over the courts' failure to request enough additional judgeships? One explanation is that the process for deciding whether to make a request is largely invisible, taking place entirely within the judiciary. In its course, a decision about requesting additional positions will be considered by the members of the court, the Circuit's Judicial Council (composed entirely of judges), and the Judicial Conference, including its various subcommittees. In Professor Hellman's words: "No one else ... [has] an opportunity to express views, to question assumptions, or to seek additional justifications or explanations for the conclusions reached at the various stages of the process."[28]

Finally, a request for additional judgeships requires extensive documentation, but the decision not to make such a request requires almost none. In other words, if the workload formula suggests a need for more judgeships, but the court makes no request, it may be required to explain its decision. But there is no review of that explanation by the Judicial Conference, and the mere statement that most of the judges oppose expansion is sufficient to end the process. As a result, Congress will be unaware of the shortfall. It will have no occasion to second-guess the judges' choice, nor typically will Congress have the opportunity to hear the views of the minority of the court that might have favored a request for additional judgeships.[29] Thus a major policy decision on resource allocation is entrusted entirely to the judges and is unlikely to provoke review or oversight by the Conference, the Congress, or anyone else.

28. *Id.* at 254.
29. *Id.* at 254, 261.

CHAPTER 12

The Need for a Small Federal Judiciary: Reasons, Arguments, and Refutations

In chapter 11, we showed that the judiciary, by a variety of means, has made a unilateral policy decision to restrict its numbers. To justify the choice, the judiciary has offered a wide array of extremely weak arguments. Nearly all of these arguments rely on factual premises with no empirical support, and some depend on assumptions contradicted by the only available studies.[1] Others rely on classic logical or statistical fallacies,[2] and still others reveal an amazing insensitivity to the needs of litigants and suggest a belief that the courts of appeals exist to provide professional satisfaction for judges rather than appellate capacity for the nation.[3]

Some of the anti-expansion arguments inveigh against creating new circuits, others oppose enlarging the existing circuits, and still others reject the establishment of nationwide courts of specialized subject matter jurisdiction. Despite the differing approaches of the anti-expansion arguments, two features unite them: they all seek to restrict the size of the federal judiciary; and nearly all of the arguments are weak, some embarrassingly so—the sort of arguments that the judges would reject out of hand had they been asserted by advocates practicing before their courts. Finally, the arguments against more judges ignore the quality of justice dispensed to litigants. In this chapter we evaluate those arguments.

1. See discussion *infra* in sections A and C.1. and 3.
2. See discussion *infra* in section C.2. and 4.
3. See discussion *infra* in section A.2., B, and chapters 13 and 14.

A. QUALITY OF THE BENCH

Some opponents of increasing judicial capacity stress the inevitable decline in the quality of the bench that would accompany expansion. Judge Newman, for example, argued:

> A federal judiciary of 3,000 to 4,000 … would also include an unacceptable number of mediocre and even a few unqualified people. Today, most observers regard the overall quality of the federal judiciary as higher than that of the average state judiciary. At a size of 3,000 to 4,000, its quality would be indistinguishable from the most pedestrian of state judiciaries.[4]

In this, its purest form (i.e., that there are not enough good judicial candidates to supply a substantial number of new judgeships), this argument is hard to take seriously. In 1960, there were 68 circuit court judgeships[5] and 285,933 attorneys,[6] yielding a ratio of 4,205 attorneys for each circuit judgeship. In 2010, judgeships had increased to 179, and total attorneys to over 1 million,[7] yielding a ratio of almost 5,600 attorneys per judgeship. Adding enough judgeships to meet the Judicial Conference's staffing model, about 40, would produce a corps of 219 judges, so there would still be over 4,500 attorneys per circuit judgeship. Doubling the size of the current circuit bench to about 360 judges would allow the courts to treat almost all cases by the traditional model of appellate justice and would still result in a ratio of almost 2,800 attorneys per judgeship. It is ridiculous to argue that none of those 2,800 attorneys is qualified to be a circuit judge.

1. The Quality of the Pool

To begin with, the average quality of this pool of 2,800 lawyers is probably higher than it was in 1960. First, the population of aspiring lawyers is much larger because of the augmentation of the pool with significant numbers of women and minorities. Second, admissions screening in law schools is much more sophisticated than it was in 1960. Additionally, law schools themselves have much better, larger libraries and computer resources, larger and more professional full-time faculties, and much more sophisticated curricula (including clinical and skills-simulation offerings)

4. *See* Jon O. Newman, *1,000 Judges—The Limit for an Effective Federal Judiciary*, 72 JUDICATURE 187, 188 (1993).

5. JUDICIAL CONFERENCE OF U.S., COMM. ON LONG RANGE PLANNING, PROPOSED LONG RANGE PLAN FOR THE FEDERAL COURTS 13 (1994), discussed in chapter 10, *supra*.

6. Statistical Abstract of the United States 210, table 637 (1994), *available at* http://www.census.gov/prod/www/abs/statab1951-1994.htm.

7. Statistical Abstract of the United States 394, table 616 (2010), *available at* http://www.census.gov/prod/2011pubs/12statab/labor.pdf.

than they did in 1960. Finally, continuing legal education after law school is much more prevalent now than it was in 1960.

Surely in this improved pool of 2,800 lawyers there is one willing and able to be a circuit court judge. Within that pool, there are 678 active federal district judges,[8] about 340 justices on state supreme courts,[9] and about 1,000 state intermediate appellate court judges.[10] It is hard to argue that such a pool could not produce enough distinguished candidates for the circuit courts. It is equally frivolous to contend that among the thousands of law professors, senior law firm partners, senior United States Attorneys, and public defenders there are not enough qualified and willing applicants.

2. Diminished Prestige

A variation on the basic dilution-of-quality argument asserts that substantial increases in the number of circuit judgeships will reduce the prestige of the position and thus diminish the pool of distinguished attorneys willing to serve on the bench.[11] Opponents of additional judgeships make this argument confidently, as though its factual premises were beyond dispute. In fact, most of the evidence is anecdotal, consisting of statements by sitting judges that they would not have accepted the position if there were more judgeships.[12] The difficulty with anecdotal evidence, of course, is that it is relatively easy to produce an opposing anecdote. Thus, other judges maintain that prestige is controlled not by the number of judges, but by the quality of the work they do. In Judge Coffin's words, "If the work is rewarding and important, there will be more than sufficient prestige."[13]

Judge Posner's version of the argument is based not on anecdote, but predictably on the tenets of the controversial law and economics school. He maintains that high-quality candidates could be found even if the number of judgeships was very high (e.g., five hundred), but only if judicial salaries were to increase to politically

8. Annual Report of the Director of the Administrative Office of the United States Courts 11, table 3, *available at* http://www.uscourts.gov/uscourts/Statistics/JudicialBusiness/2011/JudicialBusiness2011.pdf.

9. Judgepedia's Supreme Weekly: The States, *available at* http://judgepedia.org/index.php/State_Supreme_Court_justices.

10. Council of State Governments, State Intermediate Appellate Courts and General Trial Courts: Number of Judges and Terms (2011), *available at* knowledgecenter.csg.org/drupal/system/files/5.2_2.xls.

11. *See* Irving R. Kaufman, *New Remedies for the Next Century of Judicial Reform: Time As the Greatest Innovator,* 57 Fordham L. Rev. 253, 260–61 (1988).

12. *See id; see also* Lumberman's Mut. Casualty Co. v. Elbert, 348 U.S. 48, 59 (1954) (Frankfurter, J., concurring).

13. *See* Frank M. Coffin, *Research for Efficiency and Quality: Review of Managing Appeals in Federal Courts,* 138 U. Pa. L. Rev. 1857, 1867 (1990).

unacceptable levels.[14] Posner apparently believes that high-quality candidates will come disproportionately from among the group of high-income lawyers. However, for many able candidates (state judges, professors, prosecutors, and public defenders), a circuit judge's salary would come as a handsome raise.

In any case, empirical evidence is vastly better than anecdote or speculation, and there is no empirical evidence to suggest that creating additional judgeships will either reduce prestige or that reduced prestige will diminish the pool of judicial candidates. The limited empirical evidence that is available on the issue suggests just the opposite. For example, circuit judgeships have not become harder to fill as their number has increased almost threefold since 1950, nor is there a dearth of able and willing applicants. No steady diminution in prestige has accompanied the steady increase in judgeships that has occurred since the circuit courts' inception. Furthermore, vacancies in district judgeships as of 2007—totaling 678[15]—produce ample applicant pools, again suggesting that circuit judgeships could increase *threefold* without diminishing the quality or quantity of judicial candidates. Absent supporting evidence, anecdotes and speculation about whether a substantial increase in judgeships will make the positions less attractive and reduce the quality of the applicant pool should count for very little; this is an empirical question that can be investigated, and thus far it has not been.

3. Reduced Scrutiny of Appointees

Yet another variation on the dilution theme focuses on the level of scrutiny during the appointment process. The argument is that an increase in the number of appointments reduces the visibility and scrutiny of each appointment, thus permitting the political process to forward and confirm mediocre or incompetent candidates.[16] According to this line of reasoning, an appointment to a small court consisting of six or seven judges produces intense scrutiny from the bar, the press, the academy, and the public. However, the argument goes, as the court grows to twenty or thirty or fifty, vacancies will become so common that they will provoke much less attention and scrutiny.[17] This anti-expansionist argument sounds even less convincing today in an era of extreme partisan gridlock than when it was first propounded. Even before the era of gridlock, the argument depended on factual assertions utterly devoid of empirical support. Would there really be less scrutiny

14. *See* Richard A. Posner, The Federal Courts: Crisis & Reform 99 (1985).

15. Annual Report of the Director of the Administrative Office of the United States Courts, table 3, *available at* http://www.uscourts.gov/uscourts/Statistics/JudicialBusiness/2010/JudicialBusiness2010.

16. *See* Newman, *supra* note 4, at 187.

17. Note that this argument assumes that enhanced scrutiny of judicial nominees is good. Today's highly publicized confirmation process might suggest the opposite.

if appointments were more numerous, and would the diminished scrutiny really result in lower-quality judges? There is very little evidence concerning either of these issues, and the limited evidence that exists suggests that neither result would occur.

There has been no noticeable reduction in scrutiny or quality as the circuit bench has tripled in size in the last forty years. Nor does scrutiny of the many more district court nominees appear to be less rigorous than that focused at the circuit level. Furthermore, even though the circuits differ radically in size, varying from six judgeships in the First Circuit to twenty-eight in the Ninth Circuit, no clear variations in scrutiny or quality have appeared among them. Finally, even supposing that numerical increases could reduce scrutiny and thus quality, there is no indication of the relevant numbers or proportions. In other words, exactly what size increases would harm scrutiny and quality? Is there a linear and direct correlation, or are there thresholds instead? For example, a 1,000 percent increase in judgeships might have a substantial impact on scrutiny and quality, while an increase of 100 percent (the largest increase suggested so far) might have none. These questions have never been investigated, nor even seriously posed. Given this lack of evidence, it makes little sense to rely on reduced scrutiny and quality as reasons to oppose the needed increases in capacity.

An argument closely related to the reduced-scrutiny contention highlights the increased costs that additional judgeships would add to the appointments procedure itself. According to this argument, as the number of judgeships grows, the appointments process will become too burdensome for Congress and will result in confirmations occurring without thorough investigation and scrutiny.[18] This argument mistakenly assumes that the nomination and confirmation process involves a substantial amount of senatorial attention. In fact, the F.B.I. performs the investigations, and staff does most of the other work involved. Hearings usually take a few minutes.[19] Assuming a yearly 10 percent turnover rate among circuit judges, one hundred additional judgeships would require an average of ten more appointments each year—a workload unlikely to cripple the Senate.

4. The Quality of Justice

All of the foregoing quality-of-the-bench arguments suffer from an additional and very serious flaw. They all focus on the quality of the active circuit judges—not on the total average quality of the appellate justice dispensed. The two are distinctly

18. *See* Gordon Bermant et al., Fed. Judicial Ctr., Imposing a Moratorium on the Number of Federal Judges: Analysis of Arguments and Implications 33–34 (1993), *available at* http://purl.access.gpo.gov/GPO/LPS53494.
19. *Id.* at 33.

different problems, because active circuit judges are responsible for only a small part of the work of the circuit courts. To see the point clearly, recall the two-track system of justice, and first, consider Track One—the portion of the circuit courts' terminations that are decided using the traditional appellate process (oral argument, conference, published opinion)—about 20 percent of the total. Active circuit judges are responsible for only 80 percent of the participations in those cases; the remaining 20 percent is provided by senior and visiting judges.[20] Presumably, large increases in the number of active judgeships would reduce or eliminate the need for participation by senior and visiting district judges and would increase the participation by active current judges. The justice dispensed by the new, active circuit judges probably would not be lower, in average quality, than that dispensed by the visiting and senior district and circuit judges currently performing the work.

Next, consider the Track Two cases—the 80 percent of the cases that are screened out of the traditional appellate process. These cases are not argued; often there is no conference; no opinion is published; and in some cases, no opinion is even written. Track Two cases get very little attention from the judges; most of the work is done by staff attorneys and law clerks. Thus, for the great majority of the circuit courts' caseload there is already a substantial breakdown in the quality of the appellate process. If active judgeships were to increase significantly, however, the need for screening would cease or diminish, and these Track Two cases would receive much more judicial attention than they receive now. A substantial increase in active judgeships (even if it were to decrease average judge quality) would eliminate the need for visiting judges and for "screening," and thus still would substantially increase the average level of active circuit judge attention per case, thereby increasing the average quality of appellate justice dispensed by the courts.

The problem can be viewed as one of resource allocation or distributive justice. If the system creates more appellate judgeships, it is possible that the average quality of the judges may decline minimally. Accordingly, the quality of appellate justice in the cases already receiving the luxury of the full traditional appellate process might also decline somewhat. In other words, the rich may become less rich. But adding judgeships also means that the quality of justice dispensed in the cases currently screened out of plenary treatment would vastly increase. In other words, the poor would become significantly less poor. On the other hand, restricting the number of judgeships virtually insures that the poor will get poorer and that the number of poor will continue to increase in proportion to caseload. It violates modern conceptions of distributive justice to refuse to create a massive benefit for those currently deprived of quality appellate justice in order to preserve a minor benefit for those already enjoying the lion's share of the system's resources.[21] Yet that is precisely the effect of refusing to create additional appellate capacity.

20. Admin. Office of U.S. Courts, Judicial Business of the United States Courts, table S-2 (2010).

21. John Rawls, A Theory of Justice 83 (1971).

B. IT COSTS TOO MUCH

> [T]he cost of operating the judicial system is an infinitesimal part of our national expenditures .... We spend almost as much on one Stealth bomber as we do on the whole federal judicial system. We could run the entire federal judiciary for 15 years on the cost of a single space station.
>
> —Stephen Reinhardt, United States Circuit Judge, Ninth Circuit Court of Appeals[22]

Opponents of additional appellate capacity often mention, but seldom consider in depth, the cost of new judgeships.[23] The numbers do seem formidable at first glance. The annual cost of salaries, benefits (about $215,000), plus the cost of support staff and court operations (about $600,000), yields a total annual figure of about $1 million per judge.[24] If 40 new circuit judgeships are needed to generate adequate capacity (according to the Judicial Conference formula), the annual bill is just over $40 million; and to add the 150 judgeships required to handle the docket without resort to the shortcuts in appellate procedure would cost over $150 million, a considerable figure. However, these totals probably overstate the net cost considerably because full staffing of the judiciary itself would reduce the need for many quasi-judicial personnel—law clerks and central staff—and thus save millions of dollars. Nevertheless, annual expenditures in the neighborhood of $40 million or $150 million are fair estimates of the cost of a more fully staffed circuit judiciary.

These are substantial figures, but like any large number, they can be understood only through comparisons. The federal government spends between two- and three-tenths of 1 percent of the federal budget on the entire federal judiciary. This amounts to about $6.7 billion out of the total of over $3 trillion.[25] The $40 million required for forty new judgeships in turn amounts to about two-thirds of a

22. Stephen Reinhardt, *A Plea to Save the Federal Courts—Too Few Judges, Too Many Cases*, 79 A.B.A. J. 52 (Jan. 1993).

23. *See, e.g.*, PROPOSED LONG RANGE PLAN, *supra* note 5, at 32; Kaufman, *supra* note 11, at 258; *see also* THOMAS E. BAKER, RATIONING JUSTICE ON APPEAL 203 (1994); GORDON BERMANT ET AL., FED. JUDICIAL CTR., IMPOSING A MORATORIUM ON THE NUMBER OF FEDERAL JUDGES: ANALYSIS OF ARGUMENTS AND IMPLICATIONS 35–36 (1993), *available at* http://purl.access.gpo.gov/GPO/LPS53494.

24. Congressional Budget Office Cost Estimate, S. 2774, Federal Judgeship Act of 2008, *available at* http://www.cbo.gov/ftpdocs/94xx/doc9470/S2774.pdf.

25. BUDGET OF THE U.S. GOVERNMENT, FISCAL YEAR 2008, ANALYTICAL PERSPECTIVES, SUPPLEMENTAL MATERIALS 28. FEDERAL PROGRAMS BY AGENCY AND ACCOUNT (Federal Total at 157, Judicial Branch at 10). We have used the data from 2008 because it is the last year before the financial crisis caused a significant increase in the federal budget. The larger more-recent figures make our relative-cost arguments even stronger.

percent of the $6.7 billion dollar judiciary budget, and thus about .00015 percent of the federal budget. The $150 million per year required to handle the appellate caseload without resort to the shortcuts amounts to about 2.5 percent of the judiciary's budget and thus about .006 percent of the federal budget.[26]

Comparisons with other federal expenditures are also revealing. The Library of Congress spends about $76 million on books for the blind and physically handicapped.[27] The budget for the Sergeant at Arms and Doorkeeper of the Senate is $151 million,[28] and annual expenses for the National Gallery of Art and the American Battle Monuments Commission total $98 million[29] and $41 million respectively.[30] In 2005, more than forty American universities received over $180 million each in Federal Research and Development Funds,[31] and crop subsidies paid to American farmers total about $5 billion per year, with about $200 million going to owners of land that *was once but is no longer used to farm.*[32] That $200 million, allocated by bureaucrats who fully appreciate its foolishness, to landowners, who are embarrassed to receive it, would be more than adequate to fund the additional judgeships required to allow the circuit courts to return to the traditional method for judging appeals.

There is no need to belabor the point. The federal government spends vast sums of money on matters important and trivial. Given the astronomical sums spent to deal with the recent banking crisis and economic downturn, the $150 million figure for new judgeships seems almost quaint. It would not be a major expense either as a meaningful fraction of the total federal budget or the total judiciary budget, or by comparison to other uses of federal dollars or other judiciary funding requests.

Moreover, other judicial funding requests cast doubt on the sincerity of cost-based arguments against the provision of new judgeships. Thus, worries about the federal fisc have not persuaded the federal judges to share courtroom space even though many courtrooms are in use only 50 percent of the workweek.[33] Nor do the judges

26. *Id.*

27. *Id.* (Legislative Branch at 6).

28. *Id.* at 3.

29. *Id.* at 153.

30. *Id.* at 119.

31. Statistical Abstract of the United States, table 778 (2009), *available at* http://www.census.gov/prod/2008pubs/09statab/science.pdf.

32. Carolyn Lochhead, *New Farm Bill Retains Big Crop Subsidies*, S.F. Chron., Apr. 30, 2008, *available at* http://www.sfgate.com/politics/article/New-farm-bill-retains-big-crop-subsidies-3217316.php (last visited July 5, 2012) (total U.S. farm subsidy). Dan Morgan, Gilbert Gaul & Sarah Cohen, *$1.3 Billion Crop Subsidies Shelled Out to Nonfarmers*, S.F. Chron., July 2, 2006, *available at* http://www.sfgate.com/news/article/1-3-billion-crop-subsidies-shelled-out-to-2493718.php (last visited July 5, 2012) (amount paid to owners of nonfarm land).

33. *U.S. Gen. Servs. Admin., Hearing Before the Subcommittee on Economic Development, Public Buildings, and Emergency Management Committee on Transportation and Infrastructure U.S. House of Representatives* (June 22, 2006) (statement of David L. Winstead, Commissioner

seem inclined to give up any unneeded space, as there are seventy-one facilities that are occupied by the judiciary even though they house the chambers of not a single active federal judge.[34] Budgetary restraint has not stopped the judiciary from lobbying for lavish spending on federal courthouses, especially those in New York and Boston. Requests for extras such as terrazzo floors, private bathrooms, showers and kitchens, English gardens, French doors, custom lighting fixtures, English oak paneling, and a public boat dock put the projects hundreds of millions of dollars over budget.[35] An investigation by the Senate Committee on Environment and Public Works found that one out of eight dollars spent on the projects was wasted—a total of over $500 million.[36]

Nor did thriftiness stop the judiciary from petitioning Congress for funds for other resources. In its Proposed Long Range Plan,[37] the Judicial Conference included thirty separate recommendations to ensure adequate funding, including: appropriations to offset the impact on the judiciary of new legislation, funding through general appropriations rather than user fees, regular cost-of-living adjustments to judicial salaries, increased pension credit for bankruptcy judges and magistrates who later become Article III judges, increased pay for senior judges, increased resources for nomination and confirmation, increased security for judges, more technology, improved working conditions for court support personnel, and the provision of continuing education for judges.

Deference to a coordinate branch of government cannot explain the judiciary's failure to ask Congress for more judgeships. The judicial establishment shows no reluctance to tell Congress how to legislate in order to improve the quality of justice. Thus the Proposed Long Range Plan suggests that "Congress should refrain from providing federal agency or court jurisdiction over disputes involving economic or personnel relations or personal liability arising in the workplace."[38] The judiciary's willingness to provide officious advice to Congress on proper legislative goals contrasts starkly with its unwillingness to accurately inform Congress of what the judiciary needs to carry out its own mission.

The additional-judgeships-are-too-expensive argument suffers from an even more crucial flaw. Even if the extra capacity were too expensive on some platonic scale, that is a reason for Congress to decline to create the judgeships, but it is not

Public Buildings Service), http://www.gpo.gov/fdsys/pkg/CHRG-109hhrg30653/html/CHRG-109hhrg30653.htm.

34. *Id.*

35. *See* Melinda Henneberger, *Report Assails Cost Overruns for New Court*, N.Y. TIMES, Dec. 14, 1994, at B1, B7; Bob Hohler, *Senate Panel Rips Breyer over Fan Pier*, BOSTON GLOBE, Dec. 15, 1994, at 1; Sydney H. Schanberg, *A Federal Courthouse Fiasco for Foley Square*, NEWSDAY, Dec. 16, 1994, at A53

36. *See* Press Release, Senate Committee on Environment and Public Works, Courthouse Construction Costs (Dec. 15, 1994).

37. PROPOSED LONG RANGE PLAN, *supra* note 5, at 71–86.

38. *Id.* at 29.

a reason for the Judicial Conference to refuse to ask for them. Put somewhat differently, even though Congress may refuse to fund a weapons system, the generals are usually willing to ask for it. Congress certainly has not covered itself with glory by filling federal judicial vacancies promptly. Some judgeships have remained vacant for unconscionably long periods of time.[39] But why should the judges make it easy for Congress to shortchange the judiciary by understating its needs?

In the congressional funding game, each budgetary supplicant emphasizes the paramount importance of its needs to the national welfare, jockeying with the others to increase its slice of the pie. It is then the job of Congress to choose among the competing claims. The budget process thus relies on the judiciary to inform Congress of the resources needed to do the job—not to engage in self-censorship by asking for only a small fraction of the needed positions.[40] If budget cutting is later required because of more pressing national priorities, it is for Congress to weigh the requests of the judiciary, the military, the universities, the farmers, and the nonfarmers, and then to establish national value preferences. The Constitution gives the job of making these comparisons and choices to Congress—not to the courts.

The judiciary's failure to make the appropriate requests is especially damaging because Congress and the public (and even the bar) are largely ignorant of the problems of the courts of appeals. The Judicial Conference's process for generating judgeship requests is intramural and has maintained a very low profile.[41] Further, the judges have reduced the visibility of the need for increased capacity by remaining current. Instead of permitting a scrutiny-provoking backlog to develop, they have adopted the appellate screening (or triage) regime, thus decreasing the quality rather than the quantity of their output. They have screened out of the traditional process those cases that are the least likely to draw the attention of any powerful observer—social security appeals, habeas corpus cases, prisoner civil rights cases, immigration cases, and pro se litigation generally. As a result, Congress lacks the information it needs to perform its budgetary role properly. Under these circumstances, and with other constituencies constantly clamoring for a larger slice of the budgetary pie, Congress is unlikely to notice, on its own, the need for more judgeships in the courts of appeals.

In the end, of course, the question comes down to the quality of justice that the nation can afford. Economic efficiency has never been the only goal sought by American law; surely we would prize racial equality even if doing so were costly and inefficient. That does not mean racial justice will be sought at any price, but it does mean that Pareto optimality is not the only goal. The trade-off between justice and efficiency (and all of the other demands on the nation's budget) is, of

39. Carl Tobias, Symposium: *Federal Judicial Selection in the New Millennium*, 36 U.C. Davis L. Rev. 721 (2003).

40. In 2009, the Judicial Conference asked Congress to create twelve additional circuit judgeships instead of the nearly fifty called for by the Conference's own staffing model.

41. *See supra* chapter 11.

course, one for Congress to make. Moreover, that trade-off is exactly the kind of "polycentric" decision that courts are ill-equipped to handle.[42] And yet, the Judicial Conference's rules for making judgeship requests and the circuit courts' adoption of the Appellate Triage regime have made the judiciary, rather than Congress, the decision maker concerning how much appellate justice can be dispensed and how the limited supply should be apportioned.

C. UNSTABLE LAW: THE GREAT RED HERRING

One of the principal reasons cited in opposition to increases in appellate capacity is that more judges will lead to instability in the law.[43] According to this argument, if Congress adds judgeships to existing circuits, the circuit courts will decide more cases, and the law of the circuit will become muddled by "so many uncoordinated opinions from so many judges."[44] Furthermore, the argument goes, adding judges to a given circuit increases geometrically the total number of permutations of three-judge panels,[45] and thus increases the unpredictability of outcomes within that circuit. Unpredictability, in turn, promotes a higher rate of appeal as losing litigants find it increasingly worthwhile to "take their chances" by appealing. Thus, more judges means more appeals.[46]

Alternatively, Congress could add capacity and avoid intracircuit inconsistency by adding more circuits, however, anti-expansionists contend that doing so would increase intercircuit conflicts, which already are too numerous for the Supreme Court to resolve.[47] No matter how Congress adds more judges, increased capacity means more decisions. And those opposed to increased appellate capacity vehemently argue that the excess decisions will overwhelm the capacity of commentators to monitor and evaluate them, to the advantage of wealthy litigants who

42. Lon L. Fuller, *The Forms and Limits of Adjudication*, 92 HARV. L. REV. 353, 394–404 (1978).

43. *See* BAKER, *supra* note 23, at 206–07; Stephen Breyer, *Administering Justice in the First Circuit*, 24 SUFFOLK L. REV. 29, 37–40 (1990); Newman, *supra* note 4, at 188; Gerald B. Tjoflat, *More Judges, Less Justice*, 79 A.B.A. J. 70 (July 1993).

44. FED. COURTS STUDY COMM., JUDICIAL CONFERENCE OF THE UNITED STATES, REPORT OF THE FEDERAL COURTS STUDY COMMITTEE 114 (1990) [hereinafter REPORT OF THE FEDERAL COURTS STUDY COMMITTEE].

45. *See also* Frank A. Kaufman et al., Report of the American Bar Association Standing Committee on Federal Judicial Improvements, *reprinted in* The United States Courts of Appeals: Reexamining Structure and Process after a Century of Growth, 125 F.R.D. 523, 541 (1989) [hereinafter ABA Report]; Tjoflat, *supra* note 43, at 71–72.

46. BAKER, *supra* note 23 at 211; Tjoflat, *supra* note 43, at 71.

47. REPORT OF THE FEDERAL COURTS STUDY COMMITTEE, *supra* note 44, at 7; Newman, *supra* note 4, at 188. Bills in both Houses of Congress have been introduced to split the Ninth Circuit in two, thus creating an additional circuit, the Twelfth. But as of this writing, Congress has not acted definitively.

can afford to keep track of the burgeoning law and against poor litigants who cannot.[48]

This instability-of-the-law argument, however, is fatally flawed: it runs contrary to the *available empirical evidence and is subject to a powerful reductio ad absurdum* argument. Further, it ignores effective alternatives for reducing inconsistency, and it radically underestimates the costs of the present system of two-track justice.

1. Inconsistency and Circuit Size

The first of many problems with the instability-of-the-law argument is that its crucial premises lack any empirical support. There simply is no evidence that increasing the number of judgeships within a circuit reduces the stability of circuit law or increases the rate of appeal. Nor is there any evidence that increasing the number of circuits will create a serious problem of unresolved intercircuit conflicts. Indeed, the data suggest precisely the contrary.

The available evidence suggests that intracircuit inconsistency is neither a serious problem nor a function of the number of judges within the circuit. The data on these issues come from three major studies: an opinion study performed by the Federal Judicial Center in response to a Congressional mandate,[49] an A.B.A. study of circuit size,[50] and a series of case studies of the Ninth Circuit commissioned by the Executive Committee of the Ninth Circuit Conference.[51]

More than 1,400 federal judges responded to the Federal Judicial Center opinion study,[52] including 81 percent of active circuit judges and 83 percent of active district judges; the study reported that 80 percent of the responding circuit judges believed that lack of clear circuit precedent was a small or nonexistent problem. The highest percentage of judges expressing concern came from the Sixth Circuit (thirteen authorized judgeships) and the next highest from the Ninth (twenty-seven judgeships). Because circuit judges might understate the problem in order to defend their own work, the responses of the district judges are even more interesting. Sixty-eight percent of the district judges considered the problem of unclear circuit precedent to be small or nonexistent. The highest percentage of district judges expressing dissatisfaction came from the Ninth Circuit (the nation's largest), but the next highest

48. Breyer, *supra* note 43, at 39–40.

49. Federal Courts Study Committee Implementation Act of 1990, § 302(c).

50. *See Report on Federal Circuit Size,* APPELLATE PRAC. J. & UPDATE 3 (Winter 1993).

51. RESTRUCTURING JUSTICE (Arthur D. Hellman ed., 1990). *See also* Arthur D. Hellman, *Breaking the Banc: The Common Law Process in the Large Appellate Court,* 23 ARIZ. ST. L.J. 915 (1991) [hereinafter *Breaking the Banc*]; Arthur D. Hellman, *Jumboism and Jurisprudence: The Theory and Practices of Precedent in the Large Appellate Court,* 56 U. CHI. L. REV. 541 (1989) [hereinafter *Jumboism and Jurisprudence*].

52. JUDITH A. MCKENNA, FED. JUDICIAL CTR., STRUCTURAL AND OTHER ALTERNATIVES FOR THE FEDERAL COURTS OF APPEALS 2, 93–94 (1993).

came from the First Circuit (the nation's smallest, with only six authorized circuit judgeships). These results suggest that unclear precedent is not the problem that opponents of additional judgeships suppose, and moreover that there is no clear correlation between circuit size and perceptions of uncertainty.

The A.B.A. study was conducted by the Appellate Practice Committee's Subcommittee to Study Circuit Size. The subcommittee, composed of experienced appellate advocates, found "no evidence that a larger circuit necessarily causes significantly more intra-circuit conflict than a circuit of ten to fifteen judges." Accordingly, the "Subcommittee found no compelling reasons why circuit courts of various sizes—ranging from a few judges to fifty—cannot effectively meet the caseload challenge. Indeed for every argument in favor of smaller circuits, there is an equally compelling argument for larger circuits."[53]

The Ninth Circuit case studies, conducted by Professor Arthur Hellman, examined inconsistency of circuit precedent and unpredictability of decisions. Hellman examined a sample of one-fifth of the published opinions of the Ninth Circuit for 1983 and 1986.[54] He found little evidence of intracircuit conflict. In about half of the cases, there was no evidence of any contrary precedent within the circuit. When arguably contrary precedents did exist, they typically supplied only oblique support for the losing litigant's position. Even when the contrary precedent offered direct support for the losing litigant, the panel was usually able to distinguish clearly between the sample case and the contrary precedent. Most examples of inconsistency dealt with issues governed by fact-specific, multifactor, or indeterminate legal standards such as probable cause for an arrest, personal jurisdiction over a nonresident, or "rule of reason" cases. Professor Hellman concluded that these issues were likely to cause unpredictability regardless of the number of applicable precedents and, therefore, regardless of circuit size.

In a further effort to gauge uncertainty in the law of the circuit, Hellman examined separate dissenting and concurring opinions on 172 issues in the sample,[55] reasoning that such opinions were good markers of issues on which the composition of the panel could produce uncertainty of outcome. His analysis led him to conclude that the primary cause of unpredictable outcomes in the Ninth Circuit was not "a plethora of circuit precedents that point in different directions." When the panel split on the content of circuit law, the judges typically considered the same two or three relevant cases. Often the disagreements did not involve circuit precedent at all, but rather the interpretation of new statutory language or legislative history, recent Supreme Court precedent, state law, or the state of the factual record. There

53. *See Report on Federal Circuit Size*, Appellate Prac. J. & Update 3 (Winter 1993).

54. Hellman, *Breaking the Banc*, *supra* note 51, at 920–21; Hellman, *Jumboism and Jurisprudence*, *supra* note 51, at 595.

55. Hellman, *Breaking the Banc*, *supra* note 51, at 983.

were few, if any, cases in which the judges looked to conflicting circuit precedent to support their differing conclusions. Hellman concluded:

> In short, what makes for an unpredictable outcome generally is not an oversupply of circuit decisions, but the absence of a circuit precedent that is closely on point or, less commonly, a fact-specific rule of law that by its nature requires case-by-case evaluation. These conditions are no more likely to occur in the large circuit than the small; if anything, they will occur less often in the large circuit because the larger number of decisions increases the odds that there will be a precedent on point.[56]

Hellman's conclusion resonates powerfully with experience and common sense. The bitter truth known to all who do any legal research is that there is not too much law, but rather too little. Consider the law of discovery. A glance at standard treatises or casebooks reveals that many discovery issues lack any precedent at all, and that most of the decisional law comes from the district courts. Attorneys and trial judges dealing with these issues would find some guidance from the appellate courts very helpful. If having more judges leads to more precedents, trial attorneys surely would welcome that outcome. Even when there is some law, more law reinforces and clarifies the rule, and thereby makes it more certain. If there is only one circuit court opinion on an issue, another court might well feel justified in reaching a different result. However, if several panels or circuits have spoken on different variations of the issue, it will be the rare court that will take a different path. In short, having more judges will make the law more stable, not less so.

Justice Breyer[57] has advanced three variations of the unstable law argument. First, he argues that too many decisions, even if they do not produce a direct conflict between abstract legal rules, can produce uncertainty by the effect that such decisions have on "other sorts of rules, rules that grow out of the facts at hand, that arise out of the use of an example." But again, Hellman's empirical findings contradict this argument. A review of Hellman's study shows that his view of "inconsistency" is not limited to abstract legal rules, but also encompasses highly specific, fact-based rules. Indeed, his point seems even stronger in such cases; because more decisions will encompass more factual variations and examples, the law will become more, not less clear.[58]

Breyer's second argument is that more opinions will swamp the efforts of those who might criticize them. This argument is well meant but fifty years too late. The time has long since passed when even a tiny fraction of appellate decisions could receive serious scholarly attention. Further, the proliferation of specialty and practice-oriented journals and newsletters and looseleaf services means that inconsistency will not often go unnoticed.

56. *Id.* at 984.
57. Breyer, *supra* note 43, at 39.
58. Hellman, *supra* note 51, at 984.

Breyer's third argument focuses on fairness.[59] He suggests that only large law firms and institutional litigants will have the resources necessary to locate and analyze the vast, new body of law. This argument would be troubling if true. However, computer-based research tools have leveled the playing field considerably. Even if access is not equal, Breyer's argument overlooks the basic fact that more law will benefit those with scarce resources. Without clear circuit precedent on point, an advocate must guess at the law—by drawing analogies or extending dicta, by researching the law of other jurisdictions, or by reading treatises and law reviews. That is an expensive task, especially when compared to looking up existing pieces of black-letter law. Thus, research in the absence of precedent within the circuit requires much more time, expense, and resources than are often available to the small or rural practitioner.

2. Appeal Rates, Reversal Rates, and Circuit Size

A variation on the unstable law argument asserts that increasing the number of judges on a circuit court would create instability in the law of the circuit and that this instability in turn would increase the rate of appeals. The reasoning behind this argument is that because instability in the law of the circuit translates into unpredictable outcomes, appellants will "take their chances" that one of the many possible three-judge panels will reverse their trial court defeat.[60] Increasing the number of circuit court judgeships would therefore increase, rather than decrease, the workload of the courts. Proponents of this argument cite the increase in national appeal rates that has accompanied the steady growth in appellate judgeships. They point out that in 1950 (when there were 64 circuit judgeships), only one in forty district court terminations resulted in an appeal, while in 1989 (judgeships having increased to 165), the appeal rate was one in eight.[61]

This argument is a classic example of the logical fallacy: *post hoc ergo propter hoc* (i.e., if x precedes y, then x must have caused y). To see the point clearly, consider that although the number of judgeships has increased in the last thirty years, other changes in the federal appellate courts have also occurred. In that same time period, for instance, the average height of circuit judges (adjusted for gender) has increased.

59. Breyer, *supra* note 43, at 40.

60. *See, e.g.*, Tjoflat, *supra* note 43, at 71. Unanimous reversal rates apparently do show some correlation with circuit size, but oddly are inversely correlated with the courts' workloads (cases per judgeship). *See* Kevin M. Scott, *Understanding Judicial Hierarchy: Reversals and the Behavior of Intermediate Appellate Judges*, 40 LAW & SOC'Y REV. 163, 172–173 (2006). *But see* Stefanie A. Lindquist, *Bureaucratization and Balkanization: The Origins and Effects of Decision-Making Norms in the Federal Appellate Courts*, 41 U. RICH. L. REV. 659, 666 (2007).

61. BAKER, *supra* note 23, at 211.

Absent some clear causal mechanism, it makes no more sense to attribute accelerated appeal rates to additional judgeships than to increased judicial altitude. Not every correlation is a cause.

More enlightening than the historical correlation of appeal rates and appellate judgeships is a comparison of current appeal rates in circuits of various sizes. If the more-judges-creates-more-appeals argument is valid, we should expect to see a relationship between circuit size and appeal rates. In fact, however, no such correlation exists.[62] A comparison of the appeal rates of the circuits for 2009 shows the D.C. Circuit (twelve judges) to have the highest rate of appeal (52 percent) and the Third Circuit (fourteen judges) to have the lowest (8.6 percent). The largest circuit (the Ninth with twenty-eight judges) does have a high appeal rate (39 percent), but the D.C. Circuit with the highest rate of appeal (52 percent) is not large (eleven judgeships), nor are the First (six judgeships) and Second Circuits (thirteen judgeships), which have the next highest appeal rates (29 percent) after the D.C. and Ninth Circuits.

Another, and perhaps better, measure of "instability" in circuit law might be district court reversal rates, but here again there is no support for the large-courts-make-for-muddled-law argument. Thus for 2009, reversal rates show only a very weak correlation with number of circuit judgeships.[63] The Fourth Circuit, the fourth largest (with sixteen judgeships), has the lowest reversal rate (4.2 percent), and the smallest of the circuits (the First with only six judgeships) has a rate that is nearly twice as high (8.9 percent). The Ninth Circuit (twenty-nine judgeships) is almost twice as large as the Sixth (sixteen judgeships), yet the two have nearly identical reversal rates (10.9 and 10.7 percent respectively). And the Seventh Circuit with eleven judgeships has a reversal rate almost double that of the Tenth Circuit with twelve judgeships (13.2 and 6.8 percent respectively). These two sets of intercourt comparisons (rates of appeal and rates of reversal) strongly suggest that increasing the number of judgeships on a circuit court is unlikely to make circuit law more inconsistent or unstable.

So, if the increased size of the federal appellate judiciary is not responsible for the rise in rates of appeal, what is? The largest factor probably has been the growth in population along with the change in the nation's legal climate, with the forty years between 1950 and 1990 showing the most dramatic developments. During that period, the Supreme Court recognized a criminal defendant's constitutional right to counsel on appeal, legal services became available to a much larger segment of the population, pro se litigation—particularly by state prisoners—increased radically, federal appeals courts began protecting civil rights much more aggressively,

62. Appeal rate equals the number of total district court terminations divided by total circuit court filings. JUDICIAL BUSINESS OF THE UNITED STATES COURTS, tables B, C, D (2009), *available at*. http://www.uscourts.gov/statistics/JudicialBusiness.aspx#5.

63. About .09. Reversal rate equals the total merits terminations divided by total reversals. *See* JUDICIAL BUSINESS OF THE UNITED STATES, tables B, C, and D (2009).

and the substantive law (particularly new state and federal statutes) on many issues changed at unprecedented rates. It seems quite likely that these trends, rather than the increase in circuit judgeships, caused the increase in rates of appeal.

3. Intercircuit Conflict

If Congress fears intracircuit inconsistency, notwithstanding logic and empirical evidence to the contrary, it might be unwilling to add enough judgeships to the existing circuits to meet current needs. Nevertheless, it could still supply the nation with adequate appellate capacity by creating more circuits. Creating four additional circuits of ten judges each would produce forty new judgeships, almost exactly the number required to meet the Judicial Conference's staffing model of five hundred filings per three-judge panel.[64] Opponents[65] of this solution see it merely as a trade of one kind of inconsistency for another. They contend that although intracircuit conflict will not increase, intercircuit conflicts will multiply far beyond the Supreme Court's already inadequate capacity to resolve them.[66]

Once again, there is no empirical evidence to support the claim. Indeed the very limited, and now dated, empirical evidence suggests otherwise. The evidence consists of another study conducted by Professor Hellman, commissioned by the Federal Judicial Center pursuant to Congressional request.[67] Hellman examined litigants' claims of intercircuit conflict in *certiorari* petitions in order to determine the prevalence of conflicts, their tolerability, and their persistence over time. Following the suggestions of Congress and the Federal Courts Study Committee, Hellman broke down the tolerability standard into four criteria. He considered whether the conflict:

> (1) imposes economic costs or other harm on persons engaging in interstate commerce; (2) encourages forum shopping among circuits; (3) creates unfairness to litigants in different circuits, as in allowing Federal benefits in one circuit that are denied in other circuits; or (4) encourages non-acquiescence by Federal agencies in the holdings of the courts of appeals for different circuits . . . .[68]

64. See chapter 11, *supra*.

65. *See, e.g.*, Thomas G. Gee, *The Imminent Destruction of the Fifth Circuit: Or, How Not to Deal With a Blossoming Docket*, 9 TEX. TECH. L. REV. 799 (1978); John Minor Wisdom, *Requiem for a Great Court*, 26 LOY. L. REV. 787 (1980).

66. *See* BAKER, *supra* note 23, at 218; Newman, *supra* note 4, at 188.

67. *See* ARTHUR D. HELLMAN, FED. JUDICIAL CTR., UNRESOLVED INTERCIRCUIT CONFLICTS: THE NATURE AND SCOPE OF THE PROBLEM iii (1994). In making its request for the study, Congress followed the recommendation of the Federal Courts Study Committee. *See* REPORT OF THE FEDERAL COURTS STUDY COMMITTEE, *supra* note 44, at 124–25.

68. *Id.* at 123. The standards appear in REPORT OF THE FEDERAL COURTS STUDY COMMITTEE, *supra* note 44, at 125.

With the criteria in mind, Hellman developed a definition of a "tolerable conflict." A conflict was "tolerable" if it had not "resulted in differential treatment of similarly situated litigants in different parts of the country"—that is, if it had not led to contrary outcomes in subsequent cases.[69] To measure "persistence," he used the hypothesis that a conflict was not persistent if litigants stopped raising the relevant issue, one of the conflicting circuits overruled its prior "conflicting" position, the Supreme Court later resolved the questions, or subsequent legislation mooted the issue.[70]

Hellman studied 142 issues on which the Supreme Court denied review in the 1984 and 1985 Terms, despite the existence of an intercircuit conflict. Of these, he found that the persistence and tolerability tests eliminated all but forty issues. In other words, he found only forty conflicts in two Terms that "(a) [had] not been put to rest by a subsequent Supreme Court decision or otherwise; (b) [had] continued to generate litigation; and (c) [had] controlled outcomes in one or more reported cases."[71] Further, he noted that the Supreme Court had ample room on its docket to resolve those conflicts. He noted that in 1991, for example, the Court issued only 110 plenary decisions compared with an average of 153 in the 1981–1986 Terms.[72] The study shows not only that unresolved intercircuit conflict is not a serious problem, but also that the creation of several more circuits is not likely to make it one. The absolute number of persistent, intolerable unresolved conflicts is low, and the Supreme Court has ample capacity to resolve them.[73] Perhaps the addition of several new circuits might increase the number of conflicts, but the absolute number would still be low, and in a nationwide common law system it is unrealistic to insist on a "zero-tolerance" policy for conflict.

Thus, the empirical evidence against the inconsistency argument is very strong—really, one-sided. The data also are so well known that reliance on the argument by the judicial establishment (all sophisticated federal judges) seems almost perverse.

4. ***Reductio Ad Absurdum*: The Trade-Off between Consistency and Capacity**

Even if we assume, in spite of the currently available empirical evidence, that new judgeships will produce significant intracircuit or intercircuit inconsistency, it still does not follow that Congress should refuse to create them. The logical leap from

69. HELLMAN, *supra* note 67, at 113.
70. *Id.* at 105–12.
71. *Id.* at 120.
72. *Id.* at 121.
73. The capacity of the Supreme Court to resolve these conflicts actually may have grown over time. During the October Term 2009, the Court only decided seventy cases, reflecting a persistent decrease in caseload that suggests that intercircuit conflicts are decreasing.

new-judgeships-increase-inconsistency to create-no-new-judgeships is vulnerable to a powerful *reduction ad absurdum* attack. If consistency is the paramount goal of the judicial process, and fewer judgeships mean more consistency, Congress should *reduce* the number of authorized judgeships. At the very least, Congress should not have increased judgeships from the 1960 total of 68 to the current total of 179.

Yet the consequences of such a zero-growth policy would have been disastrous. Today, the circuit courts can keep current by giving full appellate process (oral argument, conference, and published, judge-authored opinion) to less than a fifth of their caseload; the remainder get no argument, no conference, and a cursory, unpublished opinion drafted by staff attorneys. If Congress had stood pat at the 1960 level of 68 judgeships, less than 10 percent of today's appellate cases would receive the traditional appellate process, with the remainder handled bureaucratically. To push the absurdity even further, if fewer judgeships means greater consistency, why not have a single three-judge panel for the nation, an option that would eliminate all uncertainty.

The answer, of course, is that consistency is not the only goal. At least as important as consistency is adequate capacity. The system needs enough judges not only to decide the cases carefully and correctly, but also to convince the litigants, the bar, and the public that each case gets the personal attention and reasoned deliberation of Article III judges. Thus, even if we assume (counterfactually) that expansion generates inconsistency, we have proved only that adequate capacity on the one hand and legal consistency on the other are competing values that must be balanced against each other, not that judgeships should be frozen at current levels.

Where then to strike the balance? In order to answer that question, we would need to know much more than we now know (or even presume to know) about the relationship between additional judgeships and legal inconsistency. Is there a straight-line correlation, with consistency decreasing proportionately to the number of new judges, or are there gradual slopes and sudden drop-offs in the curve? It is crucial to know the answer in order to generate the maximum amount of both consistency and capacity. Otherwise, there is no reason to prefer one balance of the competing goals over another. The current balance of having enough judges to give traditional appellate process only to cases involving interesting issues, high economic stakes, or powerful parties seems to satisfy the judges, but without much more data, we cannot defend it as an optimal trade-off for the courts' many other constituencies.

In the absence of data on the purported correlation, the issue turns on the burden of proof. Should that burden fall on the proponents or opponents of additional judgeships? Two arguments show that the burden belongs on the opponents. The first of these is based on the difference between known versus unknown costs and benefits. In this case, the known benefit is the traditional appellate process. The traditional appellate process with substantial personal attention by the judges to each case made the federal appellate courts great. In Judge Wyzanski's' words:

> When Brandeis understood all that there was to know about the facts, he himself … prepared his own statement of his findings and conclusions. I will remember a remark a

Justice made to me when I first entered the public service: "The reason the public thinks so much of the Justices of the Supreme Court is that they are almost the only people in Washington who do their own work."[74]

From the earliest days, federal appellate judges heard oral argument, conferred with each other, and gave reasons (oral or written) for their decisions. The reasoned decisions then served as precedent in later cases. This traditional process persisted until the 1960s when the increases in caseloads began to outstrip the growth in judgeships. Although the courts were able to compensate by becoming more bureaucratic, no one argues that bureaucratic appellate justice is intrinsically better than the traditional model. Accordingly, the burden of proof on the inconsistency/capacity trade-off belongs on those who would make permanent the change from the traditional to the bureaucratic model.

In other words, we ought not give up the proven benefits of the Learned Hand model without a very good reason. Avoiding losses in certainty and consistency might qualify as a good reason if we could be sure they would occur and we could know their orders of magnitude. It makes no sense, however, to suffer the known evil of increased bureaucratization in return for a dividend of increased consistency that is completely speculative in amount and proportion.

The second reason that the burden of proof should fall on the opponents of expansion is based on distributive justice, which deals with the allocation of costs and benefits among members of society.[75] Appellate justice—a governmental service—is not distributed evenly under the current two-track system of appellate review. Wealthy, powerful, institutional, and governmental litigants get far more of the judges' time and attention than do other litigants. Favoring consistency over capacity by restricting the number of new judgeships increases that discrepancy.

Moreover, "important" litigants are much more likely to spread out their operations geographically and to make repeated use of the appellate system over time. Thus, gains in consistency are very important to them. Consistency does not loom so large, however, for other more local, one-time litigants. Gains in capacity, on the other hand, favor poorer, weaker litigants because additional judicial capacity will increase their chances of receiving the personal attention of Article III judges.

Favoring consistency over capacity by limiting the number of judges thus sacrifices the interests of weaker litigants in favor of the interests of more powerful litigants, who already receive a disproportionate share of society's appellate resources. The current system of rationing appellate justice already favors wealthy and powerful litigants because their cases are less likely to be "screened" out of the traditional appellate process and handled via the Track Two method. Restricting

74. *See, e.g.*, CHARLES E. WYZANSKI JR., WHEREAS—A JUDGE'S PREMISES 61 (1965).
75. R.W.M. DIAS, JURISPRUDENCE 66 (4th ed. 1976).

judicial expansion merely exacerbates the current distributional discrepancy and thus violates fundamental democratic values.

5. Increasing Capacity without Losing Consistency

The increased-inconsistency argument against adding appellate capacity relies on the twin premises that (1) creating more judgeships leads to inconsistency and (2) legal consistency is our appellate system's paramount value. The preceding sections have shown that each of those premises is highly dubious. But what if we assume them to be true, does it then follow that Congress should not supply the new positions? It does not, because there are ways to safeguard consistency without permanently limiting the nation's appellate capacity. In other words, there are strategies, not yet tried, that could minimize inconsistency even if the appellate bench were considerably larger than it is now. Thus, a sensible response to the Federal Courts Study Committee's concern about "so many uncoordinated opinions from so many judges"[76] is to supply some additional coordination. The coordinating devices can be divided into those that avoid inconsistency and those that resolve it.

a. Avoidance: Better Drafting of Legislation and Judicial Opinions

Among the easiest ways to avoid inconsistency is to cut it off at its legislative source. The courts of appeals devote substantial time and effort to litigation dealing with issues of statutory construction. Statutes can be unclear or ambiguous for a variety of reasons. Sometimes the ambiguity is an intentional political compromise, but just as often it results from poor drafting and lack of foresight.

A recent notorious example of poor legislative drafting is the Supplemental Jurisdiction Statute,[77] which was designed to codify the results of *United Mine Workers v. Gibbs*[78] and *Owen Equipment and Erection Corp. v. Kroger*,[79] and also to overrule both *Finley v. United States*[80] and *Aldinger v. Howard*.[81] The idea was to permit pendent claim and pendent party jurisdiction in federal question cases but not to permit the doctrine of supplemental jurisdiction to change the rule on the complete diversity requirement or the amount in controversy requirement. Unfortunately, when Congress drafted § 1367(b), it was careless. In the section of

76. Report of the Federal Courts Study Committee, *supra* note 44, at 114.
77. 28 U.S.C. § 1367.
78. 383 U.S. 715 (1966).
79. 437 U.S. 365 (1978).
80. 490 U.S. 545 (1989).
81. 427 U.S. 1 (1976).

the statute controlling supplemental jurisdiction over claims added by plaintiffs, it specifically mentioned Federal Rules 14, 19, and 20 but omitted Rule 23; and in the section controlling other supplemental claims, it mentioned Rules 19 and 24 but omitted Rule 20.

Under the literal interpretation of the statute, these two omissions, both probably inadvertent, had the unintended consequence of overturning the jurisdictional amount aggregation rules of *Snyder v. Harris*[82] and *Zahn v. International Paper Co.*,[83] which had required that each of multiple plaintiffs separately satisfy the amount-in-controversy requirement of 28 U.S.C. § 1332. The upshot of the drafting glitch was ten additional and conflicting circuit court decisions: three by the First,[84] Third[85] and Tenth[86] Circuits (adopting the view that Congress had not intended to change the aggregation rule); and seven by the Fourth,[87] Fifth,[88] Sixth,[89] Seventh,[90] Ninth,[91] and Eleventh[92] (reading the plain language of the statute). Finally, the Supreme Court resolved the conflict in a case[93] that split the justices five to four on the perennial dilemma of statutory construction question: "plain meaning" versus "legislative intent."[94]

Congress could short-circuit statutory ambiguities before they produced inconsistent interpretations in the courts. As certain as death and taxes, for instance, is litigation to determine whether a new statute should apply retroactively, whether it should preempt state law, whether a private right of action is intended, and what the appropriate limitations period should be. These issues, as well as many others, turn entirely on legislative intent, and Congress could forestall later litigation by resolving them at the outset. To promote this development, the Federal Court Study Committee prepared a checklist of statutory construction issues for use by congressional committee staffs and the Office of Legislative Counsel in the House and Senate.[95] A further step toward coordination would be the creation of a "second look" congressional committee or office to review the progress of new legislation in

82. 394 U.S. 332 (1969).
83. 414 U.S. 291 (1973).
84. Ortega v. Star-Kist Foods, Inc., 370 F.3d 124 (1st Cir 2004).
85. Meritcare Inc. v. St. Paul Mercury Ins. Co., 166 F.3d 214, 222 (3d Cir. 1999).
86. Leonhardt v. Western Sugar Co., 160 F.3d 631, 641 (10th Cir. 1998).
87. Rosmer v. Pfizer, Inc., 263 F.3d 110 (4th Cir. 2001).
88. Free v. Abbott Lab. (*In re* Abbott Lab.), 51 F.3d 524, 529 (5th Cir. 1995).
89. Olden v. LaFarge Corp., 383 F.3d 495 (6th Cir. 2004).
90. Stromberg Metal Works, Inc. v. Press Mech., Inc., 77 F.3d 928, 930 (7th Cir. 1996); *In re* Brand Name Prescription Drugs Antitrust Litig., 123 F.3d 599 (7th Cir. 1997).
91. Gibson v. Chrysler Corp., 261 F.3d 927 (9th Cir. 2001).
92. Allapattah Servs., Inc. v. Exxon Corp., 333 F.3d 1248 (11th Cir. 2003).
93. Exxon Mobil Corp. v. Allapattah Servs., Inc. 545 U.S. 546 (2005).
94. *Id.* A majority of Justices—Kennedy, Rehnquist, Scalia, Thomas, and Souter—favored the plain meaning approach, and a dissenting minority of Justices—Ginsburg, Stevens, O'Connor, and Breyer—opted for the legislative intent theory.
95. Report of the Federal Courts Study Committee, *supra* note 44, at 91.

the courts. The goal would be to identify litigated issues that result from ambiguity or poor drafting and to resolve them in subsequent corrective legislation.[96]

Some circuits—the D.C., First, Third, Seventh, and Tenth Circuits—have experimented with this type of solution. Staff attorneys review slip opinions for cases involving statutes whose drafting glitches have produced troublesome issues of congressional intent. The court reviews these cases and selects the most appropriate ones to be forwarded to the appropriate congressional offices and committees.[97]

Another way to cut off inconsistency at its source is to clean up judicial opinions. Voices within the courts—Judge Posner prominent among them—have begun to notice that opinions are growing longer, more prolix, and overloaded with dicta and string citations.[98] Longer opinions may serve to increase the scholarly reputation of the court or the prestige of individual judges, but prolixity has its price. It increases the prevalence of poorly thought-out and extraneous dicta, general propositions quoted out of context, and needless rehearsals of basic propositions. These in turn increase the likelihood of lower court confusion and of the appearance of inconsistent precedent, when the extraneous verbiage of one bloated opinion differs from that of another. Thus cleaner, clearer, shorter opinions not only reduce law-making inconsistency, but also advance the circuit courts' central error-correction mission.

Judge Posner has ascribed the deterioration of judicial opinion writing in part to the proliferation of law clerks and staff attorneys.[99] If he is right, the ironic result is that the circuit courts have created a judicial perpetual motion machine: more clerks are needed to deal with more apparent inconsistencies created by more clerks. At bottom, the problem results from the courts' poor balancing of their two principal functions: error correction and law declaration. Disdaining cases involving only claims of error, the judges have left them largely to the staff, allowing the judges to concentrate more and more of their attention on the few "significant" cases that implicate the courts' law-making role. Professors Carrington and Cramton correctly observe that there is "a sense on the part of at least some circuit judges that lawmaking as mini-supreme court justices, or semi-super-legislators, may be the primary duty and concern of federal circuit judges."[100] Both sets of cases suffer as a result, the "trivial" appeals from too little judicial attention and the "important" cases from too much. Simply redressing this mistaken balance between the courts, two principal roles would go a long way toward reducing any inconsistency that might result from increasing the system's capacity.

96. *See* Ruth Bader Ginsburg, *A Plea for Legislative Review*, 60 S. CAL. L. REV. 995, 1012 (1987); Ruth Bader Ginsburg & Peter W. Huber, *The Intercircuit Committee*, 100 HARV. L. REV. 1417 (1987).

97. *See* BAKER, *supra* note 23, at 225–26.

98. *See, e.g.*, POSNER, *supra* note 14, at 108–09.

99. *Id.*

100. Paul D. Carrington & Roger C. Cramton, *Judicial Independence in Excess. Reviving the Judicial Duty of the Supreme Court*, 94 CORNELL L. REV. 587, 621–22 (2009).

b. Better Communication

Another relatively cost-free mechanism to limit inconsistency is to increase communication among circuit judges. The job of a circuit judge is a lonely one. With the notable exceptions of the D.C. Circuit and the Federal Circuit, the judges on most courts are geographically isolated with few, if any, colleagues in the same city.[101] Apart from sitting together on three-judge panels and meeting at circuit conferences, their communication is spotty and haphazard.[102] In some circuits, however, they have begun to increase the use of coordinated interchambers communication to avoid inconsistent holdings and dicta.[103]

There are many possible arrangements; the first to be formalized was established by the Ninth Circuit in the early 1980s.[104] Like all circuit courts, the Ninth has an en banc process to resolve intercircuit conflicts and a "first panel" rule, which provides that the first panel decision of an issue binds later panels unless overturned by an en banc decision.[105] Going further in pursuit of doctrinal consistency, the court has been a pioneer in developing an issue inventory system. Initially, staff attorneys "inventory" the case according to detailed issue codes and enter the information into a computer file. When possible, cases raising the same issues are assigned to a single three-judge panel. If that is not possible, panels hearing cases raising the same issue are so informed, and a priority-of-submission rule controls. The panel to which the issue was first submitted has priority, and other panels must await the outcome and follow the precedent established by the first panel.[106] Then, after the filing of the opinion, the panel circulates its opinion to off-panel judges who have a period of time to communicate with panel members. At the court's direction, the staff reviews all published opinions for potential conflicts and can suggest modifications to preserve consistent circuit law.

There are many possible variations on the theme, but the basic idea is that modern information technology can be used to enhance intracircuit communication and thus reduce the likelihood of inconsistency without restricting circuit size. This was true in the late 1970s when information technology consisted of note-card files and typewriters. Today, computer logging and classification of issues, cases, and parties, and the ability to conduct word searches in seconds across massive amounts of text should make consistency easy to attain. After all, law firms with thousands of

101. *See* Stephen L. Wasby, *Internal Communication in the Eighth Circuit Court of Appeals*, 58 Wash. U. L.Q. 583, 598 (1980).

102. *Id.* at 586–92.

103. *See generally* Jonathan M. Cohen, Inside Appellate Courts ch. 5 (2002).

104. Arthur D. Hellman, *Central Staff in Appellate Courts: The Experience of the Ninth Circuit*, 68 Calif. L. Rev. 937, 957–64.

105. Restructuring Justice 56 (Arthur D. Hellman ed., 1990).

106. *Id.* 58–59.

lawyers spread all over the world are able to use such systems to avoid conflicts of interest. It is difficult to see why appellate consistency should be any more resistant to technological solution.

c. Specialized Courts, Specialized Panels[107]

Specialized subject matter courts in the federal appellate system are courts of nation-wide jurisdiction over particular types of appeals and are staffed by a stable corps of judges. Examples in this country are the Court of Appeals for the Federal Circuit, the Temporary Emergency Court of Appeals, the Court of Military Appeals, and the United States Foreign Intelligence Surveillance Court of Review.[108] In other systems, specialized appellate courts and panels are the rule rather than the exception,[109] but our federal system has a prejudice against creating them *de jure*.

Apparently, that prejudice does not extend to courts or panels that have become specialized de facto. For instance, in 2007, the Second, Fifth, and Ninth Circuits had forty-nine appeals in securities cases brought by the government, while the remaining nine circuits had a total of thirteen; the Fifth Circuit had thirty-four marine injury appeals, while four circuits had none; the Ninth Circuit had fifty-eight appeals in environmental cases against the government, while eight circuits had fewer than eight.[110] And the Fifth Circuit assigns oil and gas cases to a special panel of several judges who have developed expertise in the area.[111]

There is also de facto specialization at the level of the individual judge. A recent study of opinion writing practices on the federal courts found significant variations among judges across subject areas.[112] Specialization occurred both positively

107. The literature on specialized courts and panels is extensive. *See, e.g.*, PAUL D. CARRINGTON ET AL., JUSTICE ON APPEAL (1976); Harold H. Bruff, *Specialized Courts in Administrative Law*, 43 ADMIN. L. REV. 329 (1991); Paul D. Carrington, *Crowded Dockets and the Courts of Appeals: The Threat to the Function of Review and the National Law*, 82 HARV. L. REV. 542 (1969); Rochelle Cooper Dreyfuss, *The Federal Circuit: A Case Study in Specialized Courts*, 65 N.Y.U. L. REV. 1 (1989); Erwin N. Griswold, *The Need for a Court of Tax Appeals*, 57 HARV. L. REV. 1153 (1944); Clement F. Haynsworth, *Improving the Handling of Criminal Cases in the Federal Appellate System*, 59 CORNELL L. REV. 597 (1974); Ellen R. Jordan, *Specialized Courts: A Choice*, 76 Nw. U. L. Rev. 745 (1981).

108. For the Federal Circuit, see 28 U.S.C. § 1295; for the Temporary Emergency Court of Appeals, see Economic Stabilization Act of 1970, Pub. L. No. 92–210, 85 Stat. 743, 748–50 (1971). In 1992, Congress abolished the Temporary Emergency Court of Appeals and transferred both its jurisdiction and its pending cases to the U.S. Court of Appeals for the Federal Circuit (106 Stat. 4506). For the Court of Military Appeals, see 10 U.S.C. § 867 (1994); for the FISA Court of Review, see the Foreign Intelligence Surveillance Act of 1978, 50 U.S.C. § 1803.

109. *See generally* Daniel J. Meador, *A Challenge to Judicial Architecture: Modifying the Regional Design of the U. S. Courts of Appeals*, 56 U. CHI. L. REV. 603, 610 (1989) [hereinafter *Judicial Architecture*] (describing Pennsylvania system); Daniel J. Meador, *An Appellate Court Dilemma and a Solution through Subject Matter Jurisdiction*, 16 MICH. J. L. REF. 471, 475–76 (1983) [hereinafter *An Appellate Court Dilemma*] (describing German and English systems).

110. JUDICIAL BUSINESS OF THE UNITED STATES COURTS, table B7 (2010).

111. *See* Meador, *An Appellate Court Dilemma*, *supra* note 109, at 477.

112. Edward K. Cheng, *The Myth of the Generalist Judge*, 61 STAN. L. REV. 519 (2008).

(judges who wrote a disproportionately large share of opinions in cases of a particular type) and negatively (judges who seldom wrote opinions in certain subject areas). Some of the observed specialization was predictable, such as Judges Posner and Easterbrook of the Seventh Circuit writing antitrust opinions at higher than random rates; or Judge Harry Edwards (a noted labor law scholar) of the D.C. Circuit authoring many opinions in labor and employment law cases; or Judge Douglass Ginsburg (an expert on telecommunications law), also of the D.C. Circuit, specializing in F.C.C. cases.[113] Other instances were more surprising, with criminal law cases producing the most positive *and* negative specialists. Judges who wrote often in the area typically had significant prosecutorial experience, and judges with extensive academic careers seemed to avoid criminal cases.[114]

The point here is simply that our system has no principled objection to judicial specialization when it serves other goals. Why then not use it to help solve any consistency problem that might result from increasing the number of judgeships. If the more-judges-means-greater-inconsistency thesis is correct, subject matter specialized courts can help avoid inconsistency by reducing the number of precedential decision makers in a particular area of law. Specialized courts could have nationwide jurisdiction. Or specialized panels could be subdivisions of the existing regional courts of appeals, staffed by judges who rotate through subject matter areas for terms of two to five years. In a large court like the Ninth Circuit, for example, the cases could be divided up by subject matter into five major areas, with each area handled by a panel of six judges.

The advantages of specialized panels and courts[115] are expertise, efficiency, and, most important for our purposes, consistency. Judges working in a particular area of the law learn that area well and can supply expert interpretation of the relevant statutes, case law, administrative regulations, and the policies that underlie them. Specialized judges thus work more efficiently and quickly because they do not need to learn the elementary principles of an unfamiliar subject for each new case on the docket. If the growth and inconsistency hypothesis is correct, however, the greatest advantage of specialized panels and courts would be gains in consistency. The use of relatively few decision makers means that opportunities for inconsistent holdings would be minimized and also that members of the bar could rely on a known and predictable bench. Specialized courts and panels thus combine the capacity of a large judiciary with the consistency and coherence of a much smaller one.

Opponents of increasing federal appellate capacity through specialization cite the dangers of capture, tunnel vision, boredom, and loss of prestige.[116] A highly specialized court risks capture, the argument goes, because its judges become familiar with

113. *Id.* at 541–43.
114. *Id.* at 544.
115. *Id.* at 549.
116. Meador, *An Appellate Court Dilemma, supra* note 109, at 482–84.

the specialized practitioners that routinely practice before it. Moreover, its members often will come from a part of the bar that is also specialized and thus predisposed to one view or the other on recurrent issues. Finally, because its decisions are so important to repeat litigants, appointments to the court provoke extreme lobbying efforts.

The problem of tunnel vision occurs when judges see only one particular type of case; they thus lose their perspective as generalists, develop their own jargon, and become accessible only to specialists in the bar. Finally, boredom and lack of prestige, which result from repetitive litigation before the court, ultimately make it difficult to find high-quality nominees

The favorite bête noir of the anti-specialization argument is the Commerce Court, which existed for a few years immediately prior to World War I before it succumbed to all five of the classic specialization difficulties.[117] But its design had failure stamped on it from the start. In particular, its jurisdiction consisted of review of the decisions of a single administrative agency, the Interstate Commerce Commission, which dealt recurrently with a single powerful interest group. These features suggest a substantial risk of capture or at least the risk that the bar and the public would fear its capture. It was the latter that probably caused its downfall.[118]

But there are other happier stories to tell about specialized courts. The Court of Appeals for the Federal Circuit, established by Congress in 1982, seems to function without massive controversy. Learning from the example of the Commerce Court, the Congress avoided overspecialization by supplying the court with "a varied docket spanning a broad range of legal issues,"[119] including customs and patent appeals, appeals from the Claims Court, the Court of International Trade, the International Trade Commission, the Merit Systems Protection Board, and a few other administrative agencies.[120] Moreover, the several types of de facto specialization seem to work without serious problems. From historical precedents such as these, Professor Bruff concludes that history's lesson is not that specialized courts cannot work, but only that "no specialized court should be created to oversee a single agency that deals with a single powerful interest group."[121]

A quick look at the federal appellate docket and the patterns of de facto allocation of cases among judges and between the judges and the staff suggests at least two possible specialized courts or panels. One might be composed of appeals from criminal convictions, from state and federal court denials of post-conviction relief, and cases involving state and federal prisoners' civil rights claims against their jailers. Most of the work on those cases is handled already by different personnel—the staff attorneys, not the judges. Making that subject sequestration *de jure* rather

117. The court's brief and sad history is discussed in Bruff, *supra* note 107, at 335–36.
118. *Id.* at 335–36.
119. H. R. REP. NO. 312, at 19, 31, 97th Cong., 1st Sess. (1981).
120. Bruff, *supra* note 107, at 335.
121. *Id.*

than de facto would guarantee the litigants the attention of accountable, seasoned Article III judges rather than faceless, relatively inexperienced young lawyers.

There is little danger of capture since the nation's prosecutors and its defense bar are both unlikely to invest in expensive lobbying efforts. Some may argue that such a court with a docket limited to such "mundane" matters might not attract enough qualified judicial candidates, but surely that cannot be so. The United States Attorneys and Public Defenders offices contain elite and seasoned lawyers, many of whom seek a lifelong specialty in criminal law. Nor would the docket be so terribly mundane; judges on that court would constitute the primary national law makers in several areas of constitutional law—cruel and unusual punishment, police investigatory conduct, the rights of the accused—as well as the Federal Rules of Evidence.

Another possibility is a special appellate court or special local panels for immigration appeals. In two of our current circuits, the Second and the Ninth, these constitute the fastest growing portion of the docket and the bane of the judges' existence.[122] Moreover, immigration is not a likely target for capture and is an area where national rather than regional solutions are preferable.

The point of these examples of successful specialization is that a little care in the design of a subject matter division system can avoid the classic arguments against specialized courts. The key, of course, is to resist excessively narrow jurisdictional grants. As long as a court has jurisdiction over different types of cases arising in different social contexts, it runs little risk of succumbing to the traditional specialization woes.[123] The response is even easier for specialized panels. Establishing only a few divisions per circuit assures each panel a fairly wide range of cases, and relatively short rotation periods minimize the risks of capture, lobbying, tunnel vision, and boredom.[124]

d. Resolving Inconsistency—Structural Reform

Thus far, we have concentrated on methods to avoid the inconsistencies that supposedly accompany increases in appellate capacity. Another possibility is to resolve any inconsistencies after they appear. That strategy requires, in one form or another, an additional tier in the appellate process. With another level of courts to resolve intercircuit inconsistency, more circuits could be created, allowing each of the circuit courts to remain small enough to minimize intracircuit inconsistency. Further, the resulting pyramidal structure makes sense in light of the dual function

122. Indeed, in those circuits, the staff, if not the judges, already divides the work by subject area. *See* chapter 8, *supra*.

123. *See* Bruff, *supra* note 107, at 341–42; Meador, *An Appellate Court Dilemma*, *supra* note 109, at 483; Meador, *Judicial Architecture*, *supra* note 109, at 632–40.

124. A plausible plan appears in Meador, *An Appellate Court Dilemma*, *supra* note 109, at 489–90.

of intermediate appellate courts. Error correction requires steadily increasing the number of judgeships as caseloads rise. But, according to the more-judges-creates -inconsistency argument, coherent law declaration requires fewer judgeships. The pyramid meets both needs with a relatively broad base to maximize error correction capacity and a smaller upper tier to focus law declaration.

Several different configurations are possible. The Hruska Commission suggested a single national court of appeals staffed by seven or nine life-tenure Article III judges appointed specifically to the court[125]. Another basic model would staff a single national court with judges from the existing circuit courts sitting for relatively short (two- to three-year) rotating terms.[126] Yet another configuration would consist of three or four seven-judge super-circuits, each responsible for reviewing five or six circuit courts, which, in turn, would be staffed by nine or ten judges each.[127] The judges of the super-circuit courts might be specially appointed for life terms or be recruited for rotating terms from among the judges of the circuit courts.[128] A final model, proposed by the White Commission, involves splitting the existing circuits into "divisions."[129]

Regardless of the configuration of the new court(s), a host of functional issues would arise. Would the court sit in panels or en banc; and, if it sat in panels, would there be provision for en banc rehearings? What would be the precedential effect of the decisions of the court(s), and how would the Supreme Court review those decisions? Could the new court overrule itself? Jurisdiction might be by discretionary, or in some cases mandatory, appeal from the circuit courts, by transfer from the circuit courts, or by referral from the Supreme Court. It could encompass all federal questions or instead, focus only on issues in which intercircuit conflicts exist. A functioning plan would require a decision on each of these issues and probably several more as well.

One serious disadvantage attends any plan to create an additional tier of appellate courts. A fourth layer of courts means additional expense and delay *for the litigants*; there would be one more round of briefing, one more round of argument, and months more waiting before final resolution of the case. There are, however, ways to minimize this impact. For instance, some cases could bypass the circuit court level. Thus, if the district judge or the circuit panel certified that the case raised

125. Comm'n on Revision of Fed. Court Appellate Sys., Structure and Internal Procedures: Recommendations for Change, *reprinted in* 67 F.R.D. 195 (1975).

126. Fed. Judicial Ctr., Report of the Study Group on the Caseload of the Supreme Court, *reprinted in* 57 F.R.D. 573 (1972). *See also* Baker, *supra* note 23 at 253–56 (describing the "In Banc Intercircuit Conference"); Warren E. Burger, *Annual Report on the State of the Judiciary*, 66 A.B.A. J. 442 (1983) (recommending an "Intercircuit Panel").

127. Report of the Federal Courts Study Committee, *supra* note 44, at 119–20.

128. For a discussion of this variation, see McKenna, *supra* note 52, at 117–21.

129. Named after Justice Byron White, its chair, the group's formal name was the Commission on Structural Alternatives for the Federal Courts of Appeals. For a complete discussion, see chapter 10, *supra*.

an intercircuit conflict or some other issue likely to require national law making, the case could proceed directly to the national appellate level. Another time-saving measure would be to consolidate briefing on petitions for discretionary review. If the national appellate court declined discretionary review, the submissions to that court would serve as the materials the Supreme Court would review for *certiorari*. In a four-tier system, it might be difficult to entirely eliminate additional delay and expense to the parties, but measures like those suggested could diminish the extra burden substantially.

Another disadvantage to creating an additional tier is that the appointment process could cause a political headache. If a single president appointed all members of the new court, opposition party legislators might object and retard confirmation. Relatively easy solutions to this political problem exist, however. Appointments could be staggered, or, better yet, appointment could be made automatic by seniority among current judges (perhaps subject to executive or legislative veto).

A final and trivial objection is that creation of a higher national tribunal would reduce the prestige of the existing circuit judges. Indeed, opinion surveys show overwhelming opposition from judges.[130] Opposition based on worries about prestige should count for nothing. Courts exist for the benefit of the nation, not the satisfaction of the judges. In the words of Judge Haynsworth:

> [T]hat kind of concern for personal prestige, or the prestige of one's office, can not be permitted to preclude accretions to the system which are necessary to its efficient functioning .... [A]ny reluctance on my part to look up to sixteen judges above me rather than nine should carry little weight.[131]

Suggestions like those in the last two subsections once were all the rage. Numerous appellate reform committees, commissions, studies, and plans called for a National Court of Appeals (by several names including the "intercircuit panel," or "the en banc intercircuit conference"), subdivision or consolidation of circuits, and many other types of restructuring or realigning of the federal appellate courts.[132] It seemed to be an article of faith that massive change and reorganization was inevitable. Remarkably, twenty years after the heyday of the reform proposals, none has been adopted;[133] instead, the judiciary has chosen to retain the comfortable and

130. *See* McKenna, *supra* note 52, at 121.

131. Letter from the Honorable Clement F. Haynsworth to A. Leo Levin (April 30, 1975), *in* 2 *Hearings Before the Commission on Revision of the Federal Court Appellate System*, 94th Cong., 1st Sess. 1327, 1328 (1975), *quoted in* Baker, *supra* note 23, at 251.

132. Paul D. Carrington, *A Critical Assessment of the Cultural and Institutional Roles of Appellate Courts*, 9 J. App. Prac. & Process 231 (2007) (book review); Thomas Baker, *Applied Freakonomics: Explaining the "Crisis of Volume,"* 8 J. App. Prac. & Process 101, 112 (2006); Thomas E. Baker, *A Generation Spent Studying the United States Courts of Appeals: A Chronology*, 34 U.C. Davis L. Rev. 395 (2000).

133. *Id.* 113.

familiar federal appellate structure and deal with the steady increase in caseload by relying more and more on the Appellate Triage regime. It remains to be seen whether that solution will continue until the proportion of cases that the circuit courts afford the traditional appellate process begins to approach the proportion of petitions to which the Supreme Court grants *certiorari.*

e. Structural Reform: Tradition, Proportion, and Inevitability

Any change in the structure of the federal appellate system will require abandoning or modifying some cherished traditions of the federal appellate courts. Indeed, the very notion of structural change requires a departure from the reassuring comfort of the existing order. Nevertheless, if structural alternatives are required to combat any possible inconsistency that supposedly will accompany a radical increase in appellate capacity, the gain will be worth the sacrifice.

What traditions specifically would be imperiled? Increasing appellate capacity by any means entails abandoning the tradition of a small elite federal judiciary. Further specific restructuring strategies threaten other traditions. The increased use of specialized courts or panels, for example, trenches on the historical role of federal judges as generalists. A four-tier system would have the negative effect of raising costs to litigants with additional rounds of briefing and argument and added delay. An additional level also would change the traditional judicial hierarchy, alter career trajectories, and force the Supreme Court to modify its strategy of allowing intercircuit conflicts to "percolate" before deciding to resolve them. Finally, significant increases in the number of circuits, an expedient that might be necessary to prevent the current courts from growing to unwieldy proportions, probably would require reexamining the traditional conventions of circuit alignment. Thus, in a restructuring, it might not be possible for every new circuit to contain at least three contiguous states, or a single state might need to be split between two circuits.

Those traditions of the federal appellate system are familiar and comforting, and it would be foolish to discard them without cause. Nevertheless, as familiar as they are, the threatened traditions are also peripheral. Historically, the central, defining characteristic of the federal appellate courts was that the judges did their own high-quality work. Each case received the personal attention of Article III judges; courts did not "screen" cases or ration justice according to the wealth, power, or prominence of the litigants or the importance of their dispute. That defining characteristic, of course, has been in increasingly serious jeopardy since 1970. Indeed, a whole generation of lawyers and judges has grown up accustomed to the system of Appellate Triage. Subject matter specialization or a four-tier system or an unconventional realignment of circuits could restore this defining characteristic by permitting substantial growth in capacity while retaining legal coherence. If the cost of saving the system's defining characteristic is the abandonment of some peripheral traditions, the price may be high, but it is certainly a worthwhile exchange.

Further, if the more-judges-means-greater-incoherence thesis is correct, the loss of the peripheral traditions is inevitable anyway. Because Congress is not going to reduce federal jurisdiction substantially, caseloads will continue to rise, even if not as steadily and dramatically as they have in the recent past. As they do, the system will seek to accommodate them in one of two ways. First, it could keep the number of judgeships relatively low and increase the use of screening and triage to keep pace. There are, however, political limits to that solution. At some point, Congress, the bench, the bar, and the public will rebel. Those constituencies have remained relatively docile as the courts have increased to 80 percent or more the portion of cases screened out of the traditional appellate process. But will they remain silent as the percentage rises to 90 percent? Perhaps they will, suggesting that basic rights can be eroded if done slowly and surreptitiously.

If not, the only alternative will be to increase the number of judgeships. But then, if the growth and inconsistency hypothesis is correct, the law within and among circuits will become incoherent, and structural change—specialization or a fourth tier or radical realignment—will be required anyway. In the end, both the peripheral and the central traditions of the federal appellate system will be lost. If structural modifications are required to accommodate capacity and consistency, it would be much wiser to make them now while the central value of the system can still be saved.

D. REDUCED COLLEGIALITY

Adding judges, it is sometimes argued, would reduce collegiality, thereby impairing judicial quality. Little detail accompanies this objection, and for good reason. "Collegiality" evokes the mental image of a small group of judges gathered in a library or conference room focusing on a case, trying out arguments, challenging each other's jurisprudential approaches, and, if possible, reaching consensus.[134] Reality is quite different, however; judicial collegiality in that sense appears to be a myth. One study of the Eighth Circuit, for example, found that even among judges on a particular panel, "the memorandum was the most frequently used means of communication."[135]

134. A recent encomium on the virtues of collegiality comes from the estimable Judge Edwards of the D.C. Circuit: *The Effects of Collegiality on Judicial Decision Making*, 151 U. Pa. L. Rev. 1639 (2003). Significantly, Judge Edwards' experience of collegiality has been formed on the D.C. Circuit, the only one of the twelve regional circuits whose judges all have chambers in the same city.

135. Stephen L. Wasby, *Internal Communication in the Eighth Circuit Court of Appeals*, 58 Wash. U. L.Q. 583, 589 (1980). Now, that memorandum probably arrives as an attachment to an e-mail message.

Communication with off-panel judges was "not extensive," and communication involving Track Two cases is nearly nonexistent because they usually involve no conference or, at best, a mass conference at which between thirty and fifty cases are treated in each session.[136] Moreover, the court rarely meets as a group, and individual judges are reluctant to relocate their chambers to circuit headquarters.[137]

The findings of a study of the Eighth Circuit are particularly instructive because they describe the workings of a small court, which had ten active judges at the time of the study.[138] Given judicial perceptions that the number of judges on a court somehow adversely affects communication,[139] the low level of communication in the Eighth Circuit comes as something of a surprise. However, the Eighth Circuit's experience is quite typical. Geographical dispersal of chambers, perhaps more than size, also limits collegiality. Nevertheless, even small size and the situation of chambers in the same city do not assure collegiality. Chief Justice Rehnquist and Chief Judge Wald of the D.C. Circuit, for instance, have both commented on the lack of real interchange at conferences or otherwise, even though both of their courts are relatively small and geographically compact,[140] and the Supreme Court (of course) does not even sit in panels. If collegiality does not exist on those courts, it will be hard to find anywhere. Given the low probability of producing collegiality, even on the smallest most geographically compact courts, it seems foolish to sacrifice the clear benefit of increased capacity in its name.

Even if collegiality were not a myth, it is not immediately apparent why it should be valued so highly. A possible reason is that a collegial court might operate more efficiently. If panel members know the jurisprudential views and work styles of their fellow judges from previous cases, perhaps they can spend less time getting acquainted and proceed to productive work more quickly. They might be more able to distinguish resolvable differences from deeper disagreements on fundamental principle, and thus save time spent on trying to convince colleagues whose views they know will not change. Knowing which issues are worth arguing about not only saves time, but also bruised feelings, and that could increase productivity by reducing time spent posturing, squabbling, and alliance building.

But collegiality also entails a cost. Judges who know, like, and depend on each other might be less likely to risk their personal relationship by disagreeing on matters of importance to one or the other. Over time, colleagues might accumulate

136. Richard S. Arnold, *The Federal Courts: Causes of Discontent*, 56 SMU L. REV. 767, 776 (2003).

137. Wasby, *supra* note 101, at 539, 603.

138. *Id.* at 603–04.

139. *Id.* at 602.

140. *See* WILLIAM H. REHNQUIST, THE SUPREME COURT: HOW IT WAS, HOW IT IS 294–95 (1987); Patricia M. Wald, *Some Real-Life Observations About Judging*, 26 IND. L. REV. 173, 178 (1992).

debts of deference on key issues, and subtle, unarticulated vote trading could occur. A "don't-rock-the-boat" mentality might pervade the courts.

Of course, the supposed benefits and dangers of enhanced collegiality are exactly that: supposed. There is no empirical evidence to indicate whether the postulated benefits and burdens will actually accrue. In other words, even if collegiality were a palpable public benefit, it is by no means clear that collegiality is a function of small size. A small court is not necessarily a happy one, as famous feuds on the Supreme Court attest;[141] and some quite large bodies are very collegial.[142] Today, it is plausible that increases in size might well make the courts *more collegial.* For one thing, the workload would become more manageable, leaving more time for traditional collegial decision making. Also, personal feuds could be buried in the anonymity of a larger group. Further, if there were more active circuit judges, there would be less need for visiting judges and central staff attorneys, and encounters among active circuit judges on three-judge panels would be more, rather than less, frequent.[143] But again, both sides of the argument rely on supposition; there is no empirical evidence correlating collegiality with size and, *a fortiori*, no empirical evidence on the optimal number of judges required to maximize the supposed benefits of increased collegiality and minimize its supposed dangers.

Of course, collegiality does provide one clear, unalloyed benefit: professional life on a collegial court is more pleasant for the judges. That benefit should not be discounted entirely. Happier judges are likely to be easier to recruit and retain and less likely to become ill. But those benefits are easy to over-value, especially when the judges are the ones deciding how big the courts should be; the courts, after all, exist for the good of the nation, not the professional satisfaction of the judges.

141. *E.g.*, the famous Jackson/Black feud discussed in THE OXFORD COMPANION TO THE SUPREME COURT OF THE UNITED STATES 445 (Kermit L. Hall et al. eds., 1992).

142. *E.g.*, most fire departments and many law faculties.

143. *See* discussion *supra* chapter 8.

CHAPTER 13

Jurisdictional Retrenchment: Of Babies and Bath Water

A. THE ARGUMENT

Advocates of a small, elite federal judiciary have their own solution to the problem of appellate overload—jurisdictional contraction. According to them, if Congress would just return federal jurisdiction to the proper limited scope prescribed by the Constitution, history, and federalism, the caseload of the federal courts would decrease enormously, and there would be no need for significant expansion of the judiciary.[1] The Constitution, the argument goes, contemplates a very limited role for the federal courts, and the jurisdictional statutes, at least until recently, confirm that role.[2] Continued expansion of federal jurisdiction subverts the historic role of the federal courts and usurps the powers of the state judiciaries.[3]

Further, expanding federal jurisdiction into areas of only marginal or insubstantial federal interest makes the courts less able to handle their traditional workload—major litigation involving significant national interests.[4] Finally, and perhaps most important for the anti-expansionists, the growth of federal jurisdiction has required a massive increase in the number of federal judgeships, an increase that threatens to alter the basic character of the federal judiciary as a small elite corps of judicial specialists, charged with execution of laws that are the most important to the nation's

1. JUDICIAL CONFERENCE OF U.S., COMM. ON LONG RANGE PLANNING, PROPOSED LONG RANGE PLAN FOR THE FEDERAL COURTS 19 (1994) [hereinafter PROPOSED LONG RANGE PLAN].

2. WILLIAM W. SCHWARZER & RUSSELL R. WHEELER, FED. JUDICIAL CTR., ON THE FEDERALIZATION OF THE ADMINISTRATION OF CIVIL AND CRIMINAL JUSTICE 10–11, 14–15 (Long-Range Planning Series, Paper No. 2, 1994) [hereinafter FEDERALIZATION]; GORDON BERMANT ET AL., FED. JUDICIAL CTR., IMPOSING A MORATORIUM ON THE NUMBER OF FEDERAL JUDGES: ANALYSIS OF ARGUMENTS AND IMPLICATIONS 26–27 (1993), *available at* http://purl.access.gpo.gov/GPO/LPS53494.

3. *See* FEDERALIZATION, *supra* note 2, at 17–26; William H. Rehnquist, *Welcoming Remarks: National Conference on State-Federal Judicial Relationships*, 78 VA. L. REV. 1657, 1660 (1992).

4. FEDERALIZATION, *supra* note 2, at 21; PROPOSED LONG RANGE PLAN, *supra* note 1, at 19.

welfare. Reversing the expansion of federal jurisdiction would remove the need for even greater and even more damaging expansion of the federal judiciary.

Supporters of court-capping have proposed a variety of plans to contract the jurisdiction of the federal courts,[5] but two themes predominate. The first is an inventory of types of cases that should be eliminated. Thus, for example, the Federal Courts Study Committee recommended that Congress curtail diversity jurisdiction (leaving only complex multidistrict litigation, interpleader, and suits involving aliens), prohibit removal of low dollar amount ERISA cases, require state prisoner civil rights plaintiffs to exhaust state institutional remedies, consider revising habeas corpus jurisdiction, shunt review of social security disability claims to a new Article I Court of Disability Claims, authorize the Equal Employment Opportunity Commission to arbitrate employment discrimination cases with the parties' consent, and repeal the Federal Employee's Liability Act and the Jones Act, leaving the claims of injured workers to state and federal workers compensation systems.[6]

The second theme is a generalized admonition to Congress to stop "federalizing" the civil and criminal law. According to this line of reasoning, federal law should not duplicate state law; when state law already provides civil and criminal remedies, Congress should resist the constant temptation to try to solve the nation's social and political problems with federal legislation enforced through federal court jurisdiction. Thus, proponents of this argument deplore using federal legislation and jurisdiction as a major part of the war on drugs, the attempt to control firearms, or the campaign to reduce violence against women.[7] The Committee on Long Range Planning of the Judicial Conference of the United States proposed that federal criminal jurisdiction be limited to offenses against the federal government, criminal activity with substantial interstate or international aspects, sophisticated criminal enterprises requiring federal prosecutorial resources, serious high-level or widespread state or local government corruption, and criminal cases raising highly sensitive local issues. The same committee proposed that federal civil jurisdiction be limited to cases arising under the Constitution, matters involving foreign relations, actions involving the federal government, disputes between states,

5. *See generally* Erwin Chemerinsky, Federal Jurisdiction 30–33 (5th Ed. 2007); Edward A. Purcell Jr., Symposium: II. *What Cases Belong In Federal Court? The Past and Future of Federal Court Jurisdiction: Caseload Burdens and Jurisdictional Limitations: Some Observations from The History of The Federal Courts*, 46 N.Y.L. Sch. L. Rev. 7 (2003); Proposed Long Range Plan, *supra* note 1, at 19–32; Fed. Courts Study Comm., Judicial Conference of the United States, Report of the Federal Courts Study Committee 35–67 (1990) [hereinafter Report of the Federal Courts Study Committee]; Charles Clark, *Mules and Wagons—A Plea for Jurisdictional Reform*, 14 Miss. C. L. Rev. 263, 266 (1994); Jon O. Newman, *Restructuring Federal Jurisdiction: Proposals to Preserve the Federal Judicial System*, 56 U. Chi. L. Rev. 761, 770–76 (1989).

6. Report of the Federal Courts Study Committee, *supra* note 5, at 38, 43, 48–9, 51, 55, 60–61, 62–63; *see also* Proposed Long Range Plan, *supra* note 1, at 25, 29, 48–49, 51, 27–28, 29, 19–32.

7. *See* Rehnquist, *supra* note 3, at 1660.

substantial interstate or international disputes, and matters requiring a nationally uniform rule.[8]

The jurisdictional retrenchment argument, however, like the rest of the court-capping rhetoric, is seriously flawed.

B. POWER AND HISTORY

Without saying so directly, the jurisdictional retrenchment argument suggests that some Constitutional impropriety results if Congress expands the scope of the federal courts' civil and criminal jurisdiction toward the limits in Article III. That suggestion is simply wrong. It is a matter of black-letter law that Congress has plenary power over the jurisdiction of the lower federal courts and can assign to them any matter encompassed in Article III.[9] Article III is expansive, including (among other jurisdictional grants) jurisdiction over cases "arising under"[10] the Constitution and federal statutes.

The only constitutional restriction on the ability of Congress to "federalize" civil and criminal law is the minimal limit found in the Commerce Clause. Although the Supreme Court in recent years has retreated somewhat from its very expansive reading of congressional jurisdiction, it is unlikely that the retreat will go so far as to have a noticeable impact on the caseload of the lower federal courts.

Thus the major limit on federal court jurisdiction is congressional restraint. But what if Congress fails to exercise restraint? Professors Parker and Hagin, two proponents of maintaining a small, elite federal judiciary, have suggested, in that event, the federal courts could do so on their own.[11] Citing the federal courts' power to refuse to exercise jurisdiction under the abstention and *forum non conveniens* doctrines, Parker and Hagin argue that the courts have "unilateral, inherent powers" to restrict their own jurisdiction if Congress will not control its excesses:

> The development in the federal courts of relatively distinct abstention doctrines illustrates especially well the inherent powers of the courts to respond to the excessive enlargement of federal court jurisdiction by Congress.... [C]lose attention to the basic principles infusing the abstention doctrines illuminates that, should Congress continue to create "federal" crimes and causes of action exceeding the bounds of federalism and federal court adjudicative ability, the federal courts will have no choice but to concomitantly expand the

8. Proposed Long Range Plan, *supra* note 1, at 23–29.

9. *See* Erwin Chemerinsky, Federal Jurisdiction ch. 3 (5th ed. 2007); Charles A. Wright, Law of Federal Courts 35 (4th ed. 1983).

10. U.S. Const. art. III, § 2.

11. *See* Robert M. Parker & Leslie J. Hagin, *Federal Courts at the Crossroads: Adapt or Lose!*, 14 Miss. C. L. Rev. 211, 239 (1994).

exercise of their inherent, "abstention" powers—so as to "check" the inefficient, Judiciary-subverting and federalism-thwarting excesses of the Legislature.

The argument depends upon a fundamental misunderstanding of congressional control over federal jurisdiction. There is a lively debate among scholars over whether the courts *should* exercise all of the jurisdiction conferred by Congress or should abstain in a narrow range of cases.[12] Nevertheless, no case has held and no commentator (except Parker and Hagin) has argued that the courts *could* persist in refusing to exercise jurisdiction in the face of congressional insistence. Ultimate congressional control is assumed.[13] Professor Barry Friedman goes so far as to suggest cooperative "dialogic" control, but stops well short of arguing for a "unilateral, inherent" power in the courts to refrain wholesale.[14]

Analysis of the abstention and *forum non conveniens* doctrines reveals the fundamental error in the Parker-Hagin thesis. The doctrines clearly are not of constitutional stature; either they are constructions of jurisdictional statutes or they are rules of federal common law. Either way, Congress has the power to abolish or modify both doctrines, as it has done with *forum non conveniens*.[15] Thus, if the federal courts adopt the Parker-Hagin thesis and refuse to hear "inappropriately federalized" actions, Congress may nullify that refusal and insist that the courts hear the cases. No court or commentator has ever stated that the courts could willfully refuse to hear matters within Article III in the face of Congress's explicit jurisdictional command.

With the constitutional questions removed, the jurisdictional retraction argument relies mainly on tradition. Historically, Congress has not used the full measure of its Commerce Clause power, nor has it assigned the full measure of Article III jurisdiction to the courts. But tradition can evolve as congressional perceptions of national policy and current needs change. Indeed, the reach of federal jurisdiction has repeatedly expanded and contracted in response to changing congressional appraisals of the need for federal solutions to social, political, and economic problems.

Perhaps the clearest illustration of this phenomenon is the fluctuation in criminal filings in the federal district courts, which presumably provides a gauge of the federalization of criminal law. Filings have not increased in either a linear fashion or in direct

12. *Compare* Martin H. Redish, *Reassessing the Allocation of Judicial Business between State and Federal Courts: Federal Jurisdiction and "The Martian Chronicles,"* 78 VA. L. REV. 1769, 1829 (1988), *with* David L. Shapiro, *Reflections on the Allocation of Jurisdiction between State and Federal Courts: A Response to "Reassessing the Allocation of Judicial Business between State and Federal Courts,"* 78 VA. L. REV. 1839, 1845 (1988).

13. *See, e.g.*, Shapiro, *supra* note 12, at 1845 ("[T]he legislature has the burden if it wishes to broaden or narrow the scope of this discretion in a particular area.").

14. Barry Friedman, *A Different Dialogue: The Supreme Court, Congress and Federal Jurisdiction*, 85 NW. U. L. REV. 1 (1990).

15. *See* 28 U.S.C. § 1404 (1994).

proportion to population growth. The number of filings in 2010 (just over seventy-eight thousand), for example, was about three-quarters of the all-time high reached during Prohibition. In the early 1970s, filings totaled about fifty thousand and then hit a major trough (less than thirty thousand) in the early 1980s before rising to current levels.[16] As might be expected, "federalization" (and filings numbers as a measure of federalization) has risen and fallen in response to general fluctuations in the national political perceptions of the appropriate balance between federal and state control.

In the end, the scope of federal jurisdiction has hinged less on theory and tradition and more on politics and expedience. In the words of Professor Warren:

> [T]he Federal judicial system has not been a logical development on lines of consistent theory; it has been the product of temporary necessities and emergencies, arising from ... political, sectional, and economic conditions. It has not been the embodiment of the theories of any particular party.[17]

C. REALITY AND POLITICS

The thrust of the jurisdictional retrenchment argument is that large expansions of the appellate judiciary will be unnecessary if Congress exercises proper jurisdictional restraint. Thus, the real issue in the court-capping debate is not whether jurisdictional retrenchment is a good idea, but whether it is realistic to pin hopes of reducing federal appellate caseloads on it. Given that Congress wields plenary power over federal jurisdiction, the only real question is: will Congress do it?

The prospects for such a retrenchment are bleak, to say the least. Even the most seemingly sensible federal jurisdiction reform proposals have a knack for prompting spirited opposition. Many of the Federal Courts Study Committee recommendations generated dissenting statements within the Committee. The corporate bar, for instance, opposed the abolition or restriction of diversity jurisdiction; organized labor objected to the repeal of the FELA; and the public interest bar opposed restrictions on § 1983 and habeas corpus claims by state prison inmates.[18] As a result, few of the proposals have even been introduced in Congress, let alone adopted. Summing up the Committee's work on jurisdictional contraction, Justice (then Chief Judge) Breyer observed:

> All this is simply to say that the Committee may justifiably take credit for having thought about and crafted its case removal provisions with care. But, it would surprise me to find

16. *See* FEDERALIZATION, *supra* note 2, at 51 fig. 1; PROPOSED LONG RANGE PLAN, *supra* note 1, at 7.

17. Charles Warren, *Federal Criminal Laws and the State Courts*, 38 HARV. L. REV. 545, 598 (1925).

18. *See* REPORT OF THE FEDERAL COURTS STUDY COMMITTEE, *supra* note 5, at 42–43, 63–64, 50–52.

> many of them enacted into law. If I am right, a thoughtful effort having been made, it will be difficult to advocate the door-closing solution to the federal appellate docket problem for some time to come.[19]

Further, even if those controversial proposals were passed, they would not be an effective response to appellate overload. The Federal Courts Study Committee estimated that the combined effect of its recommendations would decrease the caseload of the circuit courts by only about 17 percent.[20] A decrease of that magnitude would be wiped out by only a few years of normal caseload growth. What then would be subtracted from the jurisdiction of the federal courts so that new appellate judgeships would not be required?

Specific technical jurisdictional proposals thus are not a realistic substitute for expansion of the judiciary. But what of the more global admonitions of jurists and commentators against continued federalization of civil and criminal law?[21] At least such proposals are of the right order of magnitude; if Congress vigorously avoided new federalizations and phased out old ones, the resulting reductions in caseloads might be large enough to forestall the need for more judgeships. The probability that Congress will adopt such global restraint, however, is vanishingly small. Congress "federalizes" the civil or criminal law in response to powerful political forces, and the vision of an elite federal judiciary, unsullied by cases based on improperly federalized crimes and civil claims, has no constituency large, numerous, or powerful enough to oppose groups that favor particular federalizing legislation. On occasion, a brave and principled legislator will fall on her sword and sacrifice reelection over an important principle, but how many will do so to protect the federal courts from the growth that increasing federalization will require.

C. PRINCIPLE AND POLICY

The jurisdictional retrenchment argument is not only bad politics, but bad policy as well. Its fundamental error is to misconceive the function of federal jurisdiction. That jurisdiction exists for the good of the country—not for the good of the federal courts. If Congress believes that "federalizing" some area of the law will benefit the country by controlling the drug problem, or by reducing firearm violence, or by minimizing the victimization of some protected class, then as long as the proposed provision falls within the legislature's constitutional power, it is not merely

19. Stephen Breyer, *Administering Justice in the First Circuit*, 24 Suffolk U. L. Rev. 29, 37 (1990).

20. Report of the Federal Courts Study Committee, *supra* note 5, at 27.

21. *See, e.g.*, Proposed Long Range Plan, *supra* note 1, at 21, 24.

Congress's right, but its duty to enact it even though it might discomfort the federal judges or require additional judgeships.

Similarly, if federal prosecutors believe that federal, rather than state, prosecution would serve the national interest, they should prosecute, even though it might increase the burden on the federal courts. Some members of the judiciary disagree; the Judicial Conference Committee on Long Range Planning, for instance, recommends that "the potential for harsher federal sentencing policies and greater capacity in the federal prisons should be insufficient grounds, by themselves, to warrant prosecution under a federal, rather than a state criminal statute."[22] However, if federal prosecutors believe that stiffer federal sentences and greater prison capacity can make law enforcement more efficient, streets safer, and citizens more satisfied with government, why should they forbear?

The basic principle should be that the size of the task should control the size of the tool, not vice versa. The jurisdictional retrenchment argument, however, reverses this crucial priority. The argument starts with the premise of a small elite federal judiciary and then reasons that, because of its size, the judiciary should be allotted only a minimal core of federal jurisdiction. But surely Congress's job is to approach the problem from the front end. It must first determine, in light of changing social conditions, how much federal legislation and federal jurisdiction the nation needs. Then it must supply the federal courts with judgeships and other resources equal to the task.

Clearly, those who wish to maintain a small elite federal judiciary disagree and sometimes invoke some historic or mythic ideal conception of the federal courts to support their argument. Thus, the language of the Federal Courts Study Committee reveals its reliance on that theme: "[W]e may be approaching the limits of the *natural* growth of the federal courts, and yet the surge in case filings at both the trial and especially the appellate level continues with no cessation in sight."[23] But invoking the "nature" of an institution or equating what is "natural" with what is good is a well-known and thoroughly discredited jurisprudential fallacy.[24] There is no "natural," or *a priori,* proper size for any institution. An institution's function must dictate its appropriate form and its proper size; and in our system the function of federal jurisdiction is to meet the needs of the nation, not the judges.

Another reason to discount the jurisdictional retrenchment argument is the strong classist and elitist themes that run through it. The classism is apparent in the specific proposals to reduce federal jurisdiction. The Federal Courts Study Committee recommendations, for example, target diversity jurisdiction ("virtually eliminate" diversity jurisdiction or to raise the amount in controversy), ERISA

22. Proposed Long Range Plan, *supra* note 1, at 23.
23. Report of the Federal Courts Study Committee, *supra* note 5, at 8 (emphasis added).
24. See Jeremy Bentham, The Theory of Legislation 49–52 (Richard Hildreth trans., 1975)

cases (create a $10,000 amount in controversy requirement), prisoner civil rights litigation (require exhaustion of state remedies), social security cases (divert to an Article I court), employment discrimination suits (divert to arbitration), and the FELA and Jones Act cases (repeal the statutes).[25] These cases deal with the legal problems of the poorest and weakest of federal court litigants, groups that federal judges once took great pride in protecting.

The elitist theme is even more apparent in court-capping rhetoric than in specific proposals for jurisdictional contraction. Proponents of jurisdictional retrenchment deplore wasting the time and energy of federal courts on "small cases—against first time [drug] offenders or low-level runners,"[26] and bemoan "an ever-increasing caseload with an ever-larger percentage ... of relatively routine work which neither requires nor engages the abilities of a first-rate judge."[27] To the same effect is Judge Jones's concern that a docket of mostly routine, small-stakes cases will cause the judges to "seek ... routine methods of case disposition" and degrade their "mental and organizational flexibility, so vital for performing the federal courts' classic tasks of defending the Constitution and harmonizing federal law."[28] Moreover, the argument goes, the deterioration of the caseload, "will undoubtedly adversely affect ... [the courts'] ability to attract the people who have traditionally been drawn to this special court,"[29] and render the federal courts less effective as "forums for the big case—major commercial litigation ... and federal actions under ... laws regulating interstate commerce."[30]

The elitism of the jurisdictional retrenchment argument also appears in the proposed destination for these trivial cases—the state courts. The idea seems to be that penny-ante federal cases, while unworthy of the federal courts, are fine for the state courts.[31] The problem, of course, is that the state courts are even more overloaded than their federal counterparts, handling over fifty times the caseload with only 15 times the number of judges.[32] Nor are the state court judges clamoring for the extra

25. Report of the Federal Courts Study Committee, *supra* note 5, at 39, 43, 48, 55, 60, 62.

26. Joseph R. Biden, Setting the Stage for the Nineties—Our Mutual Obligation, Address before the Third Circuit Judicial Conference (April 19, 1993), *in* Federalization, *supra* note 2, at 30.

27. William H. Rehnquist, Remarks at the Annual Dinner of the American Bar Association (Aug. 9, 1976), *in* Carolyn Dineen King, *A Matter of Conscience*, 28 Hous. L. Rev. 955, 961 (1991).

28. Edith H. Jones, *Back to the Future for Federal Appeals Courts: Rationing Federal Justice by Recovering Limited Jurisdiction*, 73 Tex. L. Rev. 1485, 1493 (1995).

29. Report of the Judicial Conference Committee on Court Administration and Case Management to the Judicial Conference Committee on Long Range Planning 5 (Feb. 16, 1993).

30. Justice Antonin Scalia, *Remarks Before the Fellows of the American Bar Foundation and the National Conference of Bar Presidents* (Feb. 15, 1987), *in* Federalization, *supra* note 2, at 44 n.114.

31. *See* Newman, *supra* note 5, at 768.

32. See Federalization, *supra* note 2, at 23 n.60.

work or complaining that the federalizing of the civil and criminal law is usurping their prerogatives. The state court judges and prosecutors welcome the help.

The response of the jurisdictional retrenchment proponents to concerns about greater burdens on overloaded state courts is that the state courts are "already geared to handle high volume."[33] Removing seventy thousand cases from the federal courts would decrease their caseload by 30 percent, while increasing state caseloads by only 1 percent. Proponents boldly assert that the states will hardly notice! Justice (then Judge) Breyer correctly points out, however, the fallacy of that contention:

> The question is whether ... transferring several thousand cases from federal courts to state courts will help the human beings who have problems that translate into court litigation. It is difficult to see how the transfer will help. The state courts also have resource problems, often, as in Massachusetts, far more serious problems than those of federal courts in the same region. To that extent one is simply robbing Peter to pay Paul. And to suggest, as does the Committee, that the new, added burden on the far larger state systems will go unnoticed, is a bit like arguing that a new highway through Boston will cost less overall if we can convince federal, rather than state, taxpayers to pay for it.[34]

Justice Breyer could have added that there is a profound arrogance in suggesting that the way to preserve the status of the federal courts and the professional satisfaction of federal judges is to add to the burdens of state courts and judges who are even more overworked and who enjoy lower status.

The arrogance of the anti-expansionist rhetoric toward state court judges may be profound, but it is also selective, depending on the context. When advocating restriction of the growth of the federal judiciary, Judge Newman argued:

> I have seen the [weakness of the appointments process] ... at work in the filling of vacancies in a large court—the state trial bench of Connecticut. In a meeting of those with significant power over appointments, the name of someone with dubious credentials is proposed. Even the assembled politicians express dismay. "You can't be serious," one tells the candidate's sponsor. "Come off it," is the reply. "That court has 127 judges—they'll never even notice him!" The appointment is made. Few notice. The episode has been repeated in many states ....
>
> The point should not be overstated. A federal judiciary of 3,000 to 4,000 would include some extremely able people and a large number of competent people. But it would also include an unacceptable number of mediocre and even a few unqualified people. Today, most observers regard the overall quality of the federal judiciary as higher

33. Jon O. Newman, *1,000 Judges—The Limit for an Effective Federal Judiciary* 187, 194 (1993); *see* Report of the Federal Courts Study Committee, *supra* note 5, at 40–41.
34. Breyer, *supra* note 19, at 35.

than that of the average state judiciary. At a size of 3,000 to 4,000, its quality would be indistinguishable from the most pedestrian of state judiciaries.[35]

But when arguing that federal cases could be diverted to state courts without harm, Newman saw a far more worthy state judiciary:

> [S]tate courts are now authorized, indeed required, to adjudicate a vast array of claims arising under federal law, and they do so with considerable skill and faithfulness to the commands of federal statutory and constitutional law. Admittedly, the pressures arising from the need to seek reelection and even to secure reappointment present a risk to courageous decision making by state judges that federal judges enjoying life tenure do not face. But state judges have not only competence, they have courage; it would be a mistake to think that they would routinely be less protective of federal rights than would federal judges.[36]

The point is clear: the rhetoric of those who rely on jurisdictional contraction to slow the growth of the federal courts presents no coherent estimation of the quality of the state courts; rather, it assumes about them whatever it must in order to support the goal of maintaining a small federal judiciary.

The jurisdictional-retrenchment argument may seem arrogant, and at times even a bit schizophrenic, but from the judges' point of view, it is understandable. Working on low-status, low-resource cases undoubtedly seems tedious and professionally unrewarding to many circuit judges.[37] Their previous leadership positions in prestigious practice organizations and in academia permitted them to shun such work, and they see no reason to take it up upon ascending to the bench. This may help to explain why opposition to expanding federal jurisdiction and the federal courts comes mostly from the judges themselves.[38]

This limited base of support for jurisdictional retrenchment and its self-serving motivation should give Congress pause. Despite the hubris of the court-capping rhetoric, the federal courts are not an objet d'art to be appreciated aesthetically and to be protected from the profane and trivial. Nor are they learned debating societies or exclusive clubs. They are instead a national resource—supported by all the taxpayers (including those with boring, routine federal claims)—that Congress should deploy for the benefit of the nation. It may be that jurisdictional retrenchment is a good idea, but if so, it must be because of the good consequences for the country, not because it will save the judges from boring work or the federal courts from needed expansion.

35. Newman, *supra* note 33, at 187–88.

36. Newman, *supra* note 5, at 769–70.

37. Lauren K. Robel, *The Politics of Crisis in the Federal Courts*, 7 OHIO ST. J. ON DISP. RESOL. 115, 136 (1991).

38. *See* FEDERALIZATION, *supra* note 2, at 22.

CHAPTER 14

Elitism and Diversity

In the preceding pages, we have argued that judicial opposition to increasing the number of appellate judges cannot be based credibly upon concerns over doctrinal inconsistency, the quality of appointees, or cost. We have also shown that opposition to expansion cannot and should not rely upon the prospect of jurisdictional contraction. This suggests that other motives may form the true basis for judicial opposition to expansion of the federal judiciary. This chapter examines those motives as well as some likely benefits of expanding the judiciary.

A. FAMILIARITY

Even if it were possible, judges simply might not want to use the Learned Hand model in all cases. Indeed, federal judges, hardly a reticent group, seem to accept their new "administrative" role readily. No doubt part of this acceptance is due to a natural tendency to "view as appropriate that which is familiar."[1] We believe, however, that a more important consideration is that service on the new *certiorari* courts permits the judges to replicate their roles in private practice and thus to avoid cases they view with distaste.

1. Replication

Most judges come from a background in practice in which they acted as team leader rather than as solo practitioner.[2] A senior partner in today's average litigation

1. Lauren K. Robel, *Caseload and Judging: Judicial Adaptations to Caseload,* 1990 BYU L. Rev. 3, 55.

2. It is difficult to determine the practice background of judges because increasingly, the norm is that candidates for judicial appointment have prior judicial experience. Carl Tobias, Symposium, *The Judicial Appointments Process: The Bush Administration and Appeals Courts Nominees,* 10 Wm. & Mary Bill of Rts. J. (2001).

practice leads a litigation group or team that may be composed of one or two junior partners, two or three associates, and any number of paralegals and secretaries. The job of the senior partner is to supervise—she does not perform the discovery, the research, or the drafting except in the most important aspects of the most important cases. Those tasks are delegated to more junior lawyers and paralegals, with the senior partner checking only generally to see that the work is done properly—and even most of the supervision is delegated (e.g., "Mary, did you go over Joe's research?"). The chambers of an appellate judge replicates that hierarchy. The judge (the senior partner) delegates most of the work to personal clerks (junior partners), central staff attorneys (associates), and interns. Often, elbow clerks review the work of staffers and interns; the judge reviews the work of personal clerks; and serious judicial intervention is limited to the important cases.[3]

The effect of replicating pyramidical practice, however, goes beyond the administrative structure of chambers. Replication also ensures that a judge will treat most carefully those areas of the law that she knew best in practice. Few judges had much experience as attorneys with social security cases, prisoner petitions, or the routine problems of small stakes litigants. On the other hand, many judges had a good deal of experience with antitrust, securities, mass tort, or general business litigation while in private practice.[4] This observation helps explain why the former set of cases is less likely to receive the Learned Hand treatment.

2. Distaste

The judicial pyramid also ensures that judges do not have to spend a lot of time on "distasteful" cases involving such matters as employee benefits or prisoner complaints. Anyone who talks to judges knows they find those cases quite irksome. The vocation of a judge, however, is to do justice. Although it may be more interesting to read briefs prepared by great lawyers in momentous cases that will be written up in the *New York Times* than to sift through pro se petitions and immigration appeals, that should not necessarily make the "big" cases professionally more rewarding. After all, a veteran's claim that the government has improperly denied benefits should have at least as strong an appeal to a judge's sense of justice as a claim by a Fortune 500 corporate executive that his bonus was confiscated illegally.

3. Judge Wald was perhaps the first to notice this replicating effect. *See* Patricia M. Wald, *The Problem with the Courts: Black-Robed Bureaucracy or Collegiality under Challenge?* 42 MD. L. REV. 766, 778 (1984).

4. Central staff, who do most of the work on the "lesser" cases, thus develop an expertise in those "mundane" matters. Because the judges do not share this expertise, judicial deference to the work of the expert staff becomes even more likely and even more dangerous. *See supra* chapter 8.

In real life, however, appellate judges prefer the notorious insider trading case or the giant hostile acquisition case to the mundane and private world of prisoner complaints, pro se litigants, and disappointed asylum seekers. Judge Rubin once wrote that "[t]he desirability of being a federal judge is inversely proportionate to the number of routine cases brought to federal court .... The professional quality of those who seek a federal judgeship is inevitably affected by the prestige, the challenges and the responsibilities of being a federal judge."[5] Judge King has suggested that "[j]udges also resist [appointing] more judges simply because mathematics dictates that as the size of the court increases, each judge's chance of drawing an important case diminishes."[6] For many judges, apparently, the lure of the job lies primarily in handling big or sociopolitically important cases or in participating in cases that involve doctrinal development. Correcting error or just visibly assuring the litigants that justice was done in small cases—often brought by the powerless and voiceless claiming to have been victimized by the government or large corporate interests—is deemed far less desirable.

B. AN ELITE JUDICIARY

A clue as to what may really be driving some judicial opposition can be gleaned from a disturbing trend in some of the rhetoric arguing against expansion of the federal judiciary. A prime example is an article written by Chief Judge Tjoflat (the Eleventh Circuit), which marshals anecdotal and *a priori* arguments against Judge Reinhardt's (the Ninth Circuit) position that problems associated with doubling the size of the judiciary are soluble. Although Judge Reinhardt's argument is buttressed by statistical evidence and personal experience in a large court (the Ninth Circuit), Judge Tjoflat ignores the evidence and dismisses Judge Reinhardt's experience with his own jumbo court and writes:

> Those who wish to create or maintain jumbo courts do so for a variety of reasons. Some are members of the jumbo court itself. The court is their Edsel, so it's okay. Presumably, they believe that if they try hard enough to make the jumbo court work, it will work. Unfortunately, the most determined elephant will never leap like a gazelle.[7]

This kind of public discourse is rare among members of the federal bench, and Tjoflat's invective is quite instructive. Obviously, Judge Reinhardt struck an exposed nerve. Perhaps there is more at stake here than an argument over efficiency. Perhaps concerns over quality of life are central to members of the judiciary who oppose

5. Alvin B. Rubin, *Bureaucratization of the Federal Courts: The Tension between Justice and Efficiency*, 55 Notre Dame Law. 648, 655 (1981).
6. Carolyn Dineen King, *A Matter of Conscience*, 28 Hous. L. Rev. 955, 959 (1991).
7. Gerald B. Tjoflat, *More Judges, Less Justice*, 79 A.B.A. J. 70, 73 (July 1993).

expansion. Judge Tjoflat writes that "life as a judge on a jumbo court is comparable to life as a citizen in a big city—life on a smaller court to life in a small town."[8] Thus, "judges in small circuits are able to interact with their colleagues in a more expedient and efficient manner than judges on jumbo courts."[9]

Although Tjoflat's small-town imagery is attractive, reality is somewhat different. As the earlier discussion shows, interaction among judges seems to be quite minimal even on relatively small courts like Judge Tjoflat's. The small-town metaphor is also disturbing. It suggests that judges associate a "small-town" existence with comfort and that a Ninth Circuit-type experience would be less homey and less comfortable. But once again, the comfort of the judges is easily overvalued; presumably, the purpose of the federal courts is to serve the nation, not to provide professional satisfaction for the judges.

More is involved than comfort, however; status is also a serious concern of opponents of judicial expansion. Status, however, usually enters the debate through a side door. Advocates of a smaller judiciary sometimes couch their arguments in terms of a need to keep job status high in order to attract quality applicants. The Federal Courts Study Committee expressed it this way:

> The independence secured to federal judges by Article III is compatible with responsible and efficient performance of judicial duties only if federal judges are carefully selected from a pool of competent and eager applicants and only if they are sufficiently few in number to feel a personal stake in the consequences of their actions. Neither condition can be satisfied if there are thousands of federal judges.[10]

To the same effect, the ABA Report suggests that, "[s]ome distinction between harder and easier cases must be drawn ... to preserve the attractiveness and prestige of an increasingly demanding job,"[11] and Judge Newman argued that "[a]n undue increase in the number of judges will inevitably lead to a reduction in the quality of new appointees."[12]

No data support the conjecture that the judiciary will fail to attract quality candidates unless it remains a cozy, little group. A job as a federal judge is attractive for many reasons: public service, prestige, interesting colleagues and clerks, good pay and fringe benefits (especially at retirement), and perhaps of most importance these days, much less pressure than is found in practice. In fact, open judgeships

8. *Id.* at 70.
9. *Id.*
10. Fed. Courts Study Comm., Judicial Conference of the United States, Report of the Federal Courts Study Committee 7 (1990).
11. ABA Standing Comm. on Fed. Judicial Improvements, The United States Courts of Appeals: Reexamining Structure and Process After a Century of Change 548–49 (1989). For discussion of the ABA Report, see chapter 10.
12. Jon O. Newman, *1,000 Judges—The Limit for an Effective Federal Judiciary*, 76 Judicature 187, 187 (1993).

do not lack for long lines of committed capable applicants. Nor do judges leave the bench, generally. Indeed, "[a]lthough the absolute number of departures in the 1980s is large ... the rate of departure was actually lower than it was in all but three other decades in the history of the federal judiciary."[13] The ample population of would-be federal judges suggests that something other than genuine concern over the applicant pool might be at stake here.

When judges express concern over applicant quality, they really seem to be saying: "I would not have become a judge without the prestige associated with a small and elite body." Judge Wallace has written that "the call to maintain a small and exclusive federal appellate judiciary has not come from the public, or even from the bar. This sentiment appears to be championed by federal judges, and I assume it is rooted in a preference for a small-court culture."[14] Or, as then Professor Frankfurter wrote long ago: "A powerful judiciary implies a relatively small number of judges."[15]

Others are even more explicit about the relation among size, status, and power. Characteristically, Justice Scalia is very direct about his opposition to the growth of the judiciary: "It only dilutes the prestige of the office and aggravates the problem of image."[16] The themes of power, elitism, status, and image appear with distressing regularity. Judge Jones of the Eleventh Circuit provides its baldest iteration:

> [A]s the docket is "dumbed-down" by an overwhelming number of routine or trivial appeals, judges become accustomed to seeking routine methods of case disposition. Their mental and organizational flexibility, so vital for performing the federal courts' classic tasks of defending the Constitution and harmonizing federal law, inevitably suffers. The situation is like that of a competitive tennis player forced to spend the bulk of his time rallying with novices. Just as the player's competitive edge will erode from lack of peer contact, so are judges' legal talents jeopardized by a steady diet of minor appeals.[17]

13. Emily Field Van Tassel, Fed. Judicial Ctr., Why Judges Resign: Influences on Federal Judicial Service 1789 to 1992, at 9 (1993), *available at* http://bulk.resource.org/courts.gov/fjc/judgeres.pdf. For financial reasons (the ability to double dip), some judges might be opting for senior status earlier.

14. J. Clifford Wallace, *The Case for Large Federal Courts of Appeals*, 77 Judicature288 (1994).

15. Felix Frankfurter, *Distribution of Judicial Power between the United States and State Courts*, 13 Cornell L.Q. 499, 515 (1928).

16. Stuart Taylor, *Scalia Proposes Major Overhaul of United States Courts of Appeals*, N.Y. Times, Feb. 16, 1987, sec. 1 at 1.

17. Edith H. Jones, *Back to The Future for Federal Appeals Courts: Rationing Federal Justice by Recovering Limited Jurisdiction*, 73 Tex L. Rev. 1485, 1493 (1995) (reviewing Thomas E. Baker, Rationing Justice on Appeal: The Problems of the U.S. Court of Appeals (1994)).

What is so disturbing about this rhetoric is that it is grounded in a fundamental misapprehension of the purpose of the federal courts. Responding to that point of view, Judge Wallace reminds us that: "The federal courts do not exist for the benefit of judges. They exist ... solely to serve and to meet the needs of the public. Judges are, fundamentally, public servants. Judiciary policy must be dictated by concerns for the judiciary's mission, not by the personal preferences of its members."[18] Unfortunately, it is all too clear that "personal preferences" for comfort and status have driven much of the judiciary's advocacy for restricting its own size and thus ensuring the continued need for the two-track system for deciding appeals. Judge Reinhardt is brutal in his candor:

> We federal judges are simply unable to abandon our notion of the appellate courts as small, cohesive entities operating in a pristine and sheltered atmosphere. It appears that, rather than surrender this wholly unrealistic and outdated vision of the federal judiciary, many of us are willing to ration justice, to eliminate some of the best qualities we once associated with appellate decision making, and to shut the doors of the courts to the American people by severely restricting our jurisdiction.[19]

It is not only unfortunate, but also ironic, that the judges who are willing to ration justice to retain a small judiciary are the same people who have sworn to "administer justice without respect to persons, and do equal right to the poor and to the rich."[20]

C. THE ADVANTAGES OF EXPANSION

The bulk of this chapter has examined and evaluated the arguments advanced by opponents of enlarging the federal judiciary. We believe that those arguments cannot justify the continued maintenance of a small, elite corps of circuit judges. Perhaps a significant expansion of the circuit courts would produce some costs, but it would also result in substantial benefits to the courts, the profession, and society as a whole. The remainder of the chapter deals with what is to be gained by radical expansion.

Many of the benefits may be apparent from our refutations of the arguments against expansion. Even so, some of those benefits are worth a second look. Far and away the most important gain from an enlarged judiciary would be the creation of additional appellate capacity. That increase would remove much of the need for the procedural shortcuts that have come to be the norm over the last thirty years.

18. Wallace, *supra* note 14, at 288.
19. Stephen Reinhardt, *Surveys Without Solutions: Another Study of the United States Courts of Appeals*, 73 Tex. L. Rev. 1505, 1513 (1995).
20. 28 U.S.C. § 453 (1994) (judicial oath of office).

The courts would be able to hear more oral arguments, write and publish more opinions, and rely less on central staff attorneys. In other words, more cases would receive the personal attention of Article III judges. Moreover, many of the cases that would receive increased attention are those of parties with little power and wealth. That would result in more equal treatment of all litigants—rich and poor, weak and powerful. Before the basic American dream of equal justice under the law can be realized, the cases must be treated more equally and with more respect.

A second important benefit of an expanded judiciary would be the creation of more and better law. More judges, writing reasoned opinions in all of the cases brought before them, would create a vast new body of precedent. Contrary to the arguments of the advocates of nonpublication and non-citation regimes, those additional precedents would make the law more, not less, certain. At least that is the result predicted by the only available empirical evidence. Forecasts of doom from an inundation of precedent are mere speculation that runs counter to the conclusions of the most authoritative studies. More certainty, in turn would reduce, not increase, the costs of all legal consumers and increase accessibility to the law. Computer databases would continue to make this enlarged law easier to use. Because this body of precedent would be the work of judges rather than staff, by definition, it will be better, more visible, and more predictable.

Finally, enlarging the judiciary also would benefit society in a way that this Article has not yet touched upon. An enlarged judiciary would be more diverse culturally, geographically, and intellectually. The predominant view in this country is that racial, ethnic, and gender diversity is a good in itself. That certainly makes sense for the judiciary. It is hard to believe that a culturally diverse bench does not have different dynamics and thoughts from a uniform one. Achieving cultural diversity in the federal judiciary, however, is hampered by the slow turnover among the judges. Thus, as women and minority applicants begin to achieve the seniority associated with service on the federal bench, there are relatively few openings for them. A significant increase in the number of judges, however, would create more appointment opportunities and would change the makeup of the bench.

Expansion of the federal judiciary would also enhance diversity in other ways. Circuit judges traditionally have been clustered in large urban centers. The appointment of more judges would likely lead to circuit judges hailing from smaller cities or even rural areas. Those new judges would bring a different perspective to their job, a perspective that could easily affect the development of the law. Moreover, judges from cities like Toledo or Omaha would affect the attitudes of judges from bigger cities. Adding more judges would also diversify not only the geographical, but also the intellectual mix on the courts. There would be more judges coming from public agencies, public interest groups, law schools, and small firms to counter the traditional bias in favor of appointing judges from large, powerful law firms. The perspective of these representatives and of their different constituencies would surely improve the quality of justice.

Conclusion

For the first eighty years of their existence, the United State Circuit Courts of Appeals operated as traditional appellate courts—the kind that law students learn about. Sitting in panels of three, the judges heard oral argument in almost all cases, conferred, came to a unanimous or split decision, and recorded their decision in one or more opinions authored by judges appointed by the President with the advice and consent of the Senate. The author may have benefited from the assistance of one or more law clerks, recent law graduates who worked for an individual judge for a year or two between law school and law practice. The resulting opinion was published and viewed as precedent, binding on the courts within the circuit and perhaps persuasive to other courts. The responsibility of the opinion's jurist-author was to demonstrate cogently how the decision in the case at bar was consistent with prior decisions, or why the case at bar was distinguishable from the available precedents, or why the decision diverged from existing law. Then the decision, along with others of its kind, constituted the decisional law, which in turn bound or persuaded the deciders of future cases and writers of future opinions to follow its lead, distinguish the facts on which it was based, or explain why it should no longer be considered "good law."

The tradition served the nation well, acting first as a check on errors of the district courts. But it also supplied a mostly rational and predictable, yet evolving, set of rules, policies, and principles and interpretations and applications of congressional statutes and Supreme Court decisions. That body of law helped the country through history's greatest sustained economic expansion, two world wars and a Cold War, a great depression and periodic recessions, a fundamental change in the power allocation between the central government and the states, and the change from an apartheid system to *de jure* racial equality. Not bad.

Beginning in the 1960s, and in response to a geometrically increasing caseload, the circuit courts embarked on a fundamental, yet initially imperceptible, change of course. It started with a different set of procedures for habeas corpus cases and prisoner civil rights lawsuits. The judges perceived those cases as extremely burdensome, routine, largely meritless, and unlikely to produce any addition to the body of precedent. They dealt with the problem by hiring a few recent law school graduates, who worked for the court as a whole rather than an individual judge and concentrated their efforts on the habeas and civil rights cases. The memoranda that they wrote became the basis for the judicial opinions, usually issued *per curiam*, which disposed of that nettlesome slice of the docket. From the judges' point of view, it made little sense to publish those decisions or treat them as precedential for they differed fundamentally from the rest of the courts' output. Highly fact specific and prepared with less input from the judges than the typical opinion, they were unlikely to be of much use to future litigants or courts. Seeming to approve the development, the Judicial Conference directed that each of the circuit courts prepare a plan for the publication of opinions.

That modest beginning developed into a mature two-track system of appellate justice. Cases perceived to be more important continued to receive the traditional treatment, while cases of less perceived significance were consigned to an abbreviated appellate process. In those cases, oral argument was rare, the work was done mostly by the staff attorneys with little judicial input, and the decision was issued in an unpublished, nonprecedential opinion. We have called the set of new and abbreviated appellate procedures "Track Two," and we have attached the label of "Appellate Triage" to the method by which cases are diverted from the traditional process and assigned to the new truncated pathway. Through the next several decades, the quantity and variety of cases consigned to Track Two treatment have increased steadily so that today less than 20 percent of the circuit courts' caseload receives the traditional appellate process. In other words, what started as a special set of shortcuts for dealing with a small and troublesome slice of the docket has morphed into the most common way for appeals to make their way through the federal appellate system.

The change in appellate process in turn caused a major change in the circuit courts and in their opinions. The courts changed by growing much larger. While the number of judges stayed relatively constant, the corps of para-judicial personnel (law clerks and staff attorneys) increased substantially and steadily so that today they outnumber the judges by at least six to one. The courts' opinions changed in two opposite directions, developing a bimodal distribution. One set of opinions, those issued in Track One cases, became longer, more scholarly, more heavily footnoted, and more abstract until they came to resemble Supreme Court opinions or law review articles. The other set of opinions became much shorter, some consisting of barely a few conclusory lines.

Some distinguished jurists and several scholars noted the change in the courts, their staffing, and their decision procedures and decried the result as an illegitimate transformation of the courts from courts of mandatory appellate jurisdiction into de facto *certiorari* courts. Various governmental and nongovernmental committees, commissions, and study groups examined the problem over the course of a generation, and the issue was even the subject of a few contentious, published judicial opinions, but the only concrete results have been: (1) the West Publishing Company began to publish all the "unpublished" opinions in an Appendix to the

Federal Reporter, and (2) despite spirited resistance, the Federal Rules of Appellate Procedure were amended to prohibit local circuit court rules that forbid the citation of unpublished opinions. Other than those two modest steps, the trend toward Track Two treatment for larger and larger portions of the docket has been steady.

That result was not inevitable; a very simple expedient could have maintained the traditional appellate model for nearly all federal appeals; the corps of circuit judges could have been increased dramatically. Yet that simple solution has met steady resistance, not from Congress on the grounds of excessive cost, but rather from the judiciary itself. The public reasons for that resistance, expressed in a series of speeches and law review articles, have been a set of extremely weak and, at times, embarrassing arguments that have been refuted publicly and conclusively as logically flawed and empirically baseless.

The argument that expansion would reduce the quality of the bench lacks empirical support. Judgeships are highly sought after, and waiting lists are long. Moreover, even if the average quality of the judges were to decrease slightly, the average quality of appellate justice would increase because more cases would receive traditional appellate justice and fewer would be relegated to staff attorneys and clerks.

Judgeships are costly in absolute terms, but not when compared with other national expenditures. Today, in light of the vast expenditures on several foreign wars and the financial crisis, the argument from expense seems profoundly out of place, more of a bad joke than a serious argument. For the amount that the federal government wastes annually on crop subsidies for land *no longer used to farm*, circuit court capacity could be brought to adequate levels. Further, while excessive cost may be a reason for Congress to refuse to grant additional judgeships, it is not an excuse for the judiciary to refuse to ask for them. Other federal funds-seekers show no such reticence, nor do the judges themselves when it comes to expenditures for "imperial" courthouses and other forms of support.

The unstable law hypothesis, like the quality of the bench argument, is contradicted by the only available empirical studies. Moreover, the argument wrongly presupposes that legal consistency is the only goal of our appellate system; it discounts the equally important goal of maintaining enough capacity to decide all cases carefully, correctly, and visibly. Finally, the unstable law argument ignores several devices that could ensure legal consistency without sacrificing adequate capacity.

The jurisdictional retrenchment argument is a pipe dream. Congress makes changes to federal jurisdiction in response to political pressure from constituents and contributors. It is not about to make radical cuts in federal jurisdiction to accommodate the judiciary's desire to remain small, nor should it; the size of the job should dictate the size of the tool, not vice versa. The superficiality of the anti-expansion arguments suggests that they are forwarded disingenuously and that the real motivation lies elsewhere.

Occasionally, the real reasons for the resistance to expansion have peeked through the fog of overblown rhetoric. Reduced to their essentials, they are that the judges prefer to work on smaller courts, which they perceive to be more "collegial," that they prefer to devote their time to momentous rather than "trivial" cases, and that they fear an increase in their number will reduce the prestige attached to the office. In other words, they wish to remake the courts to resemble increasingly the Supreme Court and promote themselves to positions that resemble as much as possible the roles of Justices.

There is nothing intrinsically wrong with seeking collegiality and prestige; most workers prefer higher-status jobs in cordial, cooperative settings. And expansion might (although it is not clear that it will) diminish one or both of those desiderata. The important question, however, is how much should be sacrificed for the judges' prestige and collegiality, and who will do the sacrificing. High levels of prestige and collegiality inure primarily to the benefit of the judges, a relatively privileged group, while the loss of capacity is endured by the nation and the litigants—mostly the poor and powerless litigants. We can think of no principled theory of distributive justice that opts to retain a minor advantage for a privileged few at the cost of a major disadvantage for a vast underprivileged cohort.

This unjust exchange adds emphasis to one of this book's major themes—that the federal courts exist for the good of the nation, not the good of the judges. In what other enterprise, public or private, would we tolerate a permanent 50 percent capacity shortage in return for a minor fringe benefit for the workers? Try the thought experiment, substituting for the judges some other group of workers, say, janitors, or postal workers, or even congressional staffers.

After a while, the anti-expansionists stopped defending their position with public arguments. Perhaps one reason for that development was that the arguments had been exposed as bankrupt. The more important reason, however, is that the anti-expansionists realized that they could control the number of judgeships, not by reasoned argument, but through the little-known mechanics of the Judicial Conference's procedure for requesting more positions. The policy of the Conference has been that it will not request funding for an additional judgeship unless the majority of the circuit's active judges concur in the request. Thus, the anti-expansionists came to realize that sophisticated argument was not necessary and that they could carry the day with a much simpler strategy: just say no.

We are lawyers, and so to us, the relatively rapid transformation of one of the most fundamental institutions in the American legal system is intrinsically interesting. But the rest of the world could be forgiven if it perceived as trivial a largely invisible and technical change in the operating procedures of a set of intermediate appellate courts. Thus the question: So what? Why should we care?

We maintain that there are larger, more general lessons to learn from the transformation. The first and most obvious is that there is a steady force pulling on governmental institutions even in a democracy, the desires of the institution's insiders. Thus the transformation of the circuit courts provides a lesson (as if history needed one more) on how a public entity, created by society to meet a particular need, changes into one best suited to meet its own needs and those of the elites who control it.[1]

Another lesson to be drawn is one about what Hamlet called the "insolence of office," the arrogance with which public officials ignore criticism of their conduct as they sacrifice the good of the public for their own desires. The Third Branch is subject to the least popular oversight, and the judges have taken advantage of that freedom.

A third lesson is about the increasingly inequitable distribution of societal benefits; in plain terms, the rich get richer. Thus corporate officers and managers are paid a larger multiple of their employees' wages than at any time in the recent past, and the nation's GINI index (a way of measuring the unequal distribution of income) is higher than in any other industrialized democracy. The transformation of the circuit courts shows, moreover, that the inequality extends way beyond the monetary to include governmental resources that are supposed to be available to everyone. The resource, of course, is the judges' time; the rich and powerful get more of it and the poor and weak get less. And the circuit courts' transformation has exacerbated the disparity over the last fifty years. This seems especially troublesome because the judges are supposed to be the guardians of the weak and powerless. Moreover, the "rich" are probably not all that interested in getting an ever increasing share of the courts' resources. From their point of view, the result of an appeal is vastly more important than the length and scholarly excellence of the opinion. The added value of a one hundred-page opus that has gone through Judge Kosinski's eighty drafts, rather than a modest twenty-page effort that has gone through five drafts is probably an allocation of societal benefits that even the recipients do not appreciate. Winning or losing is the crucial question; the importance of everything else is insignificant in comparison.

A final and most troubling lesson is about "judicial activism." Lately, politicians and political pundits have had a good deal to say on the topic The prevailing view from both the Right and the Left seems to be that the judges are not content to limit themselves to matters purely legal. Instead, they have placed an ideological thumb on the scale in momentous cases to substitute their own policy preferences for those of the legislature. The transformation of the circuit courts represents a more pernicious form of activism for two reasons. It is one thing to shade a result for

1. This is not to say that the judges have acted to assure themselves an easy life; quite the contrary. They work long and, in some cases, inhuman hours; it is just that they do the kind of work that they please, not the kind that their enabling statute calls for. Nor have the judges acted to feather their nests financially; they are paid little compared to the ranks of lawyers from which they are selected, and they rarely lobby for raises.

policy preferences but quite another for the judges to remake their own courts to suit their own needs, contrary to statutory mandate. That is a higher order, organic form of activism.

The second reason is that judicial activism affecting political and social issues is likely to counterbalance itself. In one result, Leftist judges may be prone to forward their sociopolitical agenda, but in another, Right-Wingers will have their say. Moreover, as the political winds vary—and they have a persistent tendency to do so—the number and influence of a particular slant to judicial decisions will wax and wane. Finally, activist decisions are subject to legislative revision or reversal.

By contrast, the activism that transformed the circuit courts has attracted very little public attention; there is little political pressure to counter the judges' activism in the obscure field of judicial administration. Beyond a few scholars, who has noticed the illegitimate transformation of the circuit courts? Our hope is that this volume will increase the number and influence of those who do care and wish to return the circuit courts to the restrained, respected, and statutorily sanctioned role they played in the time of Learned Hand.

INDEX

Printed in the USA/Agawam, MA
December 16, 2014

603932.025